# Q&A
# Evidence

**Routledge Questions & Answers Series**

Each Routledge Q&A contains questions on topics commonly found on exam papers, with comprehensive suggested answers. The titles are written by lecturers who are also examiners, so the student gains an important insight into exactly what examiners are looking for in an answer. This makes them excellent revision and practice guides.

**Titles in the series:**

Q&A Company Law
Q&A Commercial Law
Q&A Contract Law
Q&A Criminal Law
Q&A Employment Law
Q&A English Legal System
Q&A Equity and Trusts
Q&A European Union Law
Q&A Evidence
Q&A Family Law
Q&A Intellectual Property Law
Q&A Jurisprudence
Q&A Land Law
Q&A Medical Law
Q&A Public Law
Q&A Torts

For a full listing, visit www.routledge.com/cw/revision

# Q&A Evidence

Charanjit Singh

Routledge
Taylor & Francis Group
LONDON AND NEW YORK

Eleventh edition published 2016
by Routledge
2 Park Square, Milton Park, Abingdon, Oxon OX14 4RN

and by Routledge
711 Third Avenue, New York, NY 10017

*Routledge is an imprint of the Taylor & Francis Group, an informa business*



First edition published by Cavendish Publishing 1994
Tenth edition published by Routledge 2013

*British Library Cataloguing in Publication Data*
A catalogue record for this book is available from the British Library

*Library of Congress Cataloging-in-Publication Data*
A catalog record for this title has been requested

ISBN: 978-1-138-82959-6 (pbk)
ISBN: 978-1-315-73765-2 (ebk)

Typeset in TheSans
by Wearset Ltd, Boldon, Tyne and Wear

# Contents


**Table of Cases** vii
**Table of Legislation** xiii
**Guide to the Companion Website** xvii

**Introduction** 1

**1** Basic Concepts 3
**2** Burden and Standard of Proof 19
**3** Presumptions, Competence and Compellability 37
**4** Hearsay I 53
**5** Hearsay II 71
**6** Hazardous Evidence 83
**7** Confessions and Ill-Gotten Evidence 99
**8** Character Evidence I 127
**9** Character Evidence II 145
**10** The Course of Testimony 171
**11** Opinion Evidence 183
**12** Privilege and Public Policy 191

**Index** 205

# Table of Cases

A (No 1) [2001] 2 WLR 1546 **10, 172**
A (No 2) [2002] 1 AC 45 **10, 87, 89, 180**
A and BC Chewing Gum Ltd *see* DPP v A and BC Chewing Gum Ltd
A and Others v Secretary of State for the Home Department [2005] UKHL 56 **123**
Abadom [1983] 1 WLR 126 **184, 186**
Agar [1989] NLJR 116; [1990] 2 All ER 442 **199, 200**
Air Canada v Secretary of State for Trade (No 2) [1983] 2 AC 394 **197**
Al-Khawaja [2006] 1 WLR 1078; [2005] EWCA Crim 2697 **55, 57, 82**
Al-Khawaja v UK [2009] All ER (D) 132 (Jan) **58, 61**
Alladice (1988) 87 Cr App R 380 **111, 113**
Allan [1969] 1 All ER 91; [1969] 1 WLR 33 **27**
Alobaydi [2007] EWCA Crim 145 **133**
Anderson [1993] Crim LR 447 **109**
Andreae v Selfridge & Co Ltd [1938] Ch 1 **14**
Andrews [1987] AC 281 **71**
Argent (1997) 2 Cr App R 27 **122**
Ashburton (Lord) v Pape [1913] 2 Ch 469 **204**
Attorney-General of Hong Kong v Lee Kwong-Kut [1993] 3 All ER 939 **23**
Aziz and Others [1995] 3 All ER 149, HL; [1996] 1 AC 41 **87, 89, 110, 181**

Bailey and Smith (1993) 97 Cr App Rep 365 **123**
Barry (Adrian Joseph) [2010] EWCA Crim 195; [2010] 2 All ER 1004 **7**
Bathurst [1968] 2 QB 99 **102, 103**
Batt [1994] Crim LR 592 **77, 100, 123**
B(C) [2004] EWCA Crim 1254; [2004] 2 Cr App Rep 570 **149, 159**
Beck [1982] 1 WLR 461 **85, 91, 92**
Beckles [2004] EWCA Crim 2766 **122**
Bentley (DW) (Deceased) [2001] 1 **27**
Betts and Hall [2001] EWCA Crim 224 **122**
Blake and Tye (1844) 6 QB 126; 115 ER 49 **100**
Blastland [1986] AC 41 **9, 80, 81, 92, 151**
Boardman *see* DPP v Boardman
Bowman v DPP [1990] Crim LR 600 **12**
Boyson [1991] Crim LR 274 **138**
Bratty v Attorney-General for Northern Ireland [1963] AC 386 **28**
Brigden [1973] Crim LR 579 **102, 103**
Britzman [1983] 1 WLR 350 **165**
Broadhurst v R [1964] AC, 441; [1964] 2 WLR 38; [1964] 1 All ER III, PC **94**
Brown; Daley (1987) 87 Cr App Rep 52 **199, 202**
Burge and Pegg [1996] 1 Cr App Rep 163 **17, 65, 85, 94, 181**
Butterwasser [1948] 1 KB 4 **169**
Byrne [1960] 2 QB 396 179 C [2006] EWCA Crim 197 **188**

C (2006) **75**
Calcraft v Guest [1898] 1 QB 759 **204**
Campbell [2007] 1 WLR 2798 **133, 135, 158, 163, 165, 167, 168–169**
Campbell v Tameside MBC [1982] QB 1065 **196**
Camplin *see* DPP v Camplin
Carr-Briant [1943] KB 607 **27**

Chalkley [1998] 2 Cr App R 79 **125**
Chard v Chard [1956] P 259; [1955] 3 All ER 721 **40, 47**
Chenia [2004] 1 All ER 543, [2003] 2 Cr App Rep 83; [2002] EWCA Cr App Rep 83; [2002] EWCA Crim 2345 **119**
Chief Constable of the West Midlands, *ex parte* Wiley [1995] AC 274 **197**
Christie [1914] AC 545 **174**
Chung [2007] EWCA Crim 328 **169**
Cokesix Lumemba; R v JP [2014] EWCA Crim 2064 and R v FA [2015] EWCA Crim 209 **38**
Coles [1995] 1 Cr App Rep 157 **183**
Commonwealth Affairs v Assistant Deputy Coroner for Inner North London [2013] EWHC 3724 (Admin) **194**
Comptroller of Customs v Western Electric Co Ltd [1966] AC 367 **64**
Condron [1997] 1 WLR 827 **122**
Constantine (Joseph) Steamship Line Ltd v Imperial Smelting Corp Ltd [1942] AC 54; [1941] 2 All ER 165 **30**
Conway v Rimmer [1968] AC 910 **193**
Cooke [1995] 1 Cr App Rep 318 **118**
Cowan [1996] QB 373; [1995] 4 All ER 939 **147, 153, 155**
Crawford [1998] 1 Cr App Rep 338 **159**
Crompton (Alfred) Amusement Machines Ltd v Customs and Excise Commissioners (No 2) [1974] AC 405 **196**

D [2009] EWCA Civ 2577 **87, 89**
Davies (1962) 1 WLR 1111 **184**
Davies v DPP [1954] AC 378 **92**
Davies v Health and Safety Executive [2002] EWCA Crim 2949 **23, 32, 35**
Dervish [2001] EWCA Crim 2789; [2002] 2 Cr App Rep 105 **114**
Desmond [1999] Crim LR 313 **166**
Devonport and Pirano (1996) 1 Cr App R 221 **78**
Dillon v R [1982] 2 WLR 538 **41**
Dix (1981) 74 Cr App Rep 306; [1982] Crim LR 302 **187**
Donald [2004] EWCA Crim 965 **138**
DPP, *ex parte* Kebilene (sub nom Kebiline) [2000] 2 AC 326; [1999] 3 WLR 972 **23, 24, 32, 35**
DPP v A and BC Chewing Gum Ltd [1968] 1 QB 159 **186, 188**
DPP v Boardman [1975] AC 421; [1974] 3 All ER 887 **139**
DPP v Camplin [1978] AC 705 **6, 8, 9**
DPP v Majewski [1977] AC 443; [1962] 3 All ER 97 **6, 8, 9**
Duff Development Co Ltd v Government of Kelantan [1924] AC 797 **13**
Duncan (1981) 73 Cr App R 359 **110**

Edwards [1975] QB 27 **33, 34**
Edwards [1991] 2 All ER 266 **172**
Edwards [2006] 1 Cr App Rep 31; [2005] EWCA Crim 1813 **128**
Elson (1994) *The Times*, 30 June **107**
Evans [1965] 2 QB 295 **92**
Exall (1866) 4 F & F 922 **144**

F [2005] EWCA Crim 493 **10**
FA [2015] EWCA Crim 209 **38, 43**
Fernandez, *ex parte* (1861) 10 CBNS 3 **43, 45, 48, 49**
Forbes [2001] 1 All ER 686 **95, 97**
Foster [2009] EWCA Crim 353 **135, 158**
Fulcher [1995] 2 Cr App R 251 **127**
Fulling [1987] QB 426 **101, 108, 114, 117**

Gadsby [2006] EWCA Crim 3206 **159**
Gayle [1999] 2 Cr App R 130 **97**
George v Davies [1911] 2 KB 445 **13–14**
Gibson (1887) 18 QBD 537 **81**
Gill [1963] 2 All ER 688 **118, 177**
Gilmore [2005] EWCA Crim 824 **166**
Glendarroch, The [1894] P 226 **31**
Goddard v Nationwide Building Society [1987] QB 670 **204**
Goss (2005) **127**
Gowland-Wynn [2002] 1 Cr App Rep 569; [2001] EWCA Crim 2715 **118–119**
Grannell (1990) 90 Cr App Rep 149 **101**
Grant (1996) 1 Cr App R 73 **6, 9, 15, 16, 78**

Grant v The Queen [2007] 1 AC 1; [2006] 2 WLR 835 **55**
Gray, Liggins, Riding and Rowlands (1995) 2 Cr App R 100 **78, 100**
Gray [2004] All ER (D) 358 **127, 130, 132**
Grayson [1993] Crim LR 864 **101**
Griffiths [1998] Crim LR 567 **9, 77**
Gummerson and Steadman [1999] Crim LR 680 **95, 97**
Gunewardene [1951] 2 KB 600 **74, 100, 102, 111**
Guney [1998] 2 Cr App R 242 **6, 9, 77**

H and Others (Minors) (Sexual Abuse: Standard of Proof), Re [1996] 1 All ER 1 **30–31**
Halpin [1996] Crim LR 112 **6, 9, 15, 17**
Hanson [2005] 1 WLR 3169 **128, 129, 130, 135, 139, 143, 144, 148, 151, 155, 158, 162, 163, 166**
Hardwicke [2000] EWCA Crim 60 **126**
Hasson [1997] Crim LR 579 **79**
Hayes [1977] 1 WLR 234 **45**
Hennessy (1978) 68 Cr App Rep 419 **200**
Hepworth [1955] 2 QB 600 **27**
Hersey [1998] Crim LR 281 **95, 97**
Hetherington v Hetherington (1887) 12 PD 12 **40**
Hickin and Others [1996] Crim LR 584 **98**
Highton [2006] 1 Cr App Rep 125; [2005] EWCA Crim 1985 **147–148, 155, 163**
Hoare [2004] EWCA Crim 784 **122**
Hornal v Neuberger Products [1957] 1 QB 247 **30**
Horncastle [2009] UKSC 14 **55, 58, 61**
Hoskyn v Commissioner of Police for the Metropolis [1979] AC 474 **50**
Howell [2003] EWCA Crim 01 **122**
Hunt [1987] AC 352 **23, 34**
Hurst [1995] 1 Cr App Rep 82 **183**

Islam [1999] 1 Cr App Rep 22 **89**
Ismail [1990] Crim LR 872 **109**

Jelen and Katz (1989) 90 Cr App Rep 456 **99, 101**
Johnson [1988] 1 WLR 1377 **199, 201**
Johnson [1995] 2 Cr App Rep 41 **91, 94, 139**
Johnstone [2003] 1 WLR 1736 **23, 24, 32, 35**
Jones and Others [1997] 2 Cr App R 119 **101**

Kearley [1992] 2 AC 228 **54, 58, 60**
Kelly [1992] Crim LR 181 **95, 97**
Khan (1981) 73 Cr App Rep 190 **45**
Khan (Sultan) [1997] AC 558; [1996] 2 **123, 125**
Knight [2003] EWCA Crim 1977 **122**
Kritz [1950] 1 KB 82 **25, 27**

L v DPP [2002] 2 All ER 854 **27, 28**
Lambert [2001] 3 All ER 577; [2002] 2 AC 545 **22, 23–24, 32, 35**
Lee [1996] 2 Cr App Rep 266 **138**
Levison v Patent Steam Carpet Cleaning Ltd [1978] QB 69 **31**
Lilley [2003] EWCA Crim 1789 **64**
Lobban v R [1995] 1 WLR 877 **118**
Lobell [1957] 1 QB 547 **28**
Loosely [2001] UKHL 53 **126**
Lovelock [1997] Crim LR 821 **79**
Lowery v R [1974] AC 85 **189**
Luca v Italy (2003) 36 EHRR 46 **55, 56, 57**
Lucas [1981] QB 720 **17, 65, 85, 94, 180, 181**
Lupien (1970) 9 DLR (3d) 1 **189**
Lydon [1987] Crim LR 407 **63, 64**

M (T) and Others [2000] 1 All ER 148 **127**
M [2009] EWCA Crim 618 **87**
Makanjuola (Oluwanfunso) [1995] 1 WLR 1348 **85, 86**
Makanjuola v Commissioner of Metropolitan Police [1992] 3 All ER 617 **197**
Makin v Attorney-General for New South Wales [1894] AC 57 **136**
Malashev [1997] Crim LR 587 **98**
Malindi v R [1967] 1 AC 439 **154, 163**
Maqsud Ali [1966] 1 QB 688 **68, 70, 123**
Marcus [2005] Crim LR 384 **98**
Marks v Beyfus (1890) 25 QBD 494 **199, 200, 201**
Martinez-Tobon [1994] 2 All ER 90; (1993) *The Times*, 1 December **102, 104**

Mason [1988] 1 WLR 139 **99, 109**
Matto v Wolverhampton Crown Court [1987] RTR 337 **121, 124, 125**
Mawaz Khan v R [1967] 1 AC 454 **63, 65, 68, 69, 91, 93**
McGovern [1991] Crim LR 124; (1990) 92 Cr App R 228 **107, 109**
McIntosh [1992] Crim LR 651 **68, 69**
McLean (1967) 52 Cr App Rep 80 **80, 81**
McQuaker v Goddard [1940] 1 KB 687 **14**
Mertens [2004] EWCA Crim 2252; [2005] Crim LR 301 **149, 159**
Michael, The [1979] 1 Lloyd's Rep 17; [1978] 1 WLR 411 **30**
Middleton [2000] All ER (D) 453 **94**
Miller v Howe [1969] 3 All ER 451 **64**
Miller v Minister of Pensions [1947] 2 All ER 372 **30**
Mills (2003) unreported **81–82**
Moghal (1977) 65 Cr App Rep 56 **92**
Mountford [1999] Crim LR 575 **118**
Mullen v Hackney LBC [1997] 1 **12**
Murray v DPP (1993) 97 Cr App **102, 104**
Murrell [2005] EWCA Crim 382 **149, 159**
Myers v DPP [1965] AC 1001 **59, 60, 80, 81**

Napper [1996] Crim LR 591 **147**
Nash [2004] EWCA Crim 2696 **96**
Neil [1994] Crim LR 441 **107, 109**
Nelson [1998] 2 Cr App Rep 399 **110**
Nickolson [1999] Crim LR 61 **119**
Nye v Niblett [1918] 1 KB 23 **14**

O [2006] 2 Cr App R 405 **181**
Oceanbulk Shipping & Trading SA v TMT Asia Ltd and Others [2010] UKSC 44 **203**
Osbourne; R v Virtue [1973] 1 All ER 649 **80, 81**
Oyesiku (1971) 56 Cr App Rep 240 **176, 177**

Paraskeva (1982) 76 Cr App Rep 162; [1983] Crim LR 186 **175**
Paris [1994] Crim LR 361; (1992) 97 Cr App Rep 99 **105, 117**
Parker [1995] Crim LR 233 **101**
Patel v Comptroller of Customs [1966] AC 356 **63, 64**
Patrick [1999] All ER (D) 532 **94**
Pattinson and Exley [1996] 1 Cr App R 51 **94, 96**
Payton [2006] EWCA Crim 1226 **127**
Pearce (1979) 69 Cr App R 365 **78**
Peart v Bolckow Vaughan & Co Ltd [1925] 1 KB 399 **13**
Petkar [2003] EWCA Crim 2668; [2004] 1 Cr App Rep 270 **91, 93, 115, 119, 122, 177**
Phillips (1936) 26 Cr App Rep 17 **174**
Pieterson [1995] 1 WLR 293 **68**
Podola [1960] 1 QB 325 **27**
Popat (1998) 2 Cr App Rep 208 **97**
Popat (No 2) [2000] Crim LR 54 **96**
Price [2004] EWCA Crim 1359; [2005] Crim LR 304 **149, 159**

Qadir [1998] Crim LR 828 **94, 96**
Quinn [1990] Crim LR 581 **109**

Rankine [1986] QBD 861 **199, 201**
Redgrave (1981) 74 Cr App Rep 10 **149, 150, 151**
Renda [2005] EWCA Crim 2826; [2006] 2 All ER 553 **128**
Rennie [1982] 1 All ER 385 **111, 113**
Reynolds [1989] Crim LR 220 **189**
Reynolds v Llanelly Tinplate Co Ltd [1948] 1 All ER 140 **12**
Rice [1963] 1 QB 857 **63, 64, 80, 81**
Roberts [1942] 1 All ER 187 **174**
Roberts [1997] 1 Cr App R 217 **99**
Robertson [1968] 3 All ER 557 **27**
Robinson [2003] EWCA Crim 2219 **122**
Robinson (Dennis) [2005] EWCA Crim 3233; [2006] 1 Cr App **149, 159**
Robinson (Wayne) [2006] Crim LR 427 **66**
Rodley [1913] 3 KB 468 **141, 142**
Rogers v Home Secretary [1973] AC 388 **196**
Romeo [2004] 1 Cr App R 417 **181**

Rowton (1865) Le & Ca 520 at 529; 169 ER 1497; [1865] All ER Rep 549 **149, 150, 151, 174**
Rudd (1948) 32 Cr App Rep 138 **102**
Rush and Tompkins Ltd v Greater London Council [1989] AC 1280 **192**
Ryder [1993] Crim LR 601 **139**

Salabiaku v France (1988) 13 EHRR 379 **20, 21, 22, 23**
Samuel [1988] QB 615; [1988] 2 WLR 920 **117**
Sang [1980] AC 402 **65, 124, 125, 128, 130, 131, 143, 145, 148, 155, 157, 162, 165**
Savage v Chief Constable of the Hampshire Constabulary [1997] 2 All ER 631 **196**
Sellick [2005] 1 WLR 3257 **55**
Selvey v DPP [1970] AC 304 **158**
Senat v Senat [1965] 2 WLR 981 **178**
Sharp [1988] 1 All ER 65 **87, 89, 101, 102, 107, 110, 111**
Shaw (1888) 16 Cox CC 503 **173, 174**
Sheldrake v DPP [2004] QB 487 **23, 24**
Silverlock [1894] 2 QB 766 **189**
Singh [2006] EWCA Crim 660 **54**
Slater [1995] 1 Cr App R 584 **94, 96**
Slowcombe [1991] Crim LR 198 **199, 200**
Somanathan [2005] EWCA Crim 2866; (2005) *The Times*, 18 November **139**
Sparks v R [1964] AC 964; [1964] 1 All ER 727 **59, 61**
Spencer [1987] AC 128; [1986] 2 All ER 928 **85**
Stagg (1994) unreported **109**
Stanton [2004] EWCA Crim 490 **96**
Stone [2005] EWCA Crim 105 **85, 91, 92**
Subramaniam v Public Prosecutor [1956] 1 WLR 965 **54**

Tahed [2004] EWCA Crim 1220 **89**
Taylor (Stuart) [2006] 2 Cr App R 14 **74**
Taylor, Weaver and Donovan (1928) 21 Cr App Rep 20 **67**
Taylor v Chief Constable of Cheshire [1987] 1 All ER 225; [1986] 1 WLR 1479 **70**
T(D) [2009] EWCA Crim 1213 **57, 61**
Teeluck and John [2005] 1 WLR 2421 **127**
Teper v R [1952] AC 480 **58, 59**
Thomas v UK (2005) 41 EHRR SE 11 **57**
Thompson (1976) 64 Cr App Rep 96 **178**
Thompson v R [1918] AC 221 **140**
Thornton [1995] 1 Cr App R 578 **94**
Tomlin v Standard Telephones and Cables Ltd [1969] 3 All ER 201 **192**
Toohey v Commissioner for Metropolitan Police [1965] AC 595 **186, 189**
Toussaint-Collins [2009] EWCA Crim 316 **69**
Tripodi v R [1961] 104 CLR 1 **100**
Truscott, Re [1967] SCR 309 **142**
Turnbull [1977] QB 224 **85, 86, 94, 96–97, 98, 137**
Turner [1975] QB 834 **8, 120, 130, 131, 187**

Valentine (1996) 2 Cr App R 213 **180, 181**
Vye [1993] 1 WLR 471 **127, 130, 132, 149, 150, 152, 153, 180**

W [2010] UKSC 12 **43**
Walsh (1989) 91 Cr App Rep 161 **113**
Walters [1979] RTR 220 **72**
Walters v R [1969] 2 AC 26 **25, 27**
Warner (1993) 96 Cr App R 324 **79**
Watkins, Watkins v Watkins, Re [1953] 1 WLR 1323 **47**
Waugh v British Railways Board [1980] AC 521 **203, 204**
Weir [2005] EWCA Crim 2866; [2006] 2 All ER 570 136 **128, 130, 131, 140**
Wetherall v Harrison [1976] 1 QB 773 **12**
Wickham (1971) 55 Cr App Rep 199 **147**
Willis [1916] 1 KB 933 **92**
Woolmington v DPP [1935] AC 462 **22**
Wright [1994] Crim LR 55 **15, 16, 17, 77**

Xhabri [2006] 1 All ER 776; [2005] EWCA Crim 3135 **55, 57**

Y [2008] EWCA Crim 10 **73, 74, 100, 118**

# Table of Legislation

## Statutes


Children Act 1989
  s 96(2) **43, 44, 45**
Civil Evidence Act 1968 **81**
Civil Evidence Act 1972 **81**
  s 1(1) **184**
  s 3(2) **184**
Civil Evidence Act 1995 **71**
  s 1(1) **53**
  s 1(2) **53**
Civil Partnership Act 2004
  s 84(1) **38**
Contempt of Court Act 1981
  s 10 **192**
Coroners and Justice Act 2009 **171**
Criminal Evidence Act 1898 **127, 167, 168, 169**
  s 1(f)(ii) **154, 155, 158, 163**
  s 1(f)(iii) **159**
Criminal Justice Act 1967
  s 10 **16**
Criminal Justice Act 1988
  s 30 **86**
  s 23 **71**
  s 24 **71**
  s 34(2) **85**
  s 139 **27**
Criminal Justice Act 2003 **55, 58, 59, 79, 81, 82, 137, 168, 169**
  Pt II
    Chap 1 **127, 129, 134, 145, 154**
    Chap 2 **53, 71**
  s 25 **71**
  s 26 **71**
  s 98 **130, 131, 134, 138, 140, 141**
  s 99(1) **159**
  s 100 **146, 174**
  s 100(1) **147**
  s 100(1)(a) **173, 174**
  s 100(1)(b) **173, 175**
  s 100(4) **147, 175**
  s 101 **138, 146**
  s 101(1) **140**
  s 101(1)(a) **128**
  s 101(1)(b) **128**
  s 101(1)(c) **127, 133, 134, 138**
  s 101(1)(d) **17, 127, 128, 130, 131, 132, 133, 135, 138, 139, 141, 143, 146, 148, 150, 151, 152, 153, 155, 156, 157, 158, 159, 161, 162, 164**
  s 101(1)(e) **128, 146, 148, 156, 157, 158, 159, 162**
  s 101(1)(f) **128, 153, 154, 155, 161, 162, 163**
  s 101(1)(g) **128, 146, 147, 148, 153, 155, 157, 158, 161, 162, 163, 164, 165, 173, 175**
  s 101(3) **128, 132, 135, 138, 148, 150, 152, 153, 155, 157, 159, 162, 163, 165**
  s 101(3)(1)(d) **163**
  s 101(3)(1)(g) **163**
  s 101(4) **128**
  s 102 **134, 138**
  s 102(1)(b) **130**
  s 103 **127, 148**
  s 103(1)(a) **17, 131, 133, 135, 157, 158, 163**
  s 103(1)(b) **130, 133, 158, 163, 164, 165**
  s 103(1)(d) **163**
  s 103(1)(f) **163**
  s 103(2) **157, 165**
  s 103(3) **141, 143, 148, 162, 163, 165**
  s 103(4)(b) **165**

s 103(5) **165**
s 104 **128, 159**
s 105 **128**
s 105(1) **153, 154**
s 105(2) **153, 154**
s 105(2)(a) **154**
s 105(3) **155, 162**
s 105(4) **154, 155**
s 105(5) **154, 155**
s 105(6) **163**
s 106 **128, 158**
s 106(1)(b) **162**
s 106(2) **165**
s 109 **139**
s 112 **130, 131, 141**
s 112(1) **134, 138, 140, 143**
s 114 **54, 57, 71, 72, 73, 118**
s 114(1) **53, 54, 74, 80**
s 114(1)(a) **74**
s 114(1)(b) **74**
s 114(1)(c) **74**
s 114(1)(d) **61, 64, 74, 100, 114**
s 114(2) **61, 74**
s 115(2) **53**
s 115(3) **53, 54, 61, 63, 65, 70**
s 116 **54, 62, 65, 71, 72, 73, 75, 87**
s 116(1) **63, 65**
s 116(1)(a) **65, 87, 88**
s 116(1)(b) **65**
s 116(2) **65**
s 116(2)(a) **88**
s 116(2)(c) **75**
s 116(2)(d) **75**
s 116(2)(e) **178**
s 116(4) **178**
s 117 **72, 73, 75**
s 117(2)(c) **75**
s 118 **71, 72, 73, 74, 91, 93**
s 118(1) **74, 92**
s 118(1)(5) **74**
s 118(1)(7) **78**
s 118(1)(a) **74**
s 118(d) **75**
s 119 **75, 171**
s 119(1) **178**
s 120 **75, 171, 180, 181**
s 120(2) **177**
s 120(3) **178**
s 120(4) **87, 88, 172, 174, 180, 181**
s 120(5) **174**
s 120(7) **87, 88, 171, 172, 180**
s 120(7)(c) **180**
s 120(7)(d) **171**
s 120(7)(e) **88, 180–181**
s 120(8) **171**
s 121 **73, 87, 88**
s 121(1) **62, 75**
s 121(1)(a) **75**
s 121(1)(b) **75**
s 121(1)(c) **75**
ss 121–125 **72**
s 126(2) **135**
s 127 **183**
s 139 **27**
s 139(1) **177, 178**
Sch 37, Part 6 **71**

Criminal Justice and Public Order Act 1994 **86**
s 32 **85**
s 34 **86, 91, 93, 102, 103, 105, 106, 114, 115, 116, 118, 119, 121, 122, 176, 177**
s 34(2A) **91, 93, 114, 118**
s 35 **102, 103, 104, 105, 161**
s 35(3) **146, 147, 161**
s 36 **102, 103, 106**
s 37 **102, 103, 106**
s 38 **102**

Criminal Procedure Act 1865
s 3 **178**
s 6 **175**

Criminal Procedure (Insanity) Act 1964
s 4(1) **27**

Criminal Procedure Investigations Act 1996
s 8 **194**

Evidence Amendment Act 1853
s 1 **43, 44, 45**

Family Law Reform Act 1969
s 26 **42, 46, 48**

Fatal Accidents Act 1976 **203**

Health and Safety at Work Act 1974
s 40 **22**

Homicide Act 1957
s 2 **184, 186, 187, 188**

Human Rights Act 1998 **20, 22, 55, 57, 58**
s 2(1)(a) **56**
Law of Property Act 1925
s 184 **46, 47**
s 184(1) **39, 41**
Magistrates' Courts Act 1980
s 101 **32, 33–34**
Marriage (Same Sex Couples) Act 2013 **49, 51**
Police and Criminal Evidence Act 1984
s 58 **109, 117**
s 58(8) **113, 117**
s 58(8)(c) **117**
s 62(10) **105**
s 62(11) **86**
s 67(11) **85**
s 71(1) **73**
s 73 **175**
s 74 **138**
s 76 **99, 102, 106, 107, 108, 109, 111, 112, 116, 117**
s 76(1) **74**
s 76(2) **101, 112**
s 76(2)(a) **101, 116, 117, 118**
s 76(2)(b) **99, 108, 111, 113, 114, 116, 117, 118**
s 76(4) **114, 116, 118**
s 76(8) **101, 108, 117**
s 76A(1) **160**
s 78 **55, 65, 85, 99, 101, 102, 107, 108, 109, 111, 112, 113, 116, 117, 118, 120, 121, 123, 124, 125, 126, 130, 131, 136, 138, 141**
s 78(1) **65, 95, 97, 117, 118, 120, 121, 122–123, 128, 129, 138, 143, 155, 163**
s 80 **38, 43, 44, 48, 49, 51**
s 80(3) **48**
s 80(3)(a) **43, 44**
s 82(1) **91, 93, 100, 107, 108, 112, 114, 117**
s 82(3) **124, 125**
Presumption of Death Act 2013 **39**
Prevention of Crime Act 1953
s 1 **25, 27**
Proceeds of Crime Act 2002
s 6 **76**
Rehabilitation of Offenders Act 1974 **157, 158**
Sexual Offences Act 2003
ss 75–77 **38**
Theft Act 1968
s 8 **44**
s 27(3) **129**
Workmen's Compensation Act 1925 **12–13**
Workmen's Compensation Act 1943 **12–13**
Youth Justice and Criminal Evidence Act 1999 **37–38, 43**
s 41 **8, 9, 10, 87, 89, 180, 182**
s 41(1) **89**
s 41(3) **88, 182**
s 41(3)(a) **182**
s 41(3)(b) **87, 89, 182**
s 41(3)(c) **87, 182**
s 41(3)(c)(i) **89**
ss 41–43 **86, 171, 172**
s 53(1) **43, 44, 91, 93**
s 53(3) **93**
ss 53–56 **38**
s 55(2) **91, 93**
s 55(2)(a) **43, 44**

## Secondary Legislation

Civil Procedure Rules 1998
r 31.20 **191, 204**
Codes of Practice (PACE)
Code C **101, 107, 112, 116**
Annex B **118**
para 3 **113, 117**
para 1.1 **109**
para 4.2 **108–109**
para 4.3 **109**
para 8.1 **113**
para 11.2 **109**
para 12.6 **117**
para 12.8 **117**
Code D **86, 94**
Annex A **85**
Annex B **85**
Annex E **85**
para 3.12 **95, 97, 98**
Code E **114**
Criminal Justice Act 2003 (Categories of Offences) Order 2004 (SI 2004/3346)
Pt I, Sched 177 **165**

## European Legislation

European Convention on the Protection of Human Rights and Fundamental Freedoms
Art 6 **10, 21, 55, 56, 57, 58, 61, 125, 199**
Art 6(2) **20, 21, 22, 24, 26, 32, 33, 35**
Art 6(3) **57**
Art 6(3)(d) **55, 56–57, 61**

# Guide to the Companion Website

## www.routledge.com/cw/revision

Visit the Law Revision website to discover a comprehensive range of resources designed to enhance your learning experience.

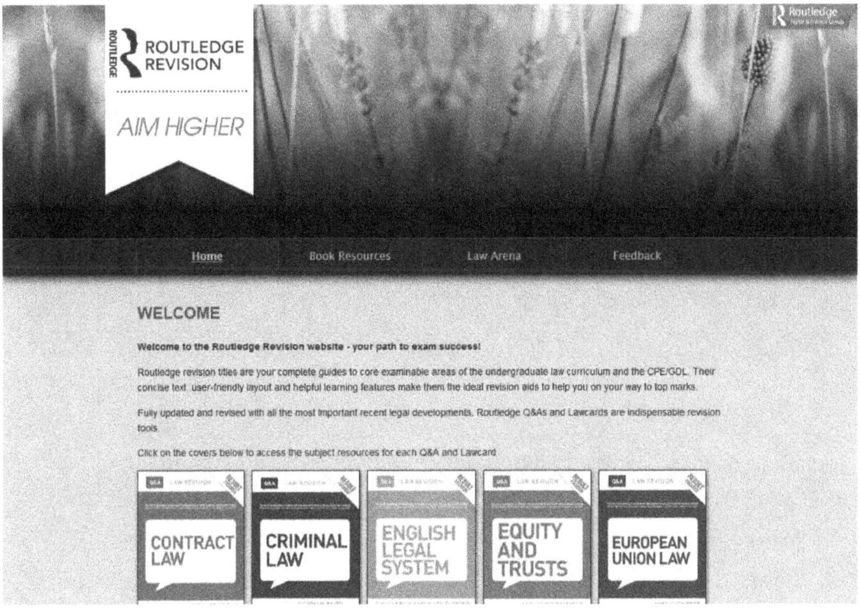


### The Good, The Fair, & The Ugly

Good essays are the gateway to top marks. This interactive tutorial provides sample essays together with voice-over commentary and tips for successful exam essays, written by our Q&A authors themselves.

### Multiple Choice Questions

Knowledge is the foundation of every good essay. Focusing on key examination themes, these MCQs have been written to test your knowledge and understanding of each subject in the book.

### Bonus Q&As

Having studied our exam advice, put your revision into practice and test your essay writing skills with our additional online questions and answers.

# Introduction

This textbook is intended to aid those students studying the law of evidence who may have acquired some knowledge, but still feel that they need more confidence in handling it correctly in assessments. You will be shown how to apply the law to both essay and problem questions. There is an emphasis on problem questions in this textbook so that you can gain as much practice as possible in reasoning with facts as well as law. The practising lawyer is concerned most of the time with facts rather than law. Even in law examinations, analysis of a factual situation is essential to the application of the law, and it is often at this stage that students go astray.

When considering problems of evidence law it may be useful to remember that these can be of two kinds. First, of course, there are questions of admissibility – a traditional concern of evidence law. But the law can also have something to say about how a trial judge should direct a jury in relation to evidence that has been admitted. This was originally a matter for the judge's discretion, but discretion has predominantly given way to rules. There are now things that a judge must say, for example, about evidence of a witness's identification, or about a defendant's silence when questioned by police. If a problem question ends with words such as, 'Discuss the evidential issues that arise', remember that this requires you to tell the examiner about judicial directions as well as admissibility. Further, you must know not only the principal occasions that require a judicial direction but also the essential elements of the appropriate direction. For example, students who tell the examiner that a *Turnbull* direction will be necessary will gain little credit unless they are able to say what is required and why. This textbook provides examples of the kind of questions that are usually asked in an examination, together with model answers and notes about their structure. I have covered the topics that are usually examined. The answers are about the length of an essay that a good student would expect to write under examination conditions. I am aware, however, that the traditional requirement of answering four questions in three hours may not be universally followed. Therefore, I have provided a fuller answer where it seemed to be useful to do so. The final chapter has some hints on revision and examination techniques.

I hope that this book may be of value as a way of achieving an overall view of this subject. The emphasis on criminal evidence is intentional; it is here that the subject is most lively and this is reflected in examination questions. I hope that the book will be useful as a means of revision, provided it is remembered that revision of particular topics should be a process that continues throughout the year.

I considered dedicating it 'to those who have better things to do', but gravitas prevailed. I like to think, though, that it will be helpful not only to those whose devotion to their mistress the law is total, but to those who spread their favours more widely: to student poets and musicians, to artists, actors and oarsmen and to many more. Nor do I forget those mature students, often with widely different concerns in their daily work, whose opportunity for study is inevitably limited. To all my readers I wish enjoyment and success.

*Dr Charanjit Singh*
*July 2015*

## Common Pitfalls

The most common mistake made when using Questions & Answers books for revision is to memorise the model answers provided and try to reproduce them in exams. This approach is a sure-fire pitfall, likely to result in a poor overall mark because your answer will not be specific enough to the particular question on your exam paper, and there is also a danger that reproducing an answer in this way would be treated as plagiarism. You must instead be sure to read the question carefully, to identify the issues and problems it is asking you to address and to answer it directly in your exam. If you take our examiners' advice and use your Q&A to focus on your question-answering skills and understanding of the law applied, you will be ready for whatever your exam paper has to offer!

# 1 Basic Concepts

## INTRODUCTION

The biggest obstacle to doing well in an evidence examination is failure to realise that this is very largely a practical subject, and that when you are faced with a problem question you need to think as carefully about the facts as about the law – perhaps even more carefully, because quite often what you think about the facts will affect the legal position. It would therefore be a good idea to make it a rule that you think about a problem question first as a story.

Somebody is trying to prove something. How is he/she doing this? First, he should have in mind a clear idea of what is to be proved. Suppose we take a famous murder trial that took place in 1910 – that of Dr Crippen. The prosecution was trying to prove that Crippen had murdered his wife. The story, according to them, was that Crippen had fallen in love with his young secretary, Ethel Le Neve, and had decided to kill his wife so as to leave him free to marry Ethel. One night, therefore, he put poison in a glass of stout – his wife's regular nightcap. The poison might have been sufficient to kill her, or it might merely have rendered her unconscious. At any rate, by the time Crippen had finished with the body she would have been dead. According to the prosecution, he cut the flesh from the bones and buried it in pieces in the cellar of the house where they lived. He burned the bones, and the head was never found. To explain his wife's absence, he told friends at first that she was staying with relations. Later, when the police began to make inquiries, he told them that she had left him and that he had been too embarrassed to tell people this. Crippen had not yet been arrested, and shortly after his interview with the police, he hurriedly left the country with Ethel Le Neve. Meanwhile, the police dug up the cellar floor and discovered the human remains that had been buried there. Crippen was followed and brought back to England to stand trial.

You will know what constitutes murder from the study of English criminal law. But from the standpoint of someone studying evidence, you must now decide precisely what it was that the prosecution had to prove in this particular case.

The first thing they had to prove was that Mrs Crippen was dead. Crippen maintained throughout that his wife had left him and that he knew nothing of the remains in the cellar. It was therefore necessary for the prosecution to establish that the remains were those of Mrs Crippen. They had also to show that her husband had killed her intentionally.

It is at this stage that the prosecution had to start thinking carefully in terms of relevance. Ideally, each item of evidence they presented should have had a probative job to do in the overall task of proving that Crippen had murdered his wife. For example, by proving that Mrs Crippen had had the mark of an operation on her body, and by showing that one of the pieces of buried flesh had the same mark, the prosecution was able to establish that the remains in the cellar were those of Mrs Crippen and that therefore she was in fact dead.

The evidence of Crippen's flight was also relevant, but it's worth pausing to consider why this was so. What probative job did this item of evidence do for the prosecution? The prosecution suggested that it showed guilty knowledge. But why should it do that? One answer is that people who suddenly leave the country when the police are making inquiries about them are likely to do so because they fear that their criminal activities are about to be discovered.

Notice two important points at this stage. The first is that if you press sufficiently the question of why an item of evidence is relevant, your explanation will often take the form of a generalisation about the way things are in the world *which itself may or may not be true*. We have tried to make our explanatory generalisation about people who run away appear true by using the words 'are likely to do so'. It leaves room for alternative explanations – they may be innocent but fear that the police will frame them; they may have a rich aunt dying in Brazil – but I put my explanation forward as one that is likely. If I am right in this, it follows that the evidence of the flight was relevant, admissible and had significant probative weight.

Now, let's look at a question of relevance in another famous murder case. Edith Thompson and her husband were not very happily married. They took in a young lodger, Freddie Bywaters. One night, when Mr and Mrs Thompson were walking home, Freddie sprang out from a place where he had been waiting and stabbed Mr Thompson to death. But the prosecution story was that Freddie was not the only culprit. He and Edith, it was alleged, were having an affair, and she had plotted the murder with him and had encouraged him to carry it out.

Among the many items of evidence relied on at trial by the prosecution was the disparity in age between Freddie and Edith. She was 28 years old at the time of the murder; he was only 20. What was the relevance of this? What probative job did this information do? At the time, nobody seems to have had any clear thoughts on the matter. But we need to ask this question: what generalisation about the way things are in the world has to be true for this item of evidence to be relevant? Here is a suggestion: 'In a sexual relationship, an older woman is likely to dominate a younger man.' That, if true, would help the prosecution because it would add to the probability that Edith persuaded Freddie to murder Mr Thompson. But *is* it true? If it is not true, and no satisfactory substitute can be found, then surely the evidence is irrelevant, and so inadmissible. (See W Twining, *Theories of Evidence: Bentham and Wigmore*, 1985, pp. 143–144; W Twining, *Rethinking Evidence: Exploratory Essays*, 1994, pp. 290–293.)

We said earlier that there were two important points to be made about the sort of answer that we suggested to the question of why evidence of Crippen's flight was relevant at his trial. One was the point that we have just been making about the *form* the answer takes – that of a generalisation. The second important point is this. The weaker a generalisation is, the more likely it is to be true. But the weaker the generalisation, the less probative weight will attach to the item of evidence in question. This may be very important where admissibility depends on assessing the probative weight of a piece of evidence and the improper prejudicial effect that it might have on a jury if they heard it. For example, some cats are Siamese. You have three cats. But, this is not much evidence that you have a Siamese cat. One or more of them *may* be a Siamese, but the likelihood is not great because there are many other breeds, as well as non-pedigree cats.

Later, you will see the importance in other areas of evidence law of the question: what is the probative job that this item of evidence is put forward to do? (Hearsay is a particularly good example. See Chapters 4 and 5.) But being able to answer this question, and being able to say why an item of evidence is relevant by pointing to an appropriate generalisation, can be done only if you have first thought carefully about the *story* the examiner is telling you in the particular problem question.

If you get a question directly on relevance in the examination, it will almost certainly be an essay question involving theory, and I have tried in the answer to Question 1 to give some idea of how such an essay might be tackled. But you don't *have* to be able to write an answer to a theoretical question about relevance to do well in an examination. What you *do* have to be able to do is understand how the idea *works*.

As well as relevance, there are a few other basic concepts that you ought to know about; we have referred to these in the Checklist and you should find them adequately dealt with in your textbook. You will find that this is a subject that has attracted quite a complicated terminology, about the use of which there is not complete agreement on the part of either judges or writers. A lot of this terminology can in practice be avoided, but you should take care to understand how the writer of the textbook you are using employs his terminology, and you should be particularly careful when reading cases to make sure that you understand what a particular judge is getting at by the language he uses.

## Checklist

**Students should be familiar with the following areas:**

- relevance;
- admissibility;
- what facts are in issue in criminal cases;
- how to discover what facts are in issue in a civil case;
- formal admissions in civil and criminal cases;
- judicial notice.

# QUESTION 1

Introducing a concept of legal relevance in the law of evidence is undesirable.

- **Discuss, with reference to examples.**

## How to Read this Question

Questions such as this often appear as essays in assessments; it requires a discussion of 'legal relevance' with examples. You are required to weigh up the *theory* with how the rules work in *practice* – thus, examples are important and a failure to include them will lose you marks.

## How to Answer this Question

This essay question requires you to discuss one of the most contentious principles in the law of evidence – relevance. Start by outlining the two different ways in which a legal concept can be 'useful': one is connected with what the law is, and the other with what the law ought to be. This essay question raises a classic problem on which Thayer and Wigmore, two great American writers on evidence, had different views; these are outlined in the answer. You should highlight the fact that there are cases where judges have laid down rules about what is or is not relevant and at least one occasion where Parliament has also tried to do so. Furthermore, mention should be made of the practice of the courts in rejecting evidence of minimal weight on the ground that it is 'irrelevant'. The main thrust of the argument is that none of this justifies acknowledging a concept of 'legal relevance' in existing law because of:

- the impossibility of defining such a concept, and
- the difficulty in developing a body of case law on the subject.

In addition, such a concept would be undesirable because:

- any body of case law that was developed would be cumbersome and restrictive, making it even more difficult than is presently the case for the law to respond to changing conditions.

In summary, your answer should make reference to the following:

- two ways in which a legal concept can be 'useful';
- give a brief outline of the argument to be put forward;
- Thayer's rejection of 'legal relevance' and Wigmore's contrary view;
- judicial decisions about relevance, for example, *DPP v Camplin* (1978) and *DPP v Majewski* (1977);
- the connection made by courts between relevance and weight;
- the apparent 'rules' on relevance: *Grant* (1996); *Halpin* (1996); *Guney* (1998);
- the difficulties presented by 'legal relevance'.

## Up for Debate

One of the major contemporary debates relates to the codification of English evidence law and the difficulties that it presents. The concept of legal relevance, defined by statute or a code, exemplifies the problems faced – highlighting this would show a greater understanding about the issues. Reading cases such as *R v Barry* (Adrian Joseph) [2010] EWCA Crim 195; [2010] 2 All ER 1004 (CA (Crim Div)) will reinforce your knowledge in relation to 'relevance'.

## Answer Structure

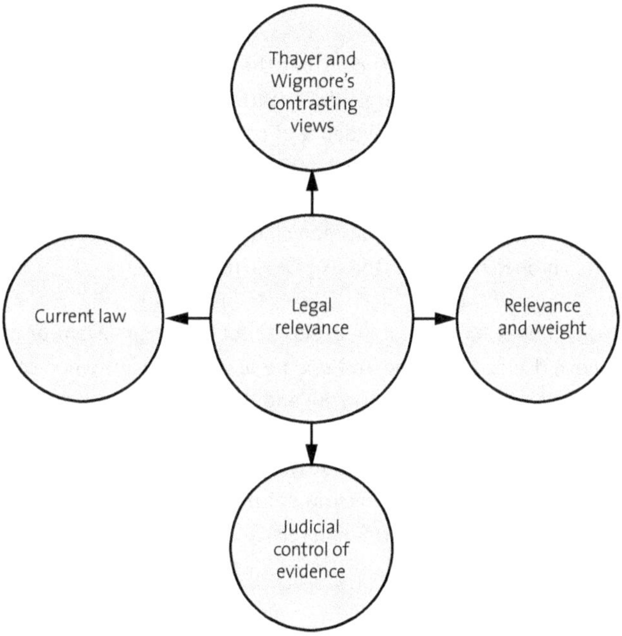


*This diagram shows the main points to consider in relation to a legal concept of relevance.*

# ANSWER

A legal concept may be useful because it serves to clarify the law as it stands and therefore our understanding of it, perhaps because it has become complex and unclear because of the piecemeal way in which it has developed, or, if it were to be introduced, it would improve the state of the law by closing any loopholes. In this essay I shall argue that a concept of legal relevance is scarcely to be found in the existing state of the law, and that it would not be useful to introduce it.[1]

1 This is a short and clear introduction that identifies the main thrust of the argument. It sets the course of the argument presented by outlining that the current law does not provide for a concept of legal relevance.

Thayer defined the law of evidence as 'a set of rules and principles affecting judicial investigations into questions of fact'. He also pointed out that these rules and principles do not regulate the process of reasoning, save to the extent that they help the selection of the factual material upon which the processes of reasoning are to operate. In addition to prescribing the manner of presenting evidence, and fixing the qualifications and privileges of witnesses, these rules and principles determine what classes of things shall not be received in evidence. However, there is one principle of exclusion that Thayer described as not so much a rule of evidence as a presupposition involved in the very conception of a rational system of evidence: that is the principle which forbids receiving anything irrelevant.[2] According to Thayer, the law furnishes no test of relevance. For this it tacitly refers to logic and general experience, with the presumption that lawyers have knowledge of these principles.

In contrast, Wigmore questioned the idea that the law furnished no test of relevance, arguing that although relevance is originally a matter of logic and common sense, there are still many instances in which the evidence of particular facts as bearing on particular issues has been so often the subject of discussion in courts of law, and so often ruled upon, that the united logic of a great many judges and lawyers may be said to furnish evidence of the sense common to a great many individuals, and so to acquire the authority of law. It is thus proper, he argued, to talk of legal relevance.[3]

In some instances judges have laid down rules about what is relevant or irrelevant. For example, they have decided that age and sex are always relevant when considering the defence of provocation (*DPP v Camplin* (1978)) and that intoxication is, as a matter of law, irrelevant in considering whether the *mens rea* for a crime of basic intent was present (*DPP v Majewski* (1977)). In **s 41** of the **Youth Justice and Criminal Evidence Act 1999**, Parliament attempted to lay down what a government minister in the House of Lords referred to as 'a statutory framework for determining relevance' in trials where a sexual offence is alleged.[4]

Other than specific rules such as these, it is necessary to take into account the practice of the courts in rejecting evidence that has minimal weight on the ground that it is therefore 'irrelevant'. The contention is that this evidence falls short of a minimum requirement of something that could be called 'legal relevance'. There are valid reasons as to why evidence of very slight weight should be excluded, whereas in other circumstances, for instance in research, such data would be justifiably used. The criminal justice system has to make some concessions in terms of what Justice Holmes referred to as 'the shortness of life', as

2 Cf. *Turner* (1975), per Lawton LJ: 'Relevance, however, does not result in evidence being admissible: it is a condition precedent to admissibility.'

3 Often students do not outline the opposing argument, making the answer less holistic. In this paragraph Wigmore's competing argument is presented; examiners will give credit for this.

4 Discussing the fact that judges have laid down which issues are relevant or irrelevant in certain circumstances demonstrates the varying practices and highlights the varying approaches that are taken to the problem that is evidential relevance and its policy considerations.

well as to the financial resources of the litigants or the legal aid fund. If the field of judicial enquiry were too wide it may make decisions more unreliable because a mass of evidence would more readily lead to complexity and confusion.[5]

It is also possible for the courts to develop something that can appear at first glance to be a rule about relevance in a particular type of situation, but which is really something else. For instance, over the last few years there has been a cluster of cases concerning the precise significance that should be attached to the discovery of large sums of cash in the possession of persons who are charged with possession of drugs with the intent to supply. The Court of Appeal stated in *Grant* (1996) that if there was any possible reason other than drug dealing for the defendant's possession of cash, then the finding of the cash was to be treated as irrelevant, and juries should be so directed.

In *Halpin* (1996) the Court of Appeal stated that evidence of a defendant's possession of large amounts of money, or of his extravagant lifestyle, could not be relevant where the issue in the case was possession, rather than intent to supply. This was later rejected in *Guney* (1998), where the Court of Appeal said that although evidence of cash or life-style might only rarely be relevant where there was a charge of simple possession of drugs, such evidence could not be excluded as irrelevant as a matter of law. The relevance of any item of evidence is to be decided 'not on abstract legal theory but on the circumstances of each individual case' (see also *Griffiths* (1998)). It appears that the courts are reluctant to acknowledge a concept of 'legal relevance' that is higher and stricter than logical relevance. In fact, there are two notable difficulties that lie in the way of such a development.[6]

The first difficulty is that such a concept would defy definition. The second is that since each case would be decided on its own facts, there would be considerable difficulty in developing a body of case law about what was legally relevant. Thus, *DPP v Camplin* and *DPP v Majewski* are better seen as cases that define the substantive law in relation to particular offences rather than in demonstrating a concept such as 'legal relevance'.[7]

Despite the language of some judges, there seems to be little support for the proposition that a concept of legal relevance can be found in the law because there appear to be good reasons why such a concept should not be recognised. There is an inherent conflict between a theory that all logically relevant evidence should be admitted unless excluded by a clear ground of policy, and a theory of legal relevance, which would require a

5 Cf. the observations of Lord Bridge in *Blastland* (1986).

6 Providing examples that the courts are unwilling or at least reluctant to acknowledge a concept of legal relevance supports the argument that the courts considered creating this as undesirable.

7 But see **s 41** of the **Youth Justice and Criminal Evidence Act 1999**. It looks very much as if the government accepted that some facts can be logically relevant, but, to preserve a 'balance' between the interests of the complainant and the defendant, they are not allowed to be legally relevant.

minimum quantity of probative value for each item of evidence in any particular case. There is a real danger that a concept of legal relevance, if consistently applied, would exclude logically relevant evidence unless legal precedent authorised its admission. If, despite these difficulties, a body of case law were to develop then it is likely to give rise to a large number of cumbersome rules and exceptions. The second reason why a concept of legal relevance ought not to be recognised relates to flexibility. Case law often results in limitation, so in terms of relevance this would make it even more difficult to adapt the law to continually changing circumstances.[8]

The decisions of judges about relevance are subjective and often reflect the prevailing value judgements of the society in which they live. Relevance can become a useful instrument for discarding arguments and evidence that challenge important, though perhaps unexpressed, values. For instance, the courts upheld a notion of freedom of contract, which allowed them to argue that an aggrieved worker could have protected his position by insisting on the inclusion of an appropriate contractual term. Here, evidence of the inequality in the bargaining power of the parties would have been ruled 'irrelevant'. This is exemplified by the problems in rape trials where judges have concluded that evidence of previous sexual behaviour may be relevant to the issue of consent (see *R v A (No. 2)* (2002) and *R v F* (2005)). The contention that relevance depends on the basic assumptions of a particular society becomes even clearer when one considers the evidential significance of marks on the bodies of those formerly suspected of witchcraft, or of the appearance in their vicinity of such creatures as a cat, a toad or a wasp.[9]

There are very few who argue cases from a standpoint wholly outside the beliefs of their own society, and it is probable that arguments relating to relevance will be constrained by the way in which the substantive law is defined. What one can reasonably hope is that the ability to argue from a critical standpoint in particular cases should not be easily frustrated. A further obstacle in the way of such arguments would be likely to emerge if a concept of legal relevance were to become fully developed in the law of evidence.[10]

A concept of legal relevance could also lead to unfairness to defendants, who might be prevented from adducing relevant and weighty evidence in support of their defence. This was recognised, in effect, by the House of Lords in *A* (2001), when the Law Lords interpreted **s 41** of the **Youth Justice and Criminal Evidence Act 1999** in the light of the **Human Rights Act 1998** and the defendant's right to a fair trial under **Art 6** of the **European Convention on Human Rights**.

8 This paragraph demonstrates good analysis of some of the pitfalls of developing a concept of legal relevance. Make sure you present both sides of an argument.

9 K Thomas, *Religion and the Decline of Magic*, 1971, p. 530.

10 See JB Thayer, *A Preliminary Treatise on Evidence at the Common Law*, 1898, chapter 6; GF James, 'Relevancy, probability and the law' (1941) 29 *California Law Review* 689, pp. 689–705; HL Trautman, 'Logical or legal relevancy: a conflict in theory' (1952) 5 *Vanderbilt Law Review* 385, pp. 385–413; WO Weyrauch, 'Law as mask: legal ritual and relevance' (1978) 66 *California Law Review* 699, pp. 699–726.

In conclusion, a concept of legal relevance would only seek to constrain the law on the admission of evidence, hindering its ability to adapt in constantly changing circumstances. It is likely that a body of rules, should they develop, would be complex, resulting in the creation of exceptions and inconsistent application. Notwithstanding these issues, some control of the evidence that is adduced in court is clearly required but perhaps not in the form of legal relevance. Thus, although the concept of relevance may be vague, it is necessarily so for it would be impossible to define a concept of legal relevance that could be consistently applied in all cases.

# QUESTION 2

How satisfactory is the law on judicial notice?

## How to Read this Question

You are required to answer a specific question: whether or not the law on judicial notice is satisfactory. Therefore, you should discuss the current law, highlight what can and cannot be judicially noted, their role and any problems posed by them.

## How to Answer this Question

The law on this subject is in a mess – albeit an interesting one. The following points should be made:

- the distinction (if any) between taking judicial notice and using local or special knowledge;
- the different rationales that have been suggested for judicial notice;
- the effect of those rationales on the way the law is viewed;
- the failure of English law to commit itself unequivocally to a single rationale;
- the ambiguity of the relationship between judicial notice and evidence.

### Up for Debate

The criticism of judicial notice relates to the fact that it allows the court to judicially notice or 'accept' notorious facts without further enquiry. The scope of the rules is not precisely determined and it is suggested that this leaves a wide discretion for the admission or exclusion of certain evidence.

## Answer Structure

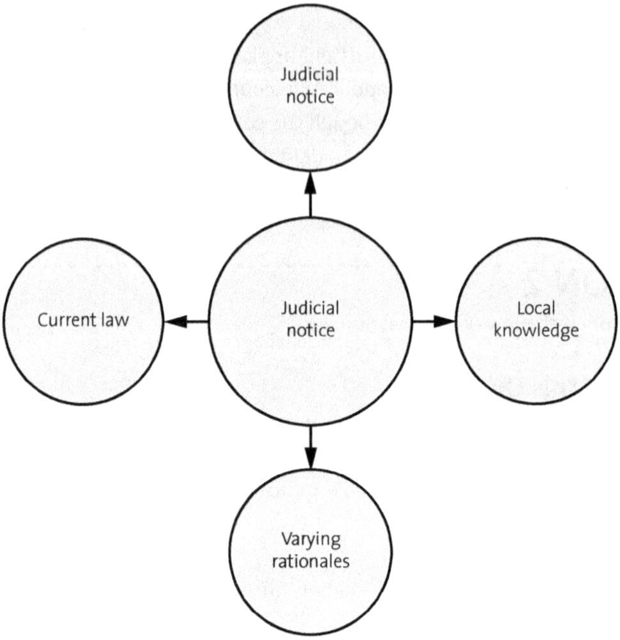


*This diagram points out the main factors to consider in relation to a question focusing on judicial notice.*

# ANSWER

The main problem with the law of judicial notice is that it is underdeveloped. As a result of this, there is confusion about the principles on which it rests and about its scope.

There is confusion about its scope because it is unclear whether a distinction should be made between taking judicial notice and using special or local knowledge. In *Wetherall v Harrison* (1976), the Divisional Court held that magistrates were entitled to use their own special or local knowledge when trying cases, but Lord Widgery CJ saw this as a necessary concession to the layman's inability to exclude such factors from his deliberations. He thought that, in this respect, magistrates were unlike trained judges and were more like members of a jury. In line with this approach, the Divisional Court in *Bowman v DPP* (1990) said that a bench of magistrates using its local knowledge of a particular piece of land was not taking 'judicial notice'. But in *Mullen v Hackney LBC* (1997), the Court of Appeal held that a county court judge had been entitled to take judicial notice of his own special or local knowledge about the defendant council's failure to honour undertakings given to the court in other cases. This decision was almost certainly wrong. There is a line of cases to the effect that county court judges can rely on their own local knowledge 'properly and within reasonable limits': see, for example, *Reynolds v Llanelly Tinplate Co Ltd* (1948). But all these cases were decided under the **Workmen's Compensation Acts**, under which the county court judge sat as an arbitrator. There is no doubt that an arbitrator can, in certain circumstances, make use of his own knowledge and experience to determine issues in dispute between the parties to the arbitration, without hearing expert evidence. This was held to be within the judge's powers under those Acts: see, for example, *Peart v Bolckow Vaughan & Co Ltd* (1925). But the cases do not establish that county court judges sitting in any other capacity have the same freedom that they had as arbitrators in workmen's compensation cases. Nor do those cases suggest that judges were taking 'judicial notice' of anything.[11]

There are two main theories about the rationale of judicial notice. On one view, it is a device for filtering out evidence about matters that are really unarguable. If you regard judicial notice in this light, you will tend to want its scope to be restricted to notorious, or readily ascertainable, facts; its application to be mandatory rather than discretionary; and the effect of its application conclusive.[12]

Another view is that judicial notice is simply a labour-saving device in litigation. If seen in this way, its scope can be wider, and its application discretionary. Its effect can even be defeasible in the light of further evidence.[13] A controversial variant of this view is that any process of judicial reasoning about facts assumes the truth of a mass of material that has not been formally proved. For example, a judge assumes that trains run on rails, that France is outside the United Kingdom and that there is a law of gravity. If this analysis is right, 'the tacit applications of the doctrine of judicial notice are more numerous and more important than the express ones'.[14] But this is a controversial view. Others have acknowledged that both judges and juries must make use of general knowledge to interpret evidence. But, they argue, this is not a question of judicial notice; it is the tribunal relying on its own experience of the ordinary course of human affairs.[15,16]

A limited view of judicial notice should require mandatory application. This line has been taken in cases relating to political and constitutional matters. For example, in *Duff Development Co Ltd v Government of Kelantan* (1924), the House of Lords said that where the question of the sovereignty of a foreign State is in issue, it is the practice of the courts to treat as conclusive the information that they obtain on the matter from a Secretary of State. But in other cases the courts have taken the view that they have discretion whether or not to take judicial notice of a particular fact. In *George v Davies* (1911), for example, it was tacitly accepted by the Divisional Court that a judge had discretion to decide whether

11 Highlighting where some of the confusion surrounding judicial notice comes from demonstrates knowledge of the concept but also provides support for the main contention of the argument that the law is confusing and unsatisfactory.

12 EM Morgan, *Some Problems of Proof under the Anglo-American System of Litigation*, 1956, p. 42.

13 Thayer, op. cit., p. 278.

14 C Tapper, *Cross & Tapper on Evidence*, 11th edn, 2007, p. 93.

15 See, for example, Sir R Eggleston, *Evidence, Proof and Probability*, 2nd edn, 1983, pp. 143–144.

16 Analysing these two opposing views and their resultant effects: whether the application of judicial notice by its nature is mandatory or discretionary demonstrates knowledge but avoids making the mistake of posing one side of such an argument.

to take judicial notice of an employment custom that had been established by evidence in earlier cases.

A further problem with judicial notice is its relationship to evidence. Where judicial notice is taken without inquiry, for example, that cats are kept for domestic purposes (*Nye v Niblett* (1918)) or that people who go to hotels do not like having their nights disturbed (*Andreae v Selfridge & Co Ltd* (1938)), it is clear that no process of proof is involved, because no material containing information is produced by either party. But is judicial notice after inquiry based on a process of proof? The opinions of judges have been divided. In *McQuaker v Goddard* (1940), at least one member of the Court of Appeal (Clauson LJ) took the view that a judge was entitled to disregard the rules of evidence and look at materials that would otherwise have been inadmissible, on the basis that he was merely 'refreshing his memory' about the ordinary course of nature – a subject of which, by a legal fiction, judges had complete knowledge.[17]

It is clearly unsatisfactory to have a situation where it is unclear whether rules about admissibility are going to be applied or not. The truth of the matter is that, in principle, scope and effect, the law about judicial notice is underdeveloped and ripe for clarification.[18]

## QUESTION 3

The police suspect that Alex and Ben are dealing separately in drugs. They lawfully search Alex's house. There they find a large quantity of cannabis resin hidden behind a wardrobe. They also find £3,420 in cash in Alex's coat pockets, and a pair of diamond earrings worth £35,000 in a jewellery box belonging to Alex's wife. Alex tells the police that he frequently smokes cannabis and that the supply was solely for his own use. He adds that he had the cash in his coat because he runs a firm of builders and had to pay his staff their wages that afternoon. He is nevertheless charged with possession of cannabis with the intent to supply.

The police lawfully search Ben's house. They find a small amount of cocaine in an old tobacco tin on a shelf in his garage, and £345 in cash in a desk in Ben's study. Ben says, 'I'd no idea there was cocaine in that old tin. Cedric must have left it there. He used to be a lodger, and I let him keep his motorcycle in the garage.' The police trace and interview Cedric, who tells them that he has never owned a motorcycle and that he never went into the garage when he was Ben's lodger. Ben is charged with possession of cocaine.

- **Discuss the evidential issues arising.**

17 This part of the answer is most interesting; it could have more directly questioned the risk of subjectivity in the facts (or knowledge) of which judges have assumed judicial notice and their construction. However, it makes a good argument in relation to the lack of a process of proof.

18 The answer ends with a clear conclusion: it answers the question. Do not be shy of suggesting debated reforms, for instance the requirement for the judicial notice of certain facts to be based only upon inquiry.

## How to Read this Question

This question requires a discussion of the potential pieces of evidence that are outlined in the scenario and the considerations that go with each one: admissibility, relevance and judicial directions (if any).

## How to Answer this Question

In this question there is no insinuation that the defendants were operating together, therefore they should be dealt with separately in the answer.

*Alex*

- ❖ You are told that the search was lawful, so there is no point to be taken about improperly obtained evidence. Obviously, evidence of finding the cannabis can be given, and it can be produced as an item of real evidence if necessary. Is there anything the prosecution could do to avoid having to produce the cannabis in court? Is there any reason for the defence to insist that it should be produced?
- ❖ The discovery of the cash in Alex's coat. You must first decide if this is relevant to the prosecution case. If it is relevant, and admissible, what directions should the judge give to the jury about the use they can make of this evidence? The cases of *Wright* (1994) and *Grant* (1996) are helpful here. A first-class answer might refer to the strength of those decisions after the passing of the **Criminal Justice Act 2003**, which has made it much easier to adduce evidence of criminal disposition on the part of the accused.
- ❖ The wife's diamond earrings. Are they relevant? Is there any other evidence of 'lavish lifestyle'? Even if there were, would it be likely to be regarded as relevant? See *Halpin* (1996).

*Ben*

- ❖ Obviously, evidence can be given of discovering the tin containing cocaine, and it can be produced at trial if necessary.
- ❖ Is the cash in Ben's desk relevant to the charge against him? Remember that although initially he was suspected of supplying, he has been charged with possession only.
- ❖ What is the significance of the evidence that Cedric can give? What direction should the judge give to the jury about it?

## Up for Debate

One factor that is often debated is whether (or to what extent) the discovery of large sums of cash or valuable items such as artworks or diamonds indicates malfeasance on the part of the accused. Consider the quality of this assertion given that the legitimacy of the accused's means to fund a lavish lifestyle will be taken into account, how the jury may receive it and why the courts will rarely allow its admission.

## Applying the Law

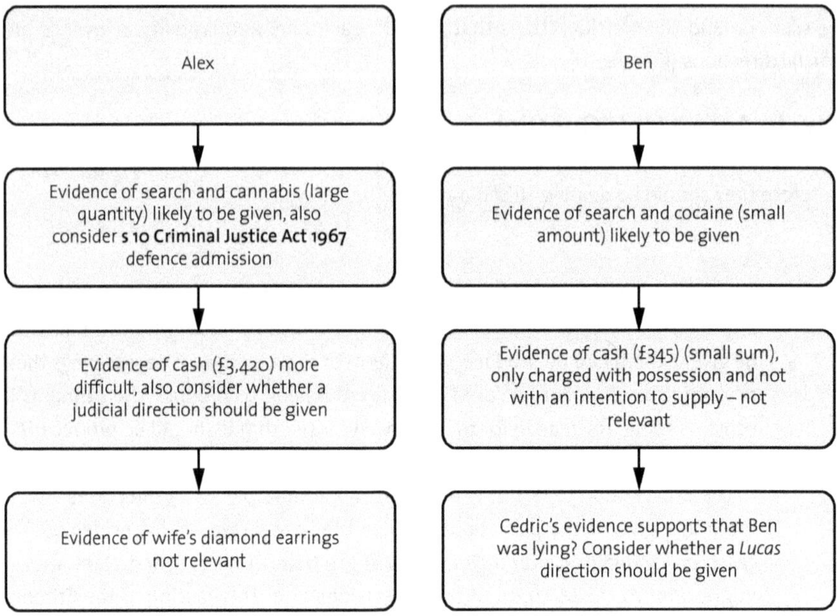


*The purpose of this diagram is to outline what evidence exists against each of the accused and its relevant evidential consideration.*

# ANSWER

The prosecution will have no difficulty in adducing evidence of the search at Alex's house or of the discovery of the cannabis, which should be produced as an item of real evidence, unless the defence is prepared to make a formal admission in respect of its discovery under **s 10** of the **Criminal Justice Act 1967**.[19]

The discovery of the cash in Alex's coat is more problematic. In *Wright* (1994) the discovery of £16,000 in cash and a gold necklace worth about £9,000 was held to be relevant and admissible where the defendant was charged with possession of cocaine with intent to supply. In *Grant* (1996) the defendant, charged with possession of crack cocaine with intent to supply, was found with just over £900 in cash in his possession. The Court of Appeal held that the finding of money in conjunction with a substantial quantity of drugs was capable of being relevant to intent to supply, and could properly be admitted as evidence. But a proper direction must be given to the jury about the use to be made of such evidence. Any innocent explanation for possession of the cash must be rejected before its possession can be relevant to the offence of possession with intent to supply. But if

19 Assuming that the crimes with which Alex and Ben have been charged are not related means the answer can be appropriately structured. Although assumptions of this nature are acceptable, avoid making up facts to support your answer.

innocent explanations are rejected, and the presence of the cash indicates not merely past dealing, but ongoing dealing in drugs, it can be taken into account in deciding whether the prosecution has proved intent to supply. It seems clear that the discovery of the cash will be relevant and admissible, but the jury will have to be satisfied that Alex did not have it for his stated purpose before they can take it into account in deciding whether the prosecution has proved intent to supply. It is unclear whether the judge should now also direct them to be satisfied that the money does not indicate merely past dealing, but is evidence of ongoing dealing. At the time when *Wright* was decided there were severe restrictions on the use of evidence of past matters to show the accused's disposition to commit the offence charged. Since the **Criminal Justice Act 2003** those restrictions have been substantially reduced,[20] and it may now be sufficiently relevant if the cash is evidence only of past dealing.[21]

The wife's diamond earrings would probably be regarded as either irrelevant, or inadmissible as possessing insufficient probative value. She is not charged, and there is no evidence even that they were a present from her husband. In *Halpin* (1996) the Court of Appeal said that a 'lavish lifestyle' would only rarely be relevant to intent to supply drugs found in the possession of the accused, and there is nothing on the facts to show that there was anything other than the earrings to indicate such a lifestyle.[22]

In Ben's case, evidence will be given of the discovery of the cocaine, which can be produced as an item of real evidence in the same way as the earlier discovery at Alex's house. It appears that Ben has given no explanation for the presence of cash in his desk. But it is a relatively small sum; he is charged with possession and not possession with intent to supply; it is difficult to see how possession of this money could be relevant to the question of whether he was also in possession of the cocaine. Cedric's denials of possession of a motorcycle or of using the garage suggest that Ben might have been lying to the police. Cedric would have to give evidence at Ben's trial and the judge would have to warn the jury, in accordance with *Lucas* (1981) and *Burge and Pegg* (1996), that before they can use Cedric's evidence against Ben, they must be satisfied that Ben had indeed lied, and was not simply mistaken, and that even if he had lied, he might have done so for an innocent reason.[23,24]

20 See **ss 101(1)(d)** and **103(1)(a)**.

21 The paragraph presents a thorough analysis of the cash in Alex's coat. Highlighting the use of this evidence in a variety of circumstances demonstrates knowledge of the statutory scheme under the **CJA 2003**.

22 Discussing *Halpin* highlights what the court considers as relevant evidence of a criminally funded lavish lifestyle, but also that other than the earrings nothing in the facts supports this contention.

23 See Chapter 6.

24 Discussion of *Lucas Directions* demonstrates knowledge. The question specifically requires the assessment of the evidence and not whether the prosecution is likely to be successful; you will often be given credit for avoiding irrelevant discussion such as the likelihood of prosecution success.

# 2 Burden and Standard of Proof

## INTRODUCTION

The burden and the standard of proof are two matters that must be kept distinct from one another. Judges have a duty to direct the jury in respect of each of them. Problems are therefore most likely to arise in criminal jury trials because a wrong direction was given, or no direction was given at all, both of which could provide successful grounds on which to appeal.

You must be able to distinguish between a legal and an evidential burden. The latter is not strictly a *burden of proof* at all. It is best seen as a rule of common sense which says that there must be *some* evidence for a particular issue to become a live one, so that it is fit for consideration by a jury or other tribunal of fact. Because of this, whether an evidential burden has been satisfied or not in a jury trial is a matter for the judge alone, and consequently there should never be a need to refer to it in a summing up.

In civil cases, it will generally be clear from the statements of case where the burden of proof lies. Although you will find fascinating cases where it was not clear at all discussed in the textbooks, do not get bogged down with them when you first approach this topic.

It is important to understand why in criminal cases it is impossible to say for certain when the well-known *Woolmington* principle will *not* apply. As you will see from the answer to Question 4, there can be no simple list of exceptions.

The *standard* of proof is less likely to occur as an essay topic because it raises too many theoretical issues. For example, should we reduce the standard of proof in (some) criminal cases if there were to be a significant increase in a particularly unpleasant type of crime? Does it make sense to talk of 'standards' of proof at all? Aren't things either proved or not, more or less easily, depending on their inherent probability? This may seem a simple task, but it is not to be attempted in the examination if you have not studied these problems as part of your course.

What you may get is a 'dud direction' question, covering both burden and standard of proof, where you are asked to examine an excerpt from the summing up and say whether there are grounds for appeal. It is important to remember that there is no magic form of words about either the burden or standard of proof that *must* be used, though judges are wise to follow one of the two accepted forms, and it is clear that some directions will not suffice. It is a good idea to look at the cases that have approved various forms of words so as to get their general sense and compare those with cases where there was held to have been a misdirection.

It is particularly important to remember that the legal burden of proof remains with the prosecution where defences such as provocation, self-defence, duress, non-insane automatism and alibi are in issue. In cases where the defendant *does* have the legal burden of proving something, that burden will be discharged if the civil standard of proof is satisfied. Remember also that where there is a burden on the defence on a particular issue, there cannot also be a burden on the prosecution on that same issue. Sometimes candidates try to have the best of both worlds and say, for example, that the defence in an offensive weapon case has to prove on the balance of probabilities that there was a reasonable excuse, and the prosecution has to prove beyond reasonable doubt that there was not. This is gibberish.

**Checklist**

**Students should be familiar with the following areas:**

- the distinction between the burden and standard of proof;
- the meaning of 'evidential burden';
- factors affecting the burden of proof in civil cases;
- the burden of proof in criminal cases;
- the standard of proof in civil and criminal cases.

# QUESTION 4

When will the imposition of a legal burden on an accused person be compatible with **Art 6(2)** of the **European Convention on Human Rights**?

## How to Read this Question

This question requires you to discuss the ramifications of imposing a legal burden on an accused to prove something and the presumption of innocence under **Art 6(2)** of the **European Convention on Human Rights**. Your discussion should explore whether a reverse burden of proof is compatible, and if yes, in what instances.

## How to Answer this Question

Note, first, that the question is about the developments after the **Human Rights Act 1998**. It should be obvious, therefore, that a discussion of the law before that Act will be irrelevant. You will waste valuable time, effort and, where you have a strict word limit, necessary text allowance if you try to make it appear relevant by saying that in order to understand recent developments it is necessary to look at the development of the law since *Woolmington*; in this question it is clearly not. The following points could be made:

- the basic principle established in *Salabiaku v France* (1988);

- the six factors that may be taken into account, supported by reference to decided cases, when deciding whether a reverse burden is compatible with the **European Convention on Human Rights**:
  - the distinction between *mala in se* and *mala prohibita* in relation to offences;
  - deference to Parliament's decision;
  - a distinction between elements of the offence and defences;
  - maximum penalties;
  - ease of proof and defendant's peculiar knowledge;
  - the presumption of innocence itself.

## Up for Debate

Although there are a number of considerations that can be discussed in an answer to this question, the problem is that authorities show that the weight given to them by the courts is unpredictable and therefore the resultant effect on the case is often difficult to decipher.

## Answer Structure

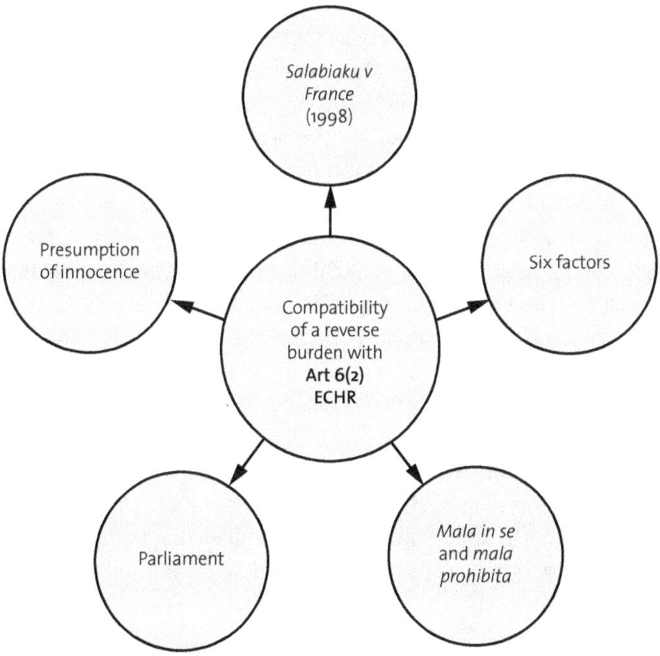


*These are the main factors you should consider in relation to the compatibility of reverse burdens of proof with* **Art 6** *of the* **ECHR.**

# ANSWER

**Article 6(2)** provides that everyone charged with a criminal offence shall be presumed innocent until proved guilty according to law. English law has not consistently followed the 'golden thread' principle referred to in *Woolmington v DPP* (1935). There are statutes expressly providing that an accused shall bear the burden of proof in relation to some matter; other statutes have in the past been interpreted as doing so by implication. Since the passing of the **Human Rights Act 1998**, it has become clear that not every reversal of the burden of proof will infringe **Art 6(2)** of the **European Convention on Human Rights**, but that each statutory provision must be considered on its merits. The European jurisprudence accepts that reverse burdens do not infringe **Art 6(2)** so long as they are confined within reasonable limits, which take into account the importance of what is at stake and maintain the rights of the defence (*Salabiaku v France* (1988)). Prediction has become an uncertain task, but Dennis has identified six elements that may be taken into account in reaching a decision where the court is faced with legislation that apparently reverses the burden of proof in any respect.[1,2]

The first element is based on a classification of offences that distinguishes, in the traditional terminology, between *mala in se* and *mala prohibita*. For example, in *Lambert* (2002) Lord Clyde said that a strict responsibility might be acceptable in the case of statutory offences that were concerned to regulate the conduct of a particular activity in the public interest. A licence could be required to carry out certain activities, or controls might be imposed to promote health and safety and avoid pollution. Such cases, he said, could properly be seen as not truly criminal. Many might be relatively trivial and carry no real social disgrace. This approach was adopted by the Court of Appeal in *Davies* (2002), where the court upheld **s 40** of the **Health and Safety at Work Act 1974**. This provision imposed a legal burden on a defendant to prove that it had not been reasonably practicable to do more than he had done to ensure that employees were not exposed to risks to their health and safety. The difficulty with classification of offences as a criterion for reverse burdens of proof is, as Dennis pointed out, that the moral quality of regulatory offences is variable. For example, where a regulatory offence leads to someone's death, as was the case in *Davies*, it might not be easy to maintain that the breach involved no real social disgrace. The same could also be true of a regulatory offence that led to widespread pollution of the environment.[3]

A second consideration is the deference that should be shown to Parliament's decision. In *Lambert* (2002) Lord Steyn said that the burden is on the state to show that the legislative means adopted were not greater than necessary. He added that there must be a 'pressing necessity' to impose a legal burden on the accused. But other judges have been more

1 I Dennis, 'Reverse onuses and the presumption of innocence: in search of principle' [2005] Crim LR 901–936.

2 Introductions should identify the main thrust of the argument, which in this answer centres on the presumption of innocence and incompatibility of a reverse burden of proof.

3 This paragraph highlights the problems with the traditional distinction as outlined in *Lambert*. Where appropriate, try to use an authority to support your argument.

inclined to give weight to the decision of the elected body that passed the legislation. For example, in *R v DPP, ex p Kebilene* (2000) Lord Hope said that such deference would be particularly appropriate where the issues involved questions of social or economic policy. In *Johnstone* (2003) Lord Nicholls pointed out that Parliament had the primary responsibility for deciding, as a matter of policy, what should be the constituent elements of a criminal offence, and courts should reach a different conclusion from the legislature only where it was apparent that the latter had attached insufficient importance to the individual's fundamental right to be presumed innocent until proved guilty.

However, in *Sheldrake v DPP* (2004) Lord Bingham doubted whether there should be an assumption that Parliament would not have made an exception to the basic rule without good reason. Such an approach might lead the court to give too much weight to the enactment under review, and too little to the presumption of innocence. Dennis has suggested that the court's approach should depend on drawing a clear distinction between the two criteria referred to in *Salabiaku*. Deference to the democratic body should be due when considering whether it was in fact pursuing a legitimate aim; less deference should be due when considering whether a reverse onus was a proportionate method of achieving that aim.

A third consideration is based on drawing a distinction between elements of the offence and available defences. For example, in *A-G of Hong Kong v Lee Kwong-Kut* (1993), a decision of the Privy Council, Lord Woolf said that if the prosecution retains responsibility for proving the essential ingredients of the offence, a reverse burden is more likely to be acceptable. But, recognising the difficulty of isolating the essential ingredients, he added that the substance and reality of the language creating the offence should be regarded, rather than its form.[4]

However, the distinction between elements of an offence and defences has often been criticised. Lord Steyn in *Lambert* said that the distinction would sometimes be 'unprincipled and arbitrary'. He observed that sometimes the distinction was based simply on the drafting technique. A constituent element of an offence can be removed from the definition and cast as a defensive issue. Further, any definition of an offence can be reformulated so as to include all possible defences within it. A good example of the difficulty in applying this criterion is *Hunt* (1987), where an element of the offence was found in what appeared at first sight to be a list of exceptions contained in a statutory instrument that had been made pursuant to powers contained in the primary legislation.

Maximum penalties are another consideration. In *Davies* (2002) Tuckey LJ said that the absence of any risk of imprisonment was 'undoubtedly an important factor' in determining whether there was a legitimate reverse burden of proof. Conversely, in *Lambert* Lord Steyn was clearly influenced by the fact that the maximum sentence was life

---

4 The discussion of these three parts demonstrates knowledge of the issues that relate to burdens of proof in terms of how they are imposed and interpreted and the standard of proof to which they are required to be discharged.

imprisonment. In *Johnstone* Lord Nicholls said that the more serious the punishment, the more compelling must be the reasons for imposing a reverse burden. But in *Sheldrake* the House of Lords upheld a reverse onus where the maximum penalty for the offence was only six months' imprisonment. Dennis has noted that maximum penalties are a very uncertain guide, and that the nature of the penalty, whether custodial or pecuniary, is not conclusive either way.

The ease of proof and the defendant's peculiar knowledge can also be taken into account. For example, in *ex p Kebilene* Lord Hope said that one of the considerations was the nature of the burden on the accused. Did it relate to something that it was likely to be difficult for him to prove, or to something likely to be within his knowledge or to which he had access? The same point was made by Lord Nicholls in *Johnstone*. On the other hand, as Dennis has pointed out, there are very many cases where the accused's state of mind is of crucial importance, but where the burden of proving it is on the prosecution.[5]

A final consideration is the presumption of innocence itself. As Lord Bingham said in *Sheldrake*, the underlying rationale of the presumption is that it is repugnant to ordinary notions of fairness for a prosecutor to accuse a defendant of crime and for the defendant to be then required to disprove the accusation, on pain of conviction and punishment if he fails to do so. The closer a legislative provision is to that situation, the more objectionable it is likely to be. Approaching the problem from a slightly different angle, Lord Nicholls in *Johnstone* said that a sound starting point for considering a reverse burden in the light of **Art 6(2)** is to remember that if a defendant is required to prove a fact on the balance of probability in order to avoid conviction, a conviction can follow in spite of the fact-finding tribunal having a reasonable doubt as to his guilt.

It will be seen that there can be no straightforward answer to the question initially posed. It is possible to identify a number of considerations, but the weight the court will give to them in any particular case is unlikely to be readily predictable. The problem is substantial. Research in 1996 showed that almost 40 per cent of offences triable in the Crown Court appeared to have violated the presumption of innocence.[6]

## QUESTION 5

Answer all FOUR parts of this question:

(a) Alice was convicted of theft. In her summing up, the judge said to the jury: 'The prosecution brings this case and it is for the prosecution to prove it. Unless, having heard all the evidence, you are sure that the defendant is guilty, she must be acquitted.' Advise Alice whether she has grounds for appeal.

5 Discussing *Kebilene* demonstrates knowledge and highlights that the courts will take into account how difficult it would be for the defendant to discharge a burden – even though this may be seen by some commentators as being unfair on the prosecution because the burden imposed on it is higher.

6 A Ashworth and M Blake, 'The presumption of innocence in English criminal law' [1996] Crim LR 306, 314.

(b) Bertha was convicted of having an offensive weapon with her in a public place, contrary to **s1** of the **Prevention of Crime Act 1953**. In her summing up, the judge said to the jury: 'Members of the jury, it is not contested that this defendant had with her an offensive weapon in a public place. But she says she had it with her for her own protection. She has to satisfy you that that was a reasonable excuse for having the weapon with her, and unless you are satisfied of that, you must convict.' Advise Bertha whether she has grounds for appeal.

(c) Charlene is charged with murder. There is medical evidence suggesting that she is under a mental disability that renders her unfit to plead and stand trial. What is the law relating to the burden and standard of proof in this situation?

(d) Dora was convicted of wounding with intent to do grievous bodily harm. In her summing up, the judge said to the jury: 'The defence in this case is self-defence. That means that the defendant has an evidential burden, but no more, to satisfy you that what she says about acting in self-defence is more probable than not.' Advise Dora whether she has grounds for appeal.

## How to Read this Question

This question has four parts to it and therefore you should ensure you answer the issues in each one separately. You should discuss the issues relating to the burden and standard of proof, the summing up and the correctness of any judicial directions.

## How to Answer this Question

Part (a) obviously deals with the burden and standard of proof. The question is whether the judge has directed the jury adequately. The answer is that she has, but note how you can show your knowledge effectively to the examiner when saying so. Without being at all irrelevant, the following points can be made:

- the need to provide a correct direction on both the burden and standard of proof;
- the proper direction on the burden of proof;
- the application of that test to what was said in this case;
- the proper direction on the standard of proof;
- it is not a particular formula but the effect of the summing up as a whole that matters;
- *Kritz* (1950) and *Walters v R* (1969).

Don't forget to advise Alice – this is done in the final sentence.

Part (b) is a bit more complicated. You need to know about **s1** of the **Prevention of Crime Act 1953**, but this is a fairly well-cited example of a statutory provision that expressly puts a burden of proof on the defendant. It is important to remember that a direction on the *burden* of proof and a direction on the *standard* of proof are two different things. The following points should be made:

- whether there has been a correct direction on the burden of proof;
- standard of proof where a burden is placed on a defendant in a criminal trial;
- ambiguity of the language used in Bertha's case.

Part (c) provides an example of the operation of different standards of proof, depending on which side raises the issue.

Part (d) requires you to make the following points:

- basic rule about burden of proof;
- self-defence available as a defence;
- no legal burden on the accused;
- the evidential burden.

## Up for Debate

You should think about the imposition of a reverse burden and its compatibility with **Art 6(2)** of the **European Convention on Human Rights**, and the potential effect of a misdirection by the trial judge.

## Applying the Law

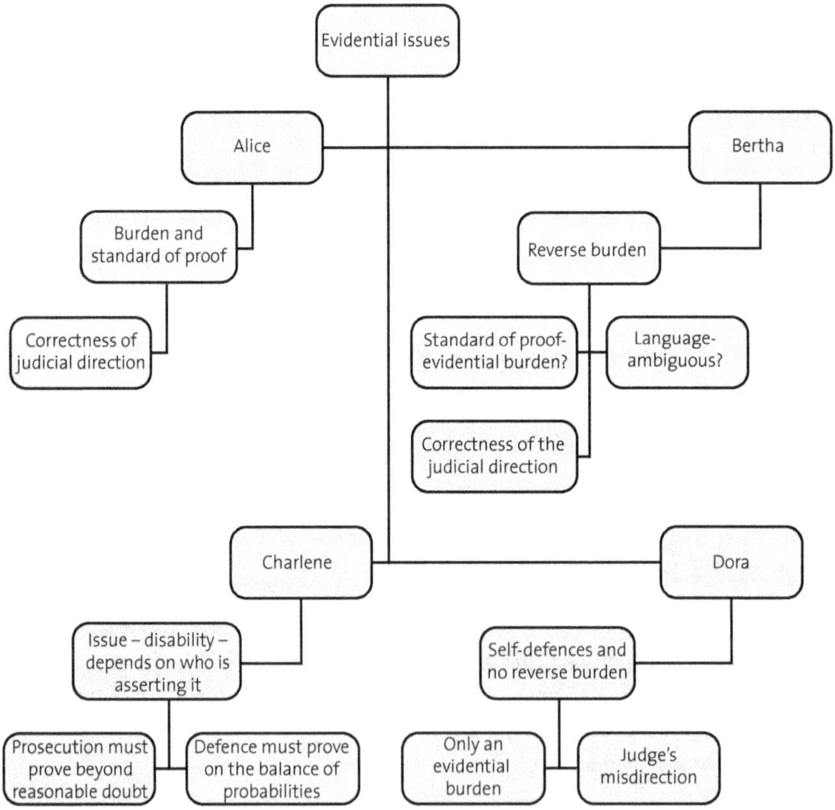


*This mind map shows the main issues that require consideration in terms of your advice to Alice, Bertha, Charlene and Dora.*

## ANSWER

(a) Every summing up should contain a correct direction on both the burden and the standard of proof (*Bentley (Deceased)* (2001)). Here, there is a direction on each. The judge has rightly told the jury, in effect, that the burden is on the prosecution. No particular form of words is necessary, and this is the clear sense of the words actually used. There has also been a correct direction on the standard of proof. Again, it is not the particular formula that matters, but the effect of the summing up (*Allan* (1969)). One of the well-established forms of direction is to tell the jury that in order to find the accused guilty they must be 'sure', or 'satisfied so that they feel sure' (*Kritz* (1950); *Walters v R* (1969)). Here, the former expression has been used. It is entirely adequate and Alice has no grounds for appeal on this part of the summing up.[7]

(b) **Section 1** of the **Prevention of Crime Act 1953** provides a defence of reasonable excuse to a charge of having an offensive weapon in a public place, but the section places the burden of proving this defence on the accused. It would be possible to argue, following *Lambert* (2002), that the effect of **s 1** is to impose only an evidential burden on defendants. But this interpretation is unlikely to be applied. In *L v DPP* (2002), the Divisional Court upheld the traditional interpretation of **s 139** of the **Criminal Justice Act 1988**, saying that there was a strong public interest in bladed articles not being carried in public without good reason, and that it was not obviously offensive to the rights of the individual to require him to prove a good reason for carrying one. The same approach is very likely to be adopted towards having an offensive weapon in a public place. The judge has almost certainly got her direction on burden right. However, in all cases where the law puts a burden of proving something on a defendant, it can be discharged merely by proof on the balance of probabilities – the civil, rather than the criminal standard (*Carr-Briant* (1943)). What has happened here is that the judge has told the jury that Bertha has to 'satisfy' them that she had a reasonable excuse. But this is ambiguous, for it could refer either to the civil or to the higher criminal standard (*Hepworth* (1955)). Thus, the jury might have applied the wrong standard in deciding whether Bertha had made out her defence. Accordingly, she has a good ground of appeal.[8]

(c) The answer depends on who raises the issue.[9] If the prosecution says that Charlene is under this disability and the defence disputes this, the burden of proof will be on the prosecution to satisfy the jury beyond reasonable doubt that its contention is correct (*Robertson* (1968)). If, on the other hand, it is the defence that puts forward this contention and the prosecution disagrees, the defence will have the burden of proof, but only to the civil standard – on a balance of probabilities (*Podola* (1960)).

---

7 This discussion of the judge's summing up demonstrates knowledge of the legal requirements. Do not be afraid to analyse its correctness.

8 This part of the answer is more complex. You should highlight the problems that are caused where the language used in a direction is ambiguous.

9 Either the prosecution or the defence may do so: see **s 4(1)** of the **Criminal Procedure (Insanity) Act 1964**.

(d) Where the defendant is charged with wounding with intent to cause grievous bodily harm, the burden of proof, as is usual in criminal cases, rests throughout on the prosecution. In certain circumstances, self-defence may be a defence to this charge, but the accused bears no legal burden on the issue. Thus, in *Lobell* (1957), where the appellant had been convicted on such a charge after the trial judge had directed the jury that it was for the defence to establish its plea of self-defence, the conviction was quashed on the ground that there had been a misdirection. What the defendant does have is an evidential burden, but this means no more than that he must be able to point to some evidence in the trial that makes self-defence a live issue for the jury's consideration. As Lord Morris put it in *Bratty v Attorney-General for Northern Ireland* (1963), where the accused bears the evidential burden alone, he must adduce such evidence as would, if believed and left uncontradicted, induce a reasonable doubt in the mind of the jury as to whether his version might not be true.[10]

Whether a party has discharged an evidential, as opposed to a legal, burden is a matter for the judge and not the jury. It was therefore wrong of the judge to refer to the evidential burden in her summing up. If possible, it was even more wrong to refer in that connection to the standard of proof that is applicable where a defendant has a *legal* burden. The jury have been misled, and Dora has a good ground of appeal.[11]

## QUESTION 6

Annie hired a removal firm, XY & Co, to move the contents of her house in Plymouth to a house that she had bought in Worcester. The removal van and all its contents were destroyed by fire in a layby just outside Exeter. Some time after the loss, Annie was told by an employee of XY & Co that the van had been deliberately set on fire so that XY & Co could claim from their insurers for its loss.

Annie is suing XY & Co for the value of her destroyed property, which she estimates to be £250,000. She claims first in respect of their deliberate destruction by the defendants; alternatively, she alleges that they were destroyed by reason of the defendants' negligence. By their defence, XY & Co deny deliberately setting fire to the van and plead that their contract with Annie had an exclusion clause, which said that they would not be liable for loss by fire provided that their servants were not negligent. They also plead that it was a term of the contract that they would not be liable for any loss in excess of £5,000. Annie says that she never agreed to this term and that XY & Co are liable for the full loss.

- **Discuss the burden and standard of proof in relation to the issues that arise.**

10 Although Lord Morris used the word 'adduce', this does not mean that the defendant must call such evidence himself. It could be obtained from prosecution witnesses under cross-examination, or it might even emerge during their examination-in-chief. See *L v DPP* (2002).

11 Erroneous directions raise a major problem, especially as they amount to grounds on which an appeal may be lodged against the court's decision. Be sure to advise the parties on the question posed.

## How to Read this Question

On establishing the claim(s) that Annie can make you must then discuss where the burden of proof lies and the standard required for that to be discharged. You must ensure that you discuss the authorities that relate to where the burden falls and how any ambiguities in the law would be settled.

## How to Answer this Question

The first step is to sort out what the issues are likely to be. A rough and ready way of doing this is to think of what matters each side would have to prove in order to win, assuming there is no response from their opponents.

Annie must prove the existence of the agreement with the defendants for the carriage of her goods, the consignment of her goods to the defendants in accordance with the agreement, the fact that non-delivery was due to deliberate destruction of the goods by the defendants, and the amount of the loss. In view of the exclusion clause, the burden of proof in relation to negligence is uncertain.

The defendants must prove the existence of the exclusion clause and, if need be, that the loss falls within it. They may also have to prove that they exercised all proper care of the goods while they were in their possession. In addition, they will have to show that the provision limiting their liability to £5,000 was part of the contract.

Broadly speaking, it will be seen that this ties in with the maxim that he who asserts must prove, but there are problems with the interpretation of the exclusion clause that require discussion of bailment.

The allegation of arson raises the question of the standard to be applied where a crime is alleged in a civil action.

## Applying the Law

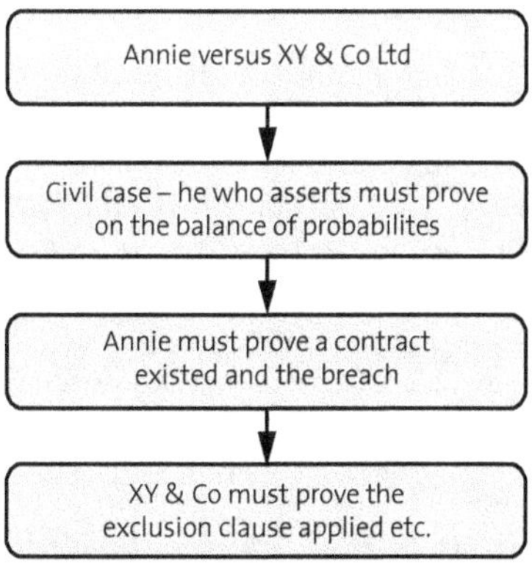


*This diagram highlights where the burden of proof rests in a civil action – in this scenario for negligence.*

## ANSWER

Although the burden of proof in any particular case depends on the circumstances under which the claim arises, in a civil action, the burden normally lies on the party who affirms something to be the case, and not upon the party who makes a denial. As Viscount Maugham said in *Constantine (Joseph) Steamship Line Ltd v Imperial Smelting Corp Ltd* (1942), it is 'an ancient rule founded on considerations of good sense and it should not be departed from without strong reasons'.[12]

Annie will therefore bear the legal burden of establishing the essential elements of her claim. With one exception, these are readily defined.

She will first have to prove the existence of a contract made between herself and the defendants for the carriage by the defendants of her goods from Plymouth to Worcester. She will then have to prove that, pursuant to this contract, she consigned her goods to the defendants. Her principal claim is that the defendants deliberately destroyed her goods by fire while they had possession of them. Clearly, the burden of proving this rests on Annie. She will also have to prove the value of the goods that have been lost.[13]

Since this is a civil action, all these matters will have to be proved according to 'the preponderance of probability' (*Miller v Minister of Pensions* (1947)). Even where Annie is alleging matters that would amount to the criminal offence of arson, she does not have to prove them beyond reasonable doubt. In *Hornal v Neuberger Products Ltd* (1957), the plaintiff was sold a lathe by the defendants. One of their directors was alleged to have stated falsely that the machine had been reconditioned by a named firm. Had this representation been made by the director with knowledge of its falsehood, he would have been guilty of fraudulent misrepresentation. In a civil action for damages for breach of warranty, alternatively for fraud, the trial judge found that the claim in respect of fraud had been proved on the balance of probabilities, but added that he would not have been satisfied had the criminal standard been applicable. The Court of Appeal held that he had correctly applied the civil standard.[14]

In *Hornal*, Denning LJ said that the more serious the allegation, the higher the degree of probability required, and in some later cases, the judge appears to have applied a slightly loaded civil standard.[15] However, Morris LJ said in *Hornal* that the gravity of the allegation was simply part of the whole range of circumstances that had to be weighed when deciding on the balance of probabilities. He did not favour variations of standard in civil cases, and current opinion prefers his view. In *Re H and Others* (1996), the majority of the House

12 Outlining that in civil disputes the burden of proof is 'he who asserts must prove that which they assert' demonstrates knowledge. Use *Constantine* to support this.

13 Approach the issues, which include whether a contract exists, the breach and the requirement to prove her losses, in this order.

14 It is important that you distinguish between the difference in the standards of proof in criminal and civil proceedings, and that even though a serious crime is alleged, that Annie does not have to prove that the acts amounted to such beyond reasonable doubt.

15 See, for example, *The Michael* (1979).

of Lords supported the view that the more serious the allegation, the less likely it was to be true, and the weightier the evidence needed for a court to find it proved. But it was emphasised that where a serious allegation was in issue, the standard of proof was not higher than the ordinary civil standard. If a third standard were to be substituted in some civil cases, it would be necessary to identify what that standard was and when it applied. Confusion and uncertainty would result. Any earlier observations to the contrary were not accurate statements of the law.[16]

As an alternative to deliberate destruction, Annie pleads negligence on the part of the defendants. Does she have the legal burden of proving this? Two arguments might be used to show that she does. It could be said that this is just another instance of the application of the basic maxim that it is for the person who affirms something to be the case to bear the burden in respect of that issue. The defendants might also argue by analogy from the way in which an exclusion clause was interpreted in *The Glendarroch* (1894). In that case, the plaintiffs claimed damages from shipowners for the latter's failure to carry goods safely. The shipowners relied on an exemption clause that excluded their liability for loss or damage occasioned by perils of the sea. It was held that the defendants had the burden of proving this provision and that the loss fell within it, but that the plaintiffs, who wished to rely on a proviso to the exemption clause that excluded its operation in the event of the shipowners' negligence, had the burden of establishing that the facts were such as to bring the proviso into effect.[17]

There is, however, an argument that, instead of Annie's having to prove negligence, the defendants have a burden to show that they used all proper care in the carriage of the goods. This is the basic common law rule in cases of bailment for reward, of which this contract is an instance. It could be argued that any ambiguity as to the burden of proof should be resolved in Annie's favour because this basic principle has not been clearly excluded, and its rationale is clearly present here: after the goods were consigned to the defendants, they, and not Annie, were in a better position to explain what happened to them. This was a consideration that proved persuasive in *Levison v Patent Steam Carpet Cleaning Ltd* (1978). In this case, the defendant carpet cleaners lost the plaintiff's Chinese carpet in unexplained circumstances. A clause in the contract would have exempted them from liability for negligence, but not for any fundamental breach of contract. The burden of proof on the latter issue was held by the Court of Appeal to lie on the defendants. They had to show that they had not been guilty of fundamental breach because they could more easily discharge this burden than could a plaintiff who had a burden to prove that there had been such a breach.

It will of course be for XY & Co to establish the existence of the exclusion clause and, if need be, that the goods were destroyed by fire. Similarly, if they wish to rely on the limitation of damages clause, they will have to prove it formed part of the contract.

16 Highlight that the current view is to prefer a single standard of proof in civil proceedings and that this avoids complexity and confusion.

17 Discuss the alternative claim and decision in *The Glendarroch* to demonstrate how burden of proof moves between the parties.

# QUESTION 7

After a vigorous press campaign prompted by a sudden increase in accidents to customers in bookshops, Parliament passes a new piece of legislation: the **Readers (Protection) Act**. **Section 1** provides: 'A bookshop owner shall be guilty of an offence if any person suffers injury while on the bookshop owner's premises.' **Section 2** provides: 'No offence is committed under **s1** if the bookshop owner took reasonable precautions to prevent the injury from occurring.' The Act provides that a bookshop owner shall be liable on conviction on indictment to an unlimited fine, the closure of his premises for such period as the court shall think fit, and to a sentence of imprisonment for a maximum of two years. Fergus, the owner of a bookshop, has been charged under **s1** of the Act after Gerald, a customer, fell downstairs and broke three ribs while moving from one floor of Fergus's shop to another. Fergus says that he took reasonable precautions to prevent injury to customers by ensuring that the stairs were well lit. He says that when he went to Gerald's assistance he could smell alcohol on Gerald's breath. He suspects that the reason for Gerald's fall was that he was unsteady on his feet after drinking too much at lunch on the day in question.

- **Advise Fergus on the burden of proof.**

## How to Read this Question

This question requires you to discuss the possible statutory imposition of a reverse burden on an accused and the effect of this in terms of the presumption of innocence provided under **Art 6(2)** of the **European Convention on Human Rights**. The discussion should include the guidance given in cases.

## How to Answer this Question

The problem raises two substantial questions of interpretation; you are going to have to be selective in the amount of law to which you refer. At the same time, you must be careful to apply the law to the facts that you have been given.

The first question to deal with is whether the statute imposes an implied reversal of the burden of proof. At this stage you do not have to consider **Art 6(2)** of the **European Convention on Human Rights**. If you can persuade the judge that the effect of **s2** is to provide an essential element of the offence, the prosecution will have to prove that Fergus failed to take reasonable precautions; there will be no burden on the defendant at all.

Start with **s101** of the **Magistrates' Courts Act 1980**, and show by reference to *Edwards* that its principles apply in this case. *Hunt* is an obvious case on which to rely so as to show that there is some flexibility in applying the **s101** principles. Refer to Lord Griffiths' guidelines and try to apply them in this situation.

Then turn to the problem that will arise if the judge holds that the effect of **s2** *is* to impose a reverse burden on the defendant. Will that be compatible with **Art 6(2)**? Again, there are guidelines to which you can refer, and which can be found in cases such as *ex p Kebilene*, *Lambert*, *Davies* and *Johnstone*. Remember to try to apply these guidelines to the facts that you have been given. You should come to some conclusion, but there can be no question of it being right or wrong. The decision could go either way.

## Up for Debate

The compatibility of the imposition of a reverse burden on an accused with **Art 6(2)** of the **European Convention on Human Rights** is much discussed. You will achieve better marks if you highlight that the main contention is that the jury could convict despite being unsure if the prosecution have proved an essential element of the offence with which the accused stands charged.

## Answer Structure

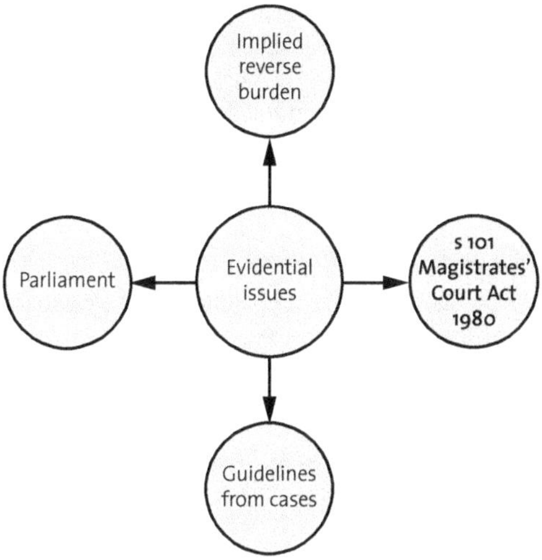


*This diagram shows those elements that you must consider in relation to the advice regarding what Fergus has to prove to defend himself against this action.*

# ANSWER

The first question that arises is whether **s1** of the **Readers (Protection) Act** creates an offence to which **s2** can be relied on as a defence, or whether the sections must be read together, so that the bookshop owner's failure to take reasonable precautions is one of the elements of the offence. If the latter is the correct interpretation, the prosecution will have the burden of proving beyond reasonable doubt that there had been a failure to take reasonable precautions. If the first suggestion is correct, the court will have to consider whether any, and if so what, burden has been imposed by Parliament on the defendant.

**Section 101** of the **Magistrates' Courts Act 1980** can be taken as a convenient starting point. Although the offence with which Fergus is charged is triable only on indictment, it was held in *Edwards* (1975) that **s101** was a statutory statement of the common law applicable in all criminal courts. **Section 101** provides that where the defendant relies for his defence on any 'exception, exemption, proviso, excuse or qualification', whether or not it is part of the description of the offence, the burden of proving such a defence shall be on him.[18]

However, as Lawton LJ observed in *Edwards*, when applying this principle it is necessary to 'construe the enactment under which the charge is laid'. This was subsequently emphasised by the House of Lords in *Hunt* (1987). In that case the prosecution proved that the defendant had been in possession of powder containing morphine, but their evidence did not prove whether the quantity of morphine was more than 0.2 per cent. The relevant legislation exempted from its provisions preparations containing not more than that quantity. The House of Lords held that, on a correct interpretation of the statute, the rule contained in **s101** of the **Magistrates' Courts Act 1980** did not apply because the 0.2 per cent provision was part of the definition of the offence. The burden therefore lay on the prosecution to prove that the powder contained more than that quantity of morphine. It was not for the defence to show that it contained only 0.2 per cent or less. In reaching this conclusion, the House of Lords said that the classification of defences was not constrained by the form of words used or their location in the statute creating the offence.[19]

Lord Griffiths suggested certain guidelines for interpretation. First, he said that courts should be very slow to classify a defence as falling within **s101**, because Parliament can never lightly be taken to have intended to impose an onerous duty on a defendant to prove his innocence. Probably the **Readers (Protection) Act** does not impose an onerous duty on owners of bookshops. They are the persons most familiar with their premises and are in the best position to do what needs to be done to ensure the safety of their customers. Making sure that your premises are safe can hardly be regarded as an onerous duty.

Second, Lord Griffiths said that the ease and difficulty to be encountered by the parties in discharging the legal burden are of great importance. Probably it is no more difficult for a bookshop owner to show what precautions he took than for the prosecution to establish that he did not take all reasonable precautions. It may indeed be easier for the bookshop owner to establish that he took all reasonable precautions because he is likely to be aware of current practices in his trade. Although following common practice will not conclusively establish that all reasonable precautions were taken, it may go some way towards doing so.

Third, the gravity of the offence should be considered. The more serious the offence, the more likely it will be that any ambiguity will be resolved in favour of the defendant. In this case we note that the offence is triable only on indictment; that an unlimited fine can be imposed; that the premises can be forced to close indefinitely; and that a sentence of

18 These first two paragraphs outline the focus of the answer; what the overall effect of **ss 1** and **2** is, and where the burden rests. Setting out the context of an answer is useful especially where fictitious legislation is utilised in a scenario.

19 Discussing the decisions in *Edwards* and *Hunt* demonstrates knowledge of how important it is to construe the provision under which the individual is charged.

imprisonment of two years can also be imposed. The financial penalties are potentially very severe; in contrast the maximum term of imprisonment is light. Taking these matters into consideration, the offence seems not to be among the gravest, though it is by no means trivial.

Although a court might well interpret **s2** as an essential element of the offence, to be proved by the prosecution, there is some danger that it will be regarded as falling within the **s101** rule. The question that would then arise is whether it imposes a legal burden on the defendant, or only an evidential burden. If the imposition of a legal burden would infringe **Art 6(2)** of the **European Convention on Human Rights**, it is likely to be interpreted as imposing an evidential burden only.[20]

It was suggested in *Lambert* (2002) and in *Davies* (2002) that a strict responsibility might be placed on a defendant where the legislation was concerned to regulate the conduct of a particular activity in the public interest, for example, to promote health and safety. This might suggest that a legal burden on Fergus would not infringe **Art 6(2)**. On the other hand, it was said in *Davies* that the absence of a risk of imprisonment was an important factor in deciding whether a reverse burden was legitimate. In this case there is a danger of imprisonment.

Deference should be shown to Parliament's decision. In *Johnstone* (2003) Lord Nicholls pointed out that Parliament had the primary responsibility for deciding what should be the constituent elements of an offence, and the courts should depart from this only if satisfied that the legislature had attached insufficient importance to the presumption of innocence. Ease of proof and a defendant's special knowledge can also be taken into account, as Lord Hope observed in *ex p Kebilene* (2000).

It seems on balance likely that if a court decides that the statute does impose a reverse burden on the defendant, it will decide that this is a legal, not just an evidential, burden.

20 Highlight the legal position where an infringement of **Art 6(2)** is likely. This demonstrates the impact of human rights law on the imposition of burdens on a defendant and the legal response to that.

# 3 Presumptions, Competence and Compellability

## INTRODUCTION

Presumptions fit awkwardly into an evidence course. When lawyers first started to write books on evidence, they used to include large amounts of substantive law on such subjects as trespass, nuisance, bailment, actions on the case and so forth. The object of these writers was to include not only what we should recognise as rules of evidence, relating to such matters as the competence of witnesses and hearsay, but rules about what had to be proved in order to establish particular claims or defences. There was no unifying principle other than the convenience of the arrangement for practitioners. (See, for example, Gilbert's *The Law of Evidence*, 2nd edn, 1760. This was the leading work on the subject in the second half of the eighteenth century; the last edition was published in 1801. See generally W Twining, 'The Rationalist Tradition of Evidence Scholarship', in *Rethinking Evidence: Exploratory Essays*, 2nd edn, 2006, pp. 35–98.)

Modern evidence textbooks deal with some, but by no means all, presumptions. (See the Checklist for details.) However, this is really no more than a hangover from the older way of writing. No successful attempts have been made to find an all-embracing theme that would make 'presumptions' a true part of evidence law. What you will be looking at will be several quite distinct bits of substantive law that have little or no connection with each other.

Because this is an area where attempts to find unifying features have been made so unsuccessfully, you may find classification confusing. When a writer refers to a presumption, you need to be sure about how he is using the word. The sort of presumption that you will be trying to learn about (of death, legitimacy, etc.) is what is often called a 'rebuttable presumption of law'. In my view, it confuses things to talk about anything else as a 'presumption'. If someone refers to a 'presumption of fact' he should mean an *inference* about facts, which is part of an ordinary reasoning process, having nothing specially to do with law at all. And, if he refers to an 'irrebuttable presumption of law', that is just the same as referring to some rule of substantive law.

Thus, to refer to 'the presumption of innocence' is the same thing as referring to the rule that places the burden of proof on the prosecution.

Questions of competence and compellability are mainly governed by statute. You should note that the **Youth Justice and Criminal Evidence Act 1999** also contains provisions that relate to the competence of witnesses and their capacity to be sworn in criminal trials (**ss 53–56**). It also amended **s 80** of the **Police and Criminal Evidence Act 1984**. Spouses and children are the obvious subjects for examination questions; for details, see Checklist.

But note that the protection originally given to spouses was also extended to civil partners by reason of the **Civil Partnership Act 2004, s 84(1)**. There is also a whole host of new authorities on how witnesses (vulnerable, those with autism or other learning disabilities) should be aided to give best evidence; see *R v Cokesix Lumemba; R v JP* [2014] EWCA Crim 2064 and *R v FA* [2015] EWCA Crim 209.

### Checklist

**Students should generally be familiar with the following areas but check your syllabus, because it may provide a narrower or wider range:**

- classifications of presumptions;
- presumption of marriage;
- presumption of legitimacy;
- presumption of death;
- presumption of regularity;
- *res ipsa loquitur*;
- conflicting presumptions;
- presumptions under **Sexual Offences Act 2003, ss 75–77**;
- general rule of universal competence and compellability;
- how a co-accused can become competent for the prosecution;
- comment on an accused's failure to testify;
- competence and compellability of an accused's spouse: for the prosecution, the accused or a co-accused;
- competence of children in civil and criminal cases.

# QUESTION 8

'The theoretical basis for recognising presumptions is that the presumed fact would, in the usual course of events, flow naturally from the existence of the primary fact, so that there is a rational connection between the two so strong that it is unnecessary to require evidence of the presumed fact in the absence of unusual circumstances.'

▶ **Discuss.**

## How to Read this Question

This question requires you to discuss presumptions. The following points should be covered: some of the instances in which they apply, the superficial effect of a presumption and the impact they have on the burden of proof.

## How to Answer this Question

This is an essay question that requires you to consider a subject that has already been referred to in the 'Introduction'. Is it possible to say something that is true about the way in which all rebuttable presumptions of law behave? If it is, is this the common factor that is to be found? It is important to emphasise that this question, like many other essay questions, cannot be answered on knowledge of statutes and cases alone. You need to have read something of the theory of the subject, and in order to answer this question, you should at least have read Colin Tapper on presumptions in *Cross & Tapper on Evidence*, 12th edn, 2010, and Paul Roberts and Adrian Zuckerman in *Criminal Evidence*, 2nd edn, 2010.

You need to cover the following topics:

- the superficial attractiveness of the proposition;
- presumptions that appear to increase artificially the probative worth of the basic facts, for example, presumption of death;
- presumptions designed simply to resolve difficulties of proof, for example, **s 184(1)** of the **Law of Property Act (LPA) 1925**;
- the argument that all presumptions may operate simply as techniques for allocating the burden of proof;
- the diversity of ways in which the 'same' presumption can operate.

The conclusion is that, at best, the quotation tells only part of the story and it may be positively misleading.

### Up for Debate

There is considerable debate in relation to the technical operation of presumptions. For instance, how the presumption of death requires a period of seven years to have elapsed and the effect that this has on the administration of an estate and the lives of those connected (legally) with that person. The law is often described as being piecemeal and criticism is levelled at legislative attempts to clarify it (see the **Presumption of Death Act 2013**). Reference to points such as this evidences wider reading and will often gain you additional credit.

## Answer Structure

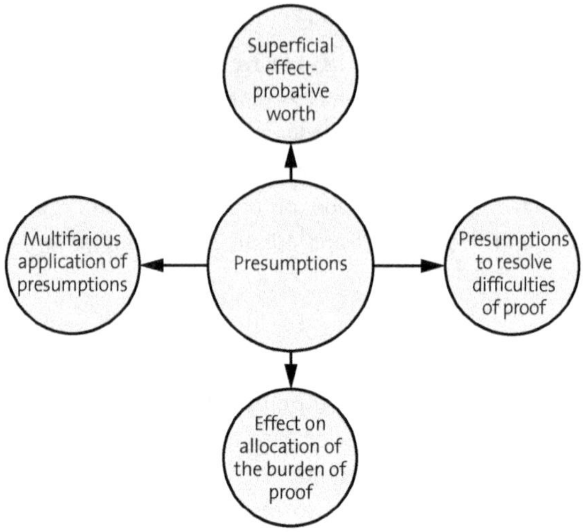


*This diagram shows the main arguments you should follow in relation to a question that asks you to critique a quotation relating to the operation and effect of rebuttable presumptions.*

# ANSWER

The theoretical basis suggested in the quotation is superficially attractive. For example, according to the presumption of legitimacy, it is presumed that a child born during lawful wedlock is legitimate in the absence of evidence to the contrary (*Hetherington v Hetherington* (1887)). Given the fact of a birth in those circumstances, it would seem most unreasonable not to presume the legitimacy of the child.

But not all presumptions provide such a ready illustration of this sort of rational process. According to the presumption of death, a person will be presumed to have died if it is proved that: (a) there is no acceptable evidence that he has been alive at some time during a continuous period of at least seven years; (b) there are persons likely to have heard of him, had he been alive, who have not heard of him during that period; and (c) all due inquiries have been made with a view to finding the person in question, but without success (*Chard v Chard* (1956)).

The presumption in this case appears to operate so as to increase artificially the probative value of the basic facts in the absence of any contrary evidence. So far as probative worth goes, other than policy considerations there is nothing special about seven years' absence as opposed, say, to one of six years. Yet, the former period gives rise to a rebuttable presumption of law, while the latter gives rise to no more than an inference of fact that may be made or not.[1]

1 Sometimes the application of the law is based on the stipulation of an arbitrarily selected period of time, here seven years. Do not be afraid to state this.

In other cases, it seems clear that a presumption has been designed simply in order to resolve a difficulty of proof. An example is **s184(1)** of the **LPA 1925**. This provides that where two or more persons have died in circumstances rendering it uncertain which of them survived the other or others, such death shall (subject to any order of the court), for all purposes affecting the title to property, be presumed to have occurred in order of seniority and, accordingly, the younger shall be deemed to have survived the elder. Here the probative worth of the basic fact is non-existent; the whole effect of the presumption is to allocate the burden of proof.[2]

It has been suggested in fact that a presumption is in all cases simply a technique whereby the substantive law distributes the risk of losing on a given issue, and that it is misleading to try to develop a rationale based on the probative force of the basic facts of the presumption. This misleading approach, it is argued, leads to the conclusion that presumptions such as that of death are simply presumptions of fact to which the law gives artificial weight. If, however, the rationale of presumptions is to be found in the allocation of the burden of proof, the charge of artificiality is misconceived. The rights of someone who has disappeared cannot remain suspended indefinitely; what the law does is to provide, by a rule affecting the burden of proof, a limitation period. The basic fact may, of course, have some probative weight, but it has this by virtue of common sense and experience rather than by virtue of the presumption.[3]

This view of presumptions as devices for allocating the burden of proof receives considerable support from the fact that a particular presumption does not always affect the burden of proof in exactly the same way; the way in which a presumption operates depends on the context in which it may be relevant. This would not be the case if, from a primary fact, there flowed naturally in the usual course of events a particular presumed fact. One would expect a rational process such as that to operate regardless of context.[4]

That this is not the case is shown by the operation of presumptions in a criminal context. According to the presumption of regularity, upon proof of the fact that some official or public act has been performed, or that a person acted in an official capacity, it is presumed that the act which was done complied with any necessary formalities, or that the person so acting had been properly appointed. In *Dillon* (1982), a police officer had been charged in Jamaica with the offence of negligently permitting two prisoners, lawfully in his custody, to escape. The prosecution failed to call any evidence to show that the officer had authority to hold the prisoners in custody, a matter which they had the burden of proving. On a defence submission of no case to answer, the magistrate held that the prosecution was entitled to rely on the presumption of regularity to establish that such authority existed. This decision was upheld by the Court of Appeal of Jamaica but rejected

2 This discussion is a good example of the operation of the law to resolve what could otherwise be an irresolvable dispute.

3 P Roberts and A Zuckerman, *Criminal Evidence*, Oxford University Press, 2004, p. 343.

4 This argument focuses on the rationale of how presumptions affect the allocation of the burden of proof and that value lies in its varying effect.

by the Privy Council, which held that the prosecution was not entitled to rely on a presumption to establish a central element of the offence.[5]

There seems little doubt that the presumption of legitimacy would also affect the burden of proof in different ways, depending on the nature of the proceedings. In a civil case, once birth in lawful wedlock is established, the court must find the child legitimate unless the party opposing legitimacy proves on the balance of probabilities that the child is illegitimate.[6] But suppose a defendant is charged with committing incest with his daughter and his defence is that, though conceived and born in wedlock, she is actually the child of another man. It is most unlikely to be held that the defendant has a legal burden of proof on that issue. It would surely be enough to raise in the minds of the jury a reasonable doubt about whether the woman in question might have been the daughter of another man.[7]

It might be objected that in these criminal examples, there is a conflict of presumptions which produces a different outcome, the presumption with which the others conflict being the presumption of innocence. But this would be to mislead by language. The so-called presumption of innocence is not a rebuttable presumption of law like the others, but is simply a way of stating the rule that in criminal cases the burden of proof is on the prosecution.

At best, therefore, it appears that the theoretical basis for recognising presumptions that is suggested in the quotation does not tell the whole story. At worst, it may be positively misleading.

# QUESTION 9

Charlie, while driving his motorcar, was involved in a collision with Doris, a cyclist aged 14, who suffered a broken leg as a result.

(a) Charlie is charged with dangerous driving. The CPS wish to call the following, both of whom have made statements to the police, as witnesses for the prosecution:

 (i) Ethel, Charlie's wife. She was travelling in the car with Charlie. Shortly after the accident, she made a statement saying that her husband was distracted by a violent argument with her just before he hit Doris's bicycle. Recently, she has been in touch with the officer in the case and has told him that she does not want to give evidence because she loves her husband despite everything.

 (ii) Freddie, aged nine, who saw the accident while he was waiting for a bus to take him to church, where he sings in the choir.

- **Advise the CPS on the competence and compellability of Ethel and Freddie.**

5 This discussion demonstrates the variety of evidential issues that operate where presumptions are concerned.

6 **Section 26** of the **Family Law Reform Act 1969**.

7 *Andrews and Hirst on Criminal Evidence*, 4th edn, 2001, para 4.17.

(b) Charlie has been prosecuted and acquitted. Civil proceedings have now been begun against him on behalf of Doris for negligence. The claimant's solicitors wish to call Ethel and Freddie as witnesses.

- **Advise the solicitors on the competence and compellability of these potential witnesses.**

## How to Read this Question

This question involves the competence and compellability of adult (Ethel) and child (Freddie) witnesses in relation to (a) criminal matters and (b) civil proceedings. You should discuss each one in turn.

## How to Answer this Question

This is one of the topics where evidence law depends on whether the proceedings are criminal or civil. Deal with the criminal trial first, and then the civil trial.

(a) *The criminal trial*

(i) *Ethel.* For competence, see **s 53(1)** of the **Youth Justice and Criminal Evidence Act (YJCEA) 1999**. For compellability, see **s 80** of the **Police and Criminal Evidence Act (PACE) 1984**, as amended by the **YJCEA 1999**. Is this a 'specified offence'? Note Doris's age at the time of the accident. How should 'involves' in **s 80(3)(a)** be interpreted?

(ii) *Freddie.* For competence, see **s 53(1)** of the **YJCEA 1999**. Note **s 55(2)(a)**.

(b) *The civil trial*

(i) *Ethel.* For competence, see *ex p Fernandez* (1861). For compellability, see **s 1** of the **Evidence Amendment Act 1853**.

(ii) *Freddie.* Note the possibility of giving sworn evidence. Your starting point will be the *Hayes* test, with **s 96(2)** of the **Children Act 1989** as a fall-back position.

## Up for Debate

Competence to give evidence relates more to the ability of a person to function as a witness. The principal objective of the court is to achieve a fair trial. Thus, there are fewer misconceptions about the ability of children to give evidence. For an example relating to family proceedings, see: *Re W* [2010] UKSC 12. Issues of competence will often only arise where the child witness has a disability. Making reference, where appropriate, to these points and cases such as *R v FA* [2015] EWCA Crim 209, where the Court of Appeal allowed live evidence through a registered intermediary, will gain you extra marks.

## Applying the Law

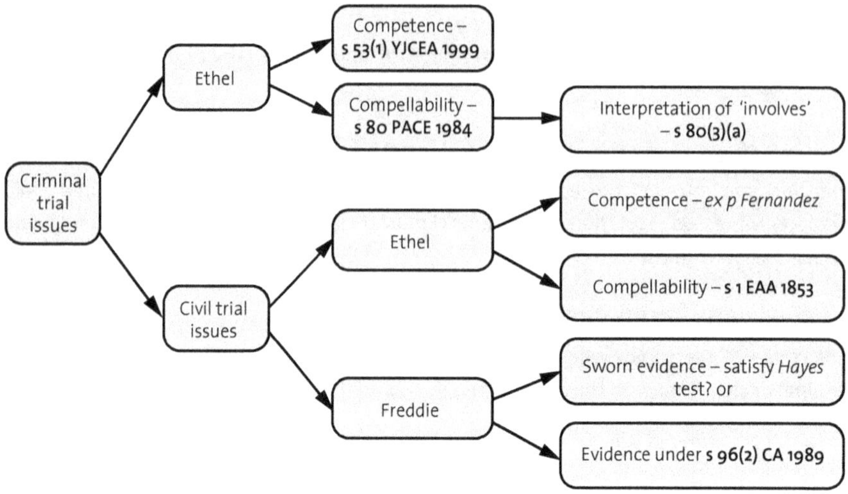


*This mind map highlights the main factors that you should consider in terms of each of the witnesses' ability to give evidence.*

# ANSWER

## THE CRIMINAL TRIAL

Ethel is competent by virtue of **s 53(1)** of the **YJCEA 1999**, which provides that, at every stage in criminal proceedings, all persons are (whatever their age) competent to give evidence. Her compellability will be governed by **s 80** of the **Police and Criminal Evidence Act (PACE) 1984**, as amended. She will be compellable only if the offence with which her husband is charged is a 'specified' offence. At the time of the accident, Doris was under the age of 16. It might be arguable that the offence fell within **s 80(3)(a)**, and so was a specified offence, because it involved injury to a person who was at the material time under the age of 16. The interpretation of 'involves' in this provision is uncertain. It might mean 'involves as a matter of legal definition', as robbery, for example, involves the use of force or a putting in fear of force.[8] If this approach is adopted, dangerous driving is clearly not a specified offence. On the other hand, 'involves' could mean 'involves as a matter of fact in the circumstances of the particular case'. If that were the interpretation adopted, the offence with which Charlie is charged would be a specified offence, and Ethel would be compellable.[9]

Freddie is in principle competent by virtue of **s 53(1)** of the **YJCEA 1999**. There is nothing to suggest that he falls into the category of persons who are not competent that is set out in **s 53(3)**. However, because he is under 14, his evidence will be given unsworn: see **s 55(2)(a)**.

8 See **s 8** of the **Theft Act 1968**.

9 This discussion demonstrates how the interpretation of an uncertain term in a provision can affect whether or not an individual can be compelled to give evidence.

## THE CIVIL TRIAL

The basic rule, set out in *ex p Fernandez* (1861), is that all persons are competent to give evidence and may be compelled to testify. By **s 1** of the **Evidence Amendment Act 1853**, it is specifically provided that the husbands and wives of the parties to civil proceedings are competent *and compellable* to give evidence on behalf of *any* of the parties to the proceedings. Ethel will therefore be a compellable witness for the claimant.[10]

Because this is a civil action, Freddie may give either sworn or unsworn evidence. The question whether he understands the nature of an oath so as to be able to give sworn evidence will presumably be decided by applying the tests formerly used when children gave evidence in criminal proceedings. The judge will question Freddie in open court before he gives evidence. In *Khan* (1981), the Court of Appeal said that although much depended on the type of child before the court, generally, inquiry should be made in the case of a child under 14. The conditions to be satisfied were stated in *Hayes* (1977) to be that the child had a sufficient appreciation of the solemnity of the occasion, and understood that an oath involved an added responsibility to tell the truth over and above the social duty to do so. Understanding of a divine sanction is not required.

If these conditions are not satisfied, Freddie may give unsworn evidence. **Section 96(2)** of the **Children Act 1989** provides that a child's evidence may be heard, even if he does not understand the nature of an oath, if he understands that it is his duty to speak the truth, and he has a sufficient understanding to justify his evidence being heard. Freddie is likely to be competent, and so also compellable (*ex p Fernandez* (1861)).

# QUESTION 10

Eight years ago, Mr and Mrs Austin set off from England to spend an indefinite period of time travelling in South America. They left behind them three adult children: Basil, Cynthia and Darren. At first Mr and Mrs Austin wrote regularly to all the children, but after a time they did so erratically and infrequently. After two years, nothing further was heard from them by any of the children. The letters that had been received showed that Mr and Mrs Austin were travelling through parts of South America where from time to time there was civil unrest and danger from natural disasters such as flooding and earthquakes.

Some years before leaving England, both Mr and Mrs Austin had made wills. Mr Austin left everything to his wife, but he also provided that, if she should predecease him, his estate should be divided equally between 'the legitimate children of my family'. Mrs Austin left everything to her husband; in the event of his predeceasing her, the estate was to be divided between various charities.

Basil and Cynthia say that their parents must by now have died and wish to know what rights of inheritance they have. They say also that Darren, though born to Mrs Austin

10 The principle from *ex p Fernandez* is relevant for the discussion in this question because it sets out the basic rule concerning competence and compellability in civil trials and their extent.

during her marriage, was not the child of Mr Austin but of a man with whom Mrs Austin was having an affair while their father was in prison.

- **Discuss the evidential issues that arise.**

## How to Read this Question

This question requires you to consider three presumptions; death, survivorship and legitimacy. You should explore the technical operation of the presumptions in relation to the available evidence.

## How to Answer this Question

Three problems of law need to be considered here:

- the presumption of death;
- the presumption of survivorship created by **s 184** of the **Law of Property Act 1925**;
- the presumption of legitimacy.

In dealing with these points, you should bear in mind the inferences that might be drawn from the evidence without the aid of presumptions, and also any gaps there may be that necessitate requests for further information.

### Up for Debate

You should highlight that the presumption of legitimacy, in terms of law, operates (in absence of rebuttal) to assure the rights of the parent as well as the child. For instance, the rights of heirs in relation to property.

## Applying the Law

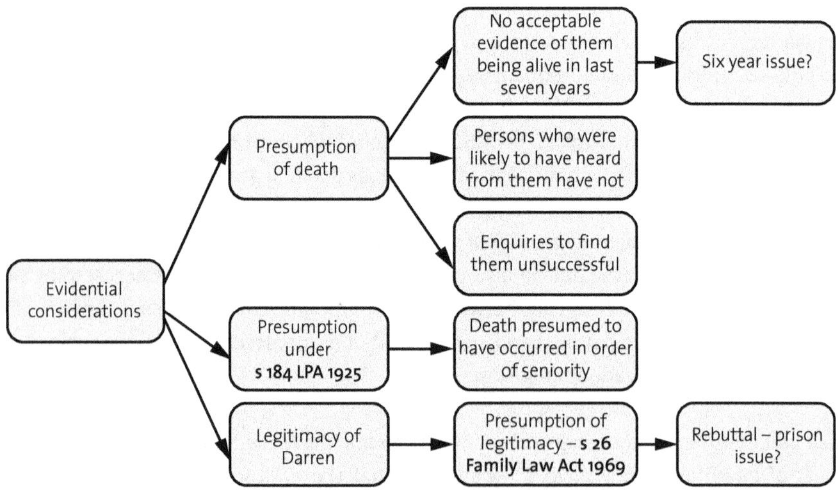


*This mind map illustrates the main evidential issues that arise in terms of a scenario of this sort and the presumptions of death and legitimacy.*

## ANSWER

A person will be presumed to have died if it is proved that:

(a) there is no acceptable evidence that he has been alive at some time during a continuous period of at least seven years;
(b) there are persons likely to have heard of him, had he been alive, who have not heard of him during that period; and
(c) all due inquiries have been made with a view to finding the person in question, but without success (*Chard v Chard* (1956)).[11]

In the case of Mr and Mrs Austin, nothing has been heard for the last six years only, so the presumption cannot be applied. In any case, it does not appear whether there are any other persons who might have heard from Mr and Mrs Austin, or what inquiries, if any, have been made. Thus, even if Basil and Cynthia were to wait for a period of seven years to have elapsed, a court might not be satisfied that all conditions for the operation of the presumption had been complied with.

Quite apart from the presumption, it would be open to a court to infer from appropriate circumstantial evidence that Mr and Mrs Austin had died, but Basil and Cynthia would have the burden of proving their parents' death on the balance of probabilities. Thus, if the evidence were sufficient, there would be no need to wait for the expiry of seven years.[12] Whether the evidence is sufficient is likely to depend largely on what inferences can be drawn as to the presence of Mr and Mrs Austin in areas of natural disaster or insurrection and their likelihood of survival in such circumstances.[13]

**Section 184** of the **Law of Property Act 1925** provides that, in all cases where two or more persons have died in circumstances rendering it uncertain which of them survived the other or others, such death shall (subject to any order of the court), for all purposes affecting the title to property, be presumed to have occurred in order of seniority, and accordingly the younger shall be deemed to have survived the elder. For the children to inherit, it would be necessary for Mr Austin to have survived his wife. By **s 184**, he will be presumed to have done so if he was the younger of the two; it will therefore be necessary to discover their respective ages. There appears to be no reason why **s 184** should not apply where the court makes a finding of death by virtue of the presumption of death.[14]

On the assumption that Mr Austin was younger than his wife and that he therefore survived her, the question of Darren's legitimacy arises. There is a presumption of legitimacy

11 Often it is useful to set out the elements of a presumption and then apply them to the facts. This ensures that you do not miss any of the elements requiring proof.

12 See, for example, *Re Watkins* (1953) for a case in which the presumption of death could not be applied, but the fact of death was nevertheless inferred.

13 This discussion demonstrates knowledge of the instance in which the seven-year rule does not strictly apply – circumstances in which death is a greater likelihood.

14 This discussion is a good example of the operation of the law in resolution of what could be an irresolvable dispute.

in respect of any child who is proved to have been born or conceived in lawful wedlock. However, **s 26** of the **Family Law Reform Act 1969** provides that this presumption may be rebutted by evidence that shows that it is more probable than not that the person in question is illegitimate or legitimate as the case may be. Darren will have the advantage of the presumption because he was born while his parents were lawfully married. It will therefore be for Basil and Cynthia to prove on the balance of probabilities that he is illegitimate in order to exclude him from sharing in the distribution of Mr Austin's estate.

One item of evidence in their favour may be the provision itself in Mr Austin's will; it suggests that he believed that there was at least one child of the family who was not legitimate. Clearly, the evidence of his imprisonment will be of the utmost importance. If, for example, Darren were conceived at a time when Mr Austin could have had no access to his wife, this would seem to rebut the presumption conclusively.

# QUESTION 11

Should spouses be compellable for the prosecution to testify against each other in criminal trials?

## How to Read this Question

This question requires you to explore the rationale that underpinned the old rule relating to making one spouse testify against another and the current position as set out in **s 80 PACE 1984**.

## How to Answer this Question

Your starting point here should be reference to the law as it stands at present. Reference to **s 80** of **PACE** is essential, and there should also be reference to the general rule of compellability, as expressed, for example, in *ex p Fernandez* (1861). To advance very far in your answer it is necessary to say something about the reasons for the old rule that one spouse could not testify against the other. These are, roughly, fourfold: the obsolete idea that husband and wife together have only one legal personality; the avoidance of 'implacable discord and dissension' between husband and wife; the harshness of compelling one spouse to testify against the other; and the public interest in maintaining stable marriages. It will help if you can tie these various arguments into decided cases, particularly if they are fairly recent. To conclude, you need to consider the arguments on each side, to realise that we are dealing with conflicting interests, and to provide reasons, in the light of this conflict, why non-compellability should prevail over compellability, or vice versa. Finally, it is worth noting that the scope of this question is a very general one. Other questions could be posed that require a more detailed consideration of the existing law; you might, for example, be asked to consider whether, if some degree of non-compellability is suitable, the existing legislation in **s 80(3)** should be amended, so as to provide a wider or narrower range of 'specified' offences where the spouse will be compellable.

## Up for Debate

To gain extra marks you can make reference to the new **Marriages (Same Sex Couples) Act 2013** and the issue of compelling one spouse to give evidence against another – this will show up-to-date knowledge.

## Answer Structure

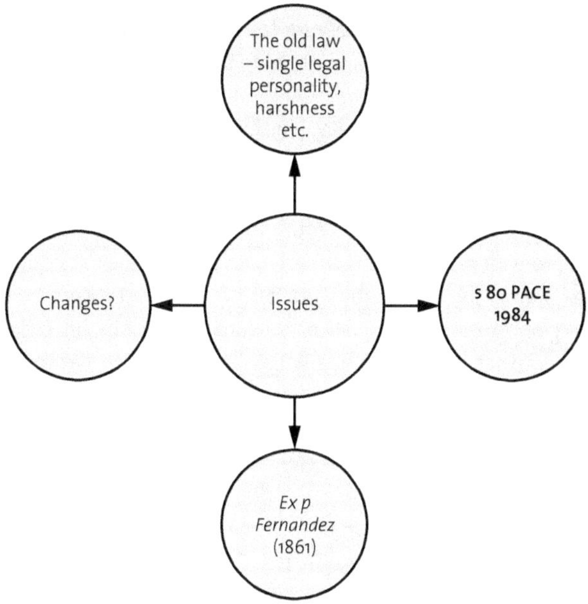


*This diagram sets out the main factors that you must consider in an essay question on the compellability of spouses and civil partners to give crown evidence.*

# ANSWER

Under **s 80** of the **Police and Criminal Evidence Act (PACE) 1984**, spouses and civil partners are compellable for the prosecution to testify against each other in only limited circumstances. In this way the Act has made some inroads on the common law privilege of spouses to refuse to testify for the prosecution against each other. The question is whether this is a privilege that should be relegated to history, so that spouses, and now civil partners as well, have no special protection against the general rule, stated for example in *ex p Fernandez* (1861), that all competent witnesses are compellable.[15]

15 This introduction highlights the current position of the law relating to the compellability of spouses. Often it is useful to set some of the major points for discussion – here it is whether this should be reformed.

The reasons for the general exception have varied to some extent over time. Originally, a wife was not even competent to testify for or against her husband, and vice versa. Thus the question of compellability did not directly arise, but the justifications expressed in that context were later used in relation to a spouse's general non-compellability for the prosecution. At least one justification, the theoretical unity of husband and wife in one person,[16] is now obsolete. Other justifications may still be operative. Coke was of the opinion that without the exception there might result 'implacable discord and dissension' between husband and wife and be 'a means of great inconvenience'. Hale, Hawkins and Blackstone followed Coke's reasoning. Gilbert provided an additional argument. According to him, it would be 'very hard' for a wife to testify against her husband because it would damage their shared interest in maintaining the marriage.

Not everyone accepted the rule uncritically. Bentham pointed out in his *Rationale of Judicial Evidence* that human families living together illustrated a variety of relationships, every one of which would be liable to suffer damage were one person to testify against another. It was illogical, he argued, to identify the relationship of husband and wife as requiring special protection, and for this situation he blamed 'the heroic dimensions given to the conjugal flame by the sentimentality of English lawyers'.[17] Its persistence amounted, he argued, to a great injustice, because it could be an encouragement to crime. The argument that it was particularly harsh for a wife by her testimony to bring about the conviction of her husband was not one that should prevent her from testifying; it was one that the husband should have had in mind as part of his likely punishment when considering whether to commit the offence.

The interests of the public in protection from crime were considered by Geoffrey Lane LJ when giving judgment in *Hoskyn* (1979) in the Court of Appeal. Even where the wife herself is a victim of the crime, there is a public element. It is in the public interest that evidence of a crime should be freely available to the court that tries the offence. In some cases it might well be that the spouse is the only person who is able to provide evidence for the prosecution. The criminal law serves a dual purpose: to help citizens who themselves seek its protection, but also to protect other citizens.[18]

At the root of the problem presented by any spousal non-compellability are certain conflicting interests. Clearly, the public has an interest in seeing that crimes are successfully prosecuted. A guilty man who goes free because of a spouse's non-compellability is likely to be encouraged in his criminal activities. To that extent, members of the public may be at risk of further crimes from him. Further, the fact that a man or woman has gone 'scot free' in this way may bring the law itself into disrepute. On the other hand, stable relationships are good for the individuals who are in them, and it is widely accepted that they

16 Co. Litt. 6 b, quoted by Lord Wilberforce in *Hoskyn v Metropolitan Police Commissioner* (1979).

17 *Rationale of Judicial Evidence*, Book 9, Part 4, Chapter 5, in *The Works of Jeremy Bentham*, edited by John Bowring (Edinburgh: William Tait, 1838–1843), vol. 7. Accessed at http://oll.libertyfund.org/title/1998/131157.

18 This discussion explains the basis of the law and the influences that impacted on it.

are good for society as a whole. It may be anomalous that two particular stable relationships, those of marriage and civil partnership, are protected when others, such as parent and child, are not. But if such relationships ought to be protected for society's good, that is an argument to extend the exception to the general rule of compellability rather than an argument for total abolition.[19]

The question must be whether the encouragement of stable marriages is so important as to outweigh the benefit to the public from securing a conviction in a proper case. Marriage today is not, in many cases, the stable relationship that it once was. Many marriages will potentially last far longer than marriages in other centuries when life expectancy was shorter. Marriages that are not harmonious can be readily dissolved. Divorce has been easily obtainable for some decades; when spousal non-compellability was initially recognised, divorce was impossible without a private Act of Parliament. There is wide recognition today that the absence of a parent can be harmful for a child and that a substitute for a missing parent is not always satisfactory. Unfortunately, modern marriages are often so fragile that to try to avoid marriage break-up by suspending the general rule about compellability is likely to strengthen the institution of marriage only minimally, but do rather more harm to society by removing an opportunity for its protection and, possibly, by bringing the law into disrepute where a case attracts sufficient publicity.[20]

It is understandable that since Parliament decided that civil partnerships should be given so far as possible the same advantages as marriages, the benefits of **s80** of **PACE** should have been extended to take this into account. It was not known what proportion of these partnerships was the basis for bringing up children, and it may have been difficult for that reason to assess the public interest in maintaining their stability. The **Marriages (Same Sex Couples) Act 2013** has legalised same-sex marriage in the UK, although note that civil partnerships are still available, it is therefore suggested in relation to both of these, that it is unlikely to be greater than the benefit of maintaining marriages, so that, on the argument above, the removal of non-compellability in those cases should also follow.

19 This paragraph demonstrates that while it is important to highlight the problems that are caused by rules of this sort, it is equally important to present both sides of the argument.

20 This question requires a discussion of the costs and benefits of reform to the law – do not be afraid to voice an objective opinion.

# 4 Hearsay I

## INTRODUCTION

**Section 1(2)** of the **Civil Evidence Act 1995** defines hearsay, for the purposes of that Act, as 'a statement made otherwise than by a person while giving oral evidence in the proceedings which is tendered as evidence of the matters stated'. That definition is, in effect, adopted in **s 114(1)** of the **Criminal Justice Act (CJA) 2003**, which states, 'In criminal proceedings a statement not made in oral evidence in the proceedings is admissible as evidence of any matter stated if, but only if...', and then goes on to set out the circumstances in which such evidence will be admissible.

Different approaches to the rule against hearsay have been taken in civil and criminal proceedings. The **Civil Evidence Act 1995** boldly enacts in **s 1(1)** that 'in civil proceedings evidence shall not be excluded on the ground that it is hearsay'. In criminal proceedings the law is governed by **Part 11, Chapter 2** of the **CJA 2003**. This does not abolish the rule against hearsay. Instead, it defines the rule and codifies the exceptions; but it achieves the latter task in a half-hearted way by preserving a number of existing common law exceptions. At least for criminal trials it is necessary to understand the scope of the rule, because it would be absurd to develop an argument that evidence should be included as a hearsay exception if the rule does not apply in the first place. It is necessary to concentrate on two features in order to understand the scope of the rule: the definitions of 'statement' and 'a matter stated', and the purpose for which evidence of an out-of-court statement is being adduced.

**Section 115(2)** of the **CJA 2003** defines a statement as 'any representation of fact or opinion made by a person by whatever means; and it includes a representation made in a sketch, photofit or other pictorial form'. The representation can therefore be made by any method. Under the common law, sketches and photofit images were held to be unaffected by the rule. This was illogical, and the Act now brings them, and representations by any other pictorial form, within the rule.

**Section 115(3)** provides as follows:

> A matter stated is one to which this Chapter applies if (and only if) the purpose, or one of the purposes, of the person making the statement appears to the court to have been –
>
> (a) to cause another person to believe the matter, or
>
> (b) to cause another person to act or a machine to operate on the basis that the matter is as stated.

The common law rule against hearsay was held in *Kearley* (1992) to cover non-assertive utterances, such as questions, commands and greetings, where the maker did not intend to communicate any information at all, but where inferences as to the existence of some fact could be drawn from what was said. The decision was widely criticised and the Law Commission recommended that this development should be reversed. **Section 115(3)** corresponds to **cl 2(3)** in the bill drafted by the Law Commission to achieve this result. Its effect is to remove 'implied assertions' from the scope of the hearsay rule by making it essential, for the operation of the rule, that the person whose words or actions are reported should have had as at least one purpose that of causing another person to believe the matter that he stated. This effect was confirmed by the Court of Appeal in *Singh* (2006).

The rule against hearsay excludes an item of evidence *only if the purpose of adducing that evidence is to establish the truth of the facts stated*. It follows that in relation to any item of evidence that you suspect may be caught by the rule, you need first to ask: 'What is the *job of proof* that this item of evidence is being put forward to do?' Only when you know what this is can you see whether the evidence is caught by the hearsay rule, which is brought into operation not by any particular form of words, but by the use that is going to be made of them. Putting it another way, you need to know the *relevance* of the evidence being considered.

Do not try to avoid the problem by saying that an item of evidence might be excluded for offending the rule against hearsay, but might be admitted to prove that the assertion was made. This will discredit you in the eyes of the examiner. If you think that somebody might want to show simply that an assertion was made, you must explain to the examiner why that is the case. For example, in a case like *Subramaniam v Public Prosecutor* (1956), you would say that the evidence ought to be admitted because any threats are likely to have affected the mind of the defendant, thus making the evidence relevant to his defence of duress.

This chapter concentrates mainly on the scope of the rule against hearsay, but some reference is also made to the unavailability exception in **s116** of the **CJA 2003** and to the 'safety-valve' exception in **s114**.

## Checklist

**Students should be familiar with the following areas:**

- the definition of hearsay reflected in **s114(1)** of the **CJA 2003**;
- the definitions of 'statement' and 'matter stated';
- statements produced by machines;
- 'negative hearsay';
- the importance of relevance in the rule against hearsay;
- justifications for excluding hearsay evidence;
- the unavailability exception in **s116** of the **CJA 2003**;
- the 'safety-valve' exception in **s114** of the **CJA 2003**.

# QUESTION 12

What effect does the **Human Rights Act 1998** have on the law relating to hearsay?

## How to Read this Question

This question requires you to explore the admission of hearsay evidence and its compatibility with the defendant's right to a fair trial under **Art 6** of the **European Convention on Human Rights**. In short, counsel for the defendant should be able to test the opposing evidence through the cross-examination of witnesses.

## How to Answer this Question

The conclusion that you are aiming for is that **Art 6** of the **ECHR** provides a right for defendants to have witnesses against them cross-examined, but it does not ban hearsay evidence, and may even permit it in certain cases where hearsay is the sole or principal evidence for the prosecution. It's particularly important to plan an essay such as this, and to spell out that plan at the beginning of your essay so that you and the reader can have clearly in mind where the argument is going. If you don't do this, it's all too easy for the essay to degenerate into 'all the cases I can remember about **Art 6**', or even 'all the cases I can half-remember about the **European Convention**'. It's very useful to summarise the argument again at the end of your essay. It will leave a clear impression of your argument in the mind of the examiner.

It would be helpful to include the following points:

- the way in which the **Convention** affects decisions of English courts;
- **Art 6(3)(d)**;
- the limited effect of the Article – *Xhabri* (2005);
- does **Art 6(3)(d)** ban hearsay evidence where it is the sole or principal evidence against a defendant? *Luca v Italy* (2003); *Sellick* (2005); *Al-Khawaja* (2005); *Grant v The Queen* (2006).

### Up for Debate

There has been discussion in relation to the contradiction between the Court of Justice of the European Union's decision in *Al-Khawaja* and the Supreme Court's decision in *Horncastle* on fairness where the case is solely or primarily based on hearsay evidence. A short discussion on this and the argument relating to how the safeguards in the **CJA 2003** and **s78** of **PACE 1984** mitigate unfairness will gain you additional credit.

## Answer Structure

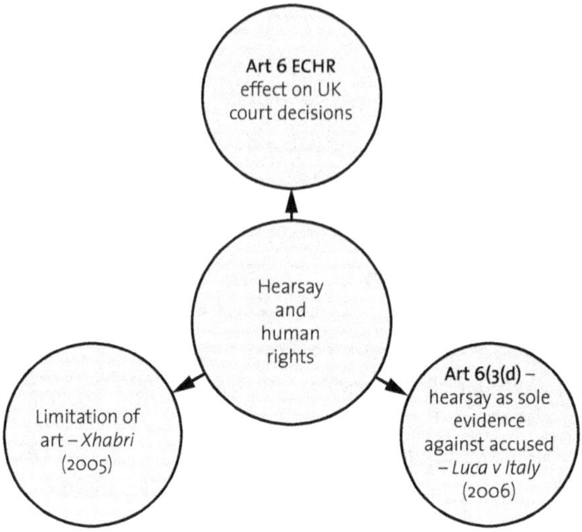


*This diagram outlines those arguments that you should include on the compatibility of the admission of hearsay evidence and the* **European Convention of Human Rights**.

# ANSWER

I shall argue in this essay that although the English courts are bound by **Art 6** of the **ECHR** to provide defendants with an opportunity to examine witnesses appearing against them, this is only one feature of the right to a fair trial. In appropriate circumstances the interest of the public in general may allow even the sole or principal evidence against a defendant to be given as hearsay. This is particularly likely to be the case where the defendant himself has been responsible for the failure of the witness to appear at trial. It follows that although the **Human Rights Act 1998** enacts principles that limit the use of hearsay evidence, such evidence is in principle admissible and may be so even where it is the sole or principal evidence against a defendant.[1]

One of the effects of the **Human Rights Act 1998** is to make the **European Convention on Human Rights** directly enforceable by English courts. Further, by **s 2(1)(a)**, a court determining a question that has arisen in connection with a **Convention** right must take into account judgments of the European Court of Human Rights. These are not binding authorities, but it is expected that English courts will follow them unless restrained from doing so by statute or binding case law.

Among the 'minimum rights' of a defendant in criminal proceedings is the right under **Art 6(3)(d)** of the **Convention** 'to examine or have examined witnesses against him'. Broadly

1 In essay questions on hearsay evidence it is useful to set out the main thrust of the argument: whether the use of such evidence is fair.

speaking, the effect of this is to give a defendant the right to have a witness who gives evidence against him called to give his testimony and be subjected to cross-examination. It amounts to a prima facie prohibition on the admission of hearsay evidence to support the prosecution case, but the considerations that support this prohibition also justify the exclusion of hearsay evidence that supports the defence case (*Thomas v UK* (2005)). In *R v T(D)* (2009) the Court of Appeal acknowledged that there was a right to confrontation under **Art 6**, which should not be departed from lightly.

The right recognised by **Art 6(3)(d)** is, however, limited in its application. First, the European Court has often said that the admissibility of evidence is a matter for national law, and that its own role is to assess the overall fairness of the criminal proceedings in question. The rights set out in **Art 6(3)** are aspects of the right to a fair trial but are not absolute in themselves. Second, the Court has recognised the need for a fair balance between the general interest of the community and the rights of individual defendants. It is unsurprising therefore that the Court of Appeal said in *Xhabri* (2005) that there is no merit in the argument that **s 114 CJA 2003** is incompatible with **Art 6**.[2]

In *Luca v Italy* (2003) there was a suggestion by the European Court that where a conviction is based solely, or to a decisive degree, on statements made by a person whom the defendant has had no opportunity to examine, the rights of the defendant will have been restricted to such an extent as to be incompatible with **Art 6**. If this is right, there would be conflict with a line of English authority to the effect that even where hearsay evidence is the sole or decisive evidence against a defendant, it is possible to admit it without infringing the defendant's right to a fair trial. In *Sellick* (2005) the Court of Appeal said that where a court was sure that a witness had been kept from giving evidence by a defendant, or by persons acting for him, there would be no infringement of **Art 6** because the defendant would have denied himself the opportunity of cross-examining the witness. It was necessary to bear in mind the rights of victims and of the public in general as well as those of the defendant. The Court said that there would be more difficulty where the evidence was not so clear-cut, so that it was only highly probable that a witness had been intimidated.

Hearsay evidence of a complainant was admitted in *Al-Khawaja* (2005). In that case the appellant had been charged with two counts of indecent assault, but one of the complainants had died by the time the trial took place. Her statement was admitted in accordance with legislation then in operation. On appeal, it was argued that this violated **Art 6(3)(d)**. The appeal was dismissed. The Court of Appeal said that the public interest in enabling the prosecution to proceed must not outweigh the defendant's right to a fair trial, but the right of cross-examination was only one element in such a trial. In that case, the appellant had been able to attack the accuracy of the deceased complainant's

2 This discussion highlights that the **HRA 1998** raises major issues relating to the admission of hearsay evidence and the fair administration of criminal proceedings. It makes the important point that the right, as set out, is not absolute and this means **s 114** of the **CJA 2003**, which makes hearsay admissible in specified circumstances, is compatible with it.

statement by exploring inconsistencies between it and evidence of recent complaints that she had made. He had also been able to adduce expert evidence to counter her allegations, and the trial judge had pointed out to the jury the difficulties presented by lack of an opportunity to cross-examine the witness. The proceedings as a whole had been fair.

The matter later came before the European Court of Human Rights, which ruled in *Al-Khawaja v UK* (2009) that hearsay was inadmissible where it was the sole or decisive evidence against a defendant. However, in *R v Horncastle* (2009) the UK Supreme Court declined to follow the European Court's decision, on the ground that the rule against using hearsay in such cases had been introduced into European jurisprudence without discussion of its underlying principles, and without consideration of whether there was justification for imposing it on common law systems. The Supreme Court said that the safeguards enacted by the **Criminal Justice Act 2003** made the rule unnecessary.[3]

For the reasons given above, it appears that although the English courts are bound by **Art 6** of the **ECHR** to provide defendants with an opportunity to examine witnesses appearing against them, this is only one feature of a fair trial. In appropriate circumstances the interest of the public in general may allow even the sole or main evidence against a defendant to be given as hearsay. This is particularly likely to be the case where the defendant himself has been responsible for the failure of the witness to appear at trial. The **Human Rights Act 1998** enacts principles that have a limiting effect on the use of hearsay evidence, but such evidence is in principle admissible.

# QUESTION 13

Has the hearsay rule been brought closer to its rationale by the reforms in the **Criminal Justice Act 2003**?

## How to Read this Question

This question requires you to consider the hearsay rule. In short, to discuss the rationale that underpins it, the issues with the application of the rule (*Kearley*) and the changes brought in by the **CJA 2003**.

## How to Answer this Question

You need to begin by stating the traditional rationale – in fact, a collection of reasons – for having a rule against hearsay. Lord Normand in *Teper v R* (1952) is a useful source. Then go on to show ways in which the rule was formerly applied, despite the fact that the rationale did not operate. It would be helpful to make some reference to challenges to the rationale, and to the effect of *Kearley* in divorcing rule from rationale. Finally, consider the effect of the new provisions in the **Criminal Justice Act (CJA) 2003**.

3 It is good practice in a question such as this to use cases that highlight how these rights have been interpreted at a European and domestic (UK) level and the subsequent conflicts that have arisen thereby.

In summary, the essay is constructed as follows:

- traditional reasons for the rule against hearsay;
- application of the rule when some reasons were absent: *Sparks v R* (1964), *Myers v DPP* (1965);
- questionable validity of some reasons against hearsay;
- effect of extending the rule to implied assertions;
- the suggested rights of confrontation and challenge;
- effect of reforms in the **CJA 2003**.

## Up for Debate

Again, mentioning whether (and how) the **CJA 2003** reconciles the right to a fair trial (**Art 6**) and the public interest will gain you credit.

## Answer Structure

*This diagram shows the factors to consider in terms of whether the statutory scheme under the* **CJA 2003** *has brought hearsay closer to its original purpose.*

# ANSWER

In *Teper v R* (1952), Lord Normand explained the rationale of the rule against hearsay in this way. Hearsay is not the best evidence, and it is not delivered on oath. The truthfulness and accuracy of the person whose words are recounted by another witness cannot be tested by cross-examination, and the light that the original speaker's demeanour would have thrown on his testimony is lost.[4]

4 In essay questions it is important to set out the issues raised by the admission of hearsay evidence.

But it is clear that the rule against hearsay has been applied when some of these criticisms have been inapplicable. In *Sparks v R* (1964), for example, the trial judge refused to allow the mother of a girl aged three to give evidence that her daughter had told her that she had been assaulted by 'a coloured boy'. The Privy Council upheld this decision. But there was no significant hearsay danger. The child's statement was unambiguous, she was unlikely to have been mistaken and the danger that she might have lied was surely non-existent.[5]

Another example is *Myers v DPP* (1965). In order to show that cars sold by the defendant had been stolen, the prosecution wished to call an employee who was in charge of records kept by the car manufacturers. These records were microfilms of cards that had been filled in by production line workers. They showed details of numbers stamped on the cylinder blocks of the cars on the production line. The House of Lords held that this evidence was hearsay, and so inadmissible. But the manufacturers' records must have been far more reliable than the memories of the workers, even if they could have been identified and called.

It is arguable that the hearsay rule became divorced from some elements of its rationale because those elements had become obsolete, or at least questionable. The argument that hearsay is not the best evidence has always been unsatisfactory. Where hearsay is the only evidence of some matter, it will be the best evidence of that matter. The Law Commission concluded that there is no clear evidence that an oath or affirmation in itself promotes truthful testimony.[6] Wigmore thought that the oath added little to cross-examination, which he thought was the real test.[7] In any case, the argument that hearsay is not on oath addresses only the danger that the person reported might have made a false statement deliberately. It can be no safeguard against an original observation that was mistaken. Opinions have differed about the value of a witness's demeanour in testing reliability.[8] The difficulty in recapturing the emphasis and tone of voice of the original utterance may be a more significant objection to admissibility. The main element in Lord Normand's explanation that survives today is the absence of an opportunity to cross-examine the original speaker.[9]

The extension of the hearsay rule to implied assertions in *Kearley* (1992) divorced the rule even from the rationale based on absence of cross-examination. Lord Normand's objection was that the truthfulness and accuracy of someone whose words are reported by another witness cannot be tested. But where the words relied on are non-assertive, they cannot have a truth-value, and this objection cannot apply. The real objection here is that

5 The case of *Sparks* highlights how the strict application of the rule may lead to otherwise relevant evidence being excluded from the jury's consideration.

6 Law Com No 245, Cm 3670, para 3.13.

7 *Wigmore on Evidence*, 3rd edn, 1940, vol 5, para 1, 362.

8 Law Com No 245, Cm 3670, paras 3.9–3.12.

9 This discussion demonstrates knowledge through the analysis of the main reasons for seeking to exclude hearsay evidence from trials; what is quite rightly deduced is that the main issue is with the lack of opportunity to subject this evidence to cross-examination.

the original speaker may be mistaken (though hardly dishonest) in the underlying belief that prompted the non-assertive utterance. If Sheetal is overheard asking James, 'Have you any bananas for sale today?' that utterance cannot be true or false. What is true or false is Sheetal's underlying belief that James is in the business of selling bananas.

Lord Normand's explanation of the rule against hearsay relies solely on the limited probative weight to be given to hearsay evidence. A different kind of argument is based not on rectitude of decision, but on concern for procedural rights.[10] There are two rights that may be relied on in support of the hearsay rule. One is the right of confrontation, by which evidence cannot be given against a defendant behind his back. The other is the right of challenge to witnesses. Although these rights make for rectitude of decision, they also maximise the defendant's participation in his own trial and so promote the legitimacy of the verdict in his eyes and in the eyes of the public generally.

Hearsay evidence appears to infringe both the right of confrontation and the right of challenge. There is no absolute right of physical confrontation in English law. Evidence may be given by video link, for example. And European decisions show that hearsay evidence can be used against defendants in certain circumstances, despite **Art 6(3)(d)** of the **European Convention on Human Rights**, which provides that everyone charged with a criminal offence has the right to examine or have examined witnesses against him. Nevertheless, in *R v T(D)* (2009) the Court of Appeal said that there is a right of confrontation under **Art 6** of the **ECHR**, which should not be departed from lightly. In *Al-Khawaja v UK* (2009) the European Court held that hearsay was inadmissible where it was the sole or decisive evidence against a defendant. However, in *R v Horncastle* (2009) the UK Supreme Court declined to follow the European Court's decision, on the ground that the rule against using hearsay in such cases had been introduced into European jurisprudence without discussion of its underlying principles, and without consideration of whether there was justification for imposing it on common law systems.[11]

One of the major reforms effected by the **CJA 2003** was, as the Court of Appeal acknowledged in *Singh* (2006), to remove the concept of 'implied assertions' from the scope of the rule against hearsay. This was done by the definition of 'a matter stated' in **s 115(3)**. In this way the new legislation closed a gap between rule and rationale that the decision in *Kearley* had opened. Further, the decision in *Sparks v R* would almost certainly not be the same today. The reason for this is the existence of the 'safety-valve' contained in **s 114(1)(d)** of the Act, whereby a hearsay statement is admissible either for the prosecution or the defence if the court is satisfied that it is in the interests of justice for it to be admissible. The court must have regard to the factors set out in **s 114(2)**, but this list is intended to focus attention on whether the circumstances surrounding the making of the hearsay statement show that it can be treated as sufficiently reliable to be admitted, despite the fact that its maker cannot be cross-examined. The fact that Parliament, or at least the

10 See IH Dennis, *The Law of Evidence*, 3rd edn, 2007, sections 16.5–16.7.

11 The discussion of *Al-Khawaja* and *Horncastle* highlights the conflict between the interpretation of the right at a European and domestic (UK) level and the subsequent issue that has arisen as a result of this.

Law Commission, was conscious of the real dangers of unreliability is shown by the special provisions relating to multiple hearsay contained in **s121(1)**. The hearsay rule was made to accord more with its rationale by the provisions permitting documentary hearsay in the **Criminal Justice Act 1988**. But the position of oral hearsay remained unchanged until **s116** of the **CJA 2003** allowed oral as well as written statements to be admissible where a witness was unavailable.[12]

In these respects at least, the **CJA 2003** has brought the law relating to hearsay closer to the traditional rationale for exclusion.

# QUESTION 14

Oliver Mellors is charged with the murder in London of Connie Chatterley. The case for the prosecution is that they met at Connie's house, and that during a quarrel Oliver struck Connie repeatedly with a cricket bat, thereby causing her death. There is medical evidence that Connie died between 1 pm and 2 pm. The police found a gold cigarette case engraved with the initials 'OM' beside the body. They subsequently interviewed Mellors, who claimed to have been in France on the day that Connie was killed. Later, a neighbour told the police that she had seen Mellors in London on the day in question, but no written statement was taken and the witness cannot now be traced. Connie's gardener has told the police that at about 10.30 am on that day he overheard a conversation between Connie and a man. He did not see either of them, but he recognised Connie's voice and he thought he recognised that of Mellors. He says that Connie said: 'Don't forget to buy some fish, Oliver.' The man replied, 'I'll get some on the way home.'

- **Discuss the evidential issues that arise.**

## How to Read this Question

This question requires you to consider the relevance of the evidence presented and whether each poses any hearsay issues for the purposes of admission. For example, the cigarette case is original evidence but what issues (if any) does the engraving pose?

## How to Answer this Question

You must first decide what items of evidence have to be discussed. They are as follows:

- The discovery of the cigarette case. What is its relevance? Is there a hearsay problem? If there is, can it be avoided?
- The relevance of a false alibi. Is hearsay involved in relating what Mellors said about being in France?
- Can evidence be adduced of what the neighbour said to establish that the alibi was false?
- The gardener's evidence. What is its relevance?

12 This discussion demonstrates knowledge relating to some of the fundamental changes brought in by the **CJA 2003**.

## Up for Debate

The admission of hearsay where the witness is not available (for whatever reason) to give evidence has been widely criticised – consider the right to a fair trial. Briefly exploring the impact that the unavailability of a witness has will gain you credit. Read the Law Commission's paper called 'Evidence in Criminal Proceedings: Hearsay and Related Topics' for a greater insight.

## Applying the Law

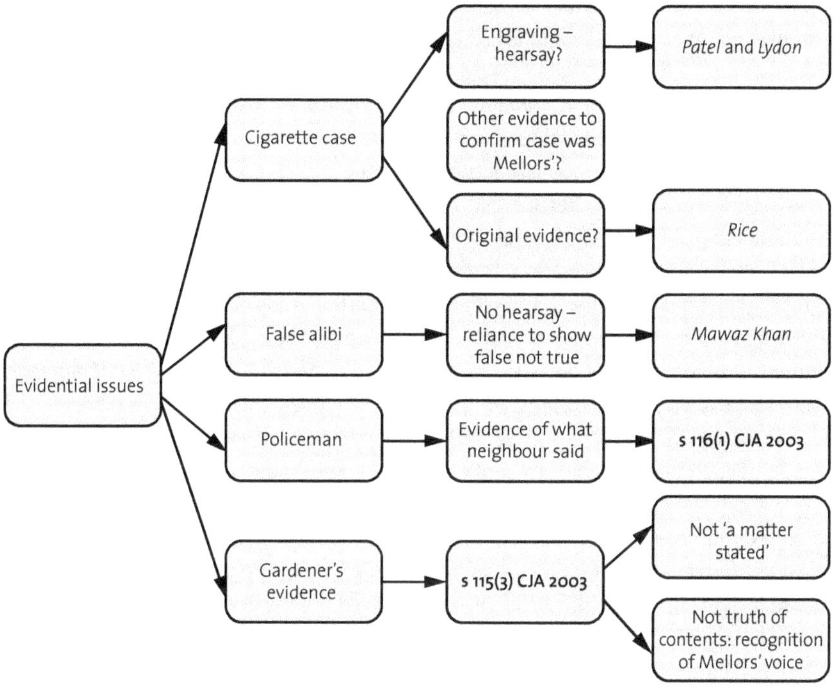


*This mind map shows the main factors around the evidence against Mellors and whether it can be adduced.*

# ANSWER

The first issue concerns the discovery of the engraved cigarette case. This may assist the prosecution by showing that the defendant was present at the scene of the crime at about the time when the murder took place. For this purpose, it would have to be established that the cigarette case belonged to the defendant, and the engraved initials suggest that this was so. But is there a hearsay problem? It is arguable that the context in which the initials appear shows that their function is to assert ownership; this appears to make the prosecution rely on a statement for the truth of its contents, contrary to the rule against hearsay. A similar situation arose in *Patel v Comptroller of Customs* (1966), where labels on goods that stated the country of origin were held by the Privy Council to be inadmissible as proof of where the goods came from.[13]

The country of origin of the goods was one of the matters in issue in the case of *Patel*, and this serves to distinguish it from *Lydon* (1987). In the latter case, the prosecution wished to adduce evidence that a piece of paper bearing the words 'Sean rules' had been found near the scene of the crime. This was alleged to be relevant because it tended to connect the defendant, whose first name was Sean, with the commission of the offence. The Court of Appeal held that this evidence was admissible because although the words on the paper constituted an assertion, it was not in itself an assertion of anything that was relevant to the facts in issue. The fact that something relevant to a fact in issue might be inferred from this item of evidence did not affect admissibility.

Here, however, the inscription arguably does amount to an assertion of a matter, which the prosecution wishes to establish as part of its case – the ownership of the cigarette case. In principle, therefore, admissibility seems to be in doubt because of the rule against hearsay. However, it may be possible for the prosecution to rely on evidence from acquaintances of Mellors who can recognise the cigarette case as one that Mellors used to carry. *Miller v Howe* (1969) suggests that something that is written will not be caught by the rule against hearsay when it is an identifying part of an object, the identity of which is in issue, and not merely an assertion of a characteristic of the object. This was a case where the question arose whether a particular breath-testing device had been the one approved by the Home Secretary, an 'Alcotest 80'. The Court of Appeal indicated that a label to that effect on the device would have been sufficient evidence of its identity, and that even the presence of such a label on the box containing the device would have been enough.

The prosecution could also try to rely on the decision in *Rice* (1963) in order to argue that the cigarette case was admissible as an item of original, as opposed to hearsay, evidence, because a cigarette case with those initials engraved on it is likely to belong to someone with those initials. A more recent case is *Lilley* (2003), where the Court of Appeal held that the words 'Sharon's book' on the cover of an exercise book, which had been used to practise forging signatures, were not caught by the rule against hearsay. They operated simply as evidence of the defendant's connection with a conspiracy to defraud.[14]

A last resort would be the 'safety-valve' exception to the rule against hearsay provided by **s 114(1)(d)** of the **Criminal Justice Act (CJA) 2003**.

The giving of a false alibi may be an indication of guilt. The prosecution will have no difficulty in adducing evidence that Mellors told the police that he was in France on the day of

13 See also *Comptroller of Customs v Western Electric Co Ltd* (1966).

14 This discussion demonstrates the relative importance of the purpose for adducing a piece of hearsay evidence, something that has been one of the main arguments for its admission and for having safeguards in place for this. This also shows how prejudicial hearsay evidence is.

the murder. No breach of the rule against hearsay is involved because the prosecution wishes to rely, as in *Mawaz Khan* (1967), not on the truth of what was said, but on its falsity.[15,16]

The policeman to whom the neighbour spoke might be able to give evidence of what he was told by virtue of the unavailability exception in **s116(1)** of the **CJA 2003**. The neighbour, had she been available, could have given evidence of having seen Mellors in London on the relevant day, thus satisfying **s116(1)(a)**. It is assumed that the neighbour can be identified (even though they cannot trace her) so as to satisfy **s116(1)(b)**. In the absence of identification the evidence could not be given. The remaining question would then be whether any of the five conditions mentioned in **s116(2)** is satisfied. The obvious condition on which to rely is condition (d). It would be necessary to show that 'such steps as it is reasonably practicable to take' have been taken to find the neighbour. But even if what the neighbour told the police was admissible in principle under **s116**, it would be open to the defence to ask the judge to exclude it in the exercise of his discretion, either under the principle confirmed in *R v Sang* (1980), or under **s78(1)** of the **Police and Criminal Evidence Act 1984**. Since evidence of identification is regarded as peculiarly hazardous, such an application might well succeed on the basis that the absence of opportunity to cross-examine the identifying witness about the circumstances of the identification would make the proceedings unfair.[17]

The probative force of the gardener's testimony is that Mellors was not in France, but with Connie in London on the day in question. Two factors suggest this. First, the fact that Connie addressed 'Oliver' suggests that it was Mellors to whom she was talking. The fact that the words 'Don't forget to buy some fish, Oliver' were not intended as a statement but as an exhortation, or perhaps a command, means that the words would not offend the rule against hearsay, because the purpose of uttering them was not to cause the person to whom they were addressed to believe any matter. The words did not, therefore, constitute 'a matter stated' within **s115(3)** of the **CJA 2003**.

Second, however, the fact that the gardener heard a voice that he thought he recognised as that of Mellors also suggests that the latter was in London and not in France. What is relied on here to prove that Mellors was present is not the truth of what the man who made a reply to Connie said, but the fact that whatever words were uttered were in tones which the gardener identified as those of Mellors. No hearsay problem

15 For the directions that a judge must give in relation to lies told by a defendant, see *Lucas* (1981), *Burge and Pegg* (1996) and Chapter 6.

16 The discussion in this paragraph is a good example of how the rule can be bypassed by adducing hearsay evidence but with an alternative purpose – to prove a falsity rather than a truth.

17 This discussion demonstrates knowledge of the provisions made by the **CJA 2003**, namely **s116**, in facilitating admission of hearsay evidence where the maker of the statement is unavailable. It also highlights how such evidence, although admissible, could be excluded using the judicial discretion to exclude under *Sang* or **s78** of **PACE 1984**.

arises, and the gardener should be able to testify that he heard, at the time and place referred to, the voice of Connie and a voice which he thought he recognised as that of Mellors.[18]

## QUESTION 15

Percy is being prosecuted for the murder of Edith. He is an Australian visitor to England who was staying in a flat on the third floor of a block known as Shearman Court in West London. Edith lived alone in another flat on the ground floor. The prosecution says that Percy and Edith were having an affair, but that on the evening of 14 July, there was a quarrel between them at Edith's flat, during which Percy strangled her.

Percy was first implicated in the crime when a police tracker dog led detectives to his flat on the third floor. In a properly conducted police interview, he told the police that he had not killed Edith, had never had an affair with her and had never been inside her flat.

Curtis, who lived in another flat on the ground floor of Shearman Court, told police that on the evening of the murder, he had heard a loud argument going on in Edith's flat between Edith and a man with an Australian accent.

When the police lawfully searched Percy's flat, they found an opened letter in a desk drawer. It was addressed to Percy and read as follows: 'Don't be fooled by that tart Edith. She's been sleeping with Frederick for the last month. Give her up – she's not worth it. With love from Rose.' The prosecution does not wish to call Rose, but it wants to put the letter in evidence as part of its case against Percy.

Lilian, a friend of Edith, was interviewed by Percy's solicitor. She told him that after the murder, she took away from Edith's flat a parrot called Max, which Edith had kept as a pet, in order to look after it. She said that during the day Max was silent, but that when evening came, the bird repeatedly called out, 'Frederick, no, no, no!'.

- **Discuss the evidential issues that arise.**

### How to Read this Question

This question has five parts, you are required to discuss the evidence outlined in the scenario; its relevance and whether it poses any hearsay (or other) issues in terms of admissibility.

### How to Answer this Question

The first thing to emphasise is that all the evidence you have been asked to consider is circumstantial and highly inconclusive, *but it is not, merely for this reason, inadmissible*. If you think about it, there is no evidence that proves something conclusively, for there will always exist possible alternative explanations for the item of evidence in question. Far too

18 For the difficulties with voice identification, see the commentary on *Robinson (Wayne)* (2006) **Crim LR 427**.

many students think that a defendant cannot be convicted on purely circumstantial evidence, or at least that such evidence is bound by its very nature to be less substantial than direct evidence, such as the evidence given by a witness of what he saw or heard. This too is completely wrong. In *Taylor, Weaver and Donovan* (1928), Lord Hewart CJ said: 'It is no derogation of evidence to say that it is circumstantial.' His words should be remembered.

With this in mind, you need to consider five points:

- *Tracker dog evidence*. There is an English authority on this. Note what has to be proved to establish the reliability of such evidence. Of course, there is no hearsay problem here.
- *What Percy said to the police*. What is the purpose of adducing this in evidence? The answer to that question will solve any hearsay difficulties.
- *Curtis's evidence*. Again, what will the prosecution be adducing this to prove? Your answer should be: (a) There was a quarrel that night; (b) It took place at Edith's flat; (c) It was between Edith and a man; (d) The man was Australian. None of this, of course, points inevitably to Percy, but see the opening paragraph above, and remember that this is only a part of the prosecution case.
- *The letter*. This is an example of what is sometimes called the distinction between hearsay and real evidence. If you treat these expressions as labels that can be instinctively slapped on various items of evidence, you are heading for disaster. The starting point, as always, is not the *label* but the *job of proof* that the evidence can do. Putting it another way, the problem of admissibility can be solved only if you consider carefully what inferences can be drawn from the evidence in question. As part of its case, the prosecution wants to prove a number of propositions. Which of those propositions, if any, does the letter support? The answer to this will tell you if it is relevant. What arguments are needed to move from the letter to the propositions that the prosecution wants to prove? The answer to this will tell you about admissibility.
- *Lilian's evidence*. Is it relevant? Is there a hearsay problem? If it is relevant and there is no hearsay problem, what is to stop it from being admitted?

## Up for Debate

Mentioning the fact that a case based on circumstantial evidence will satisfy the CPS test for prosecution will gain you credit. Discussing the reliability of, for instance, the tracker dog evidence will also attract marks. Highlighting the debate that surrounds prosecutions based on purely circumstantial evidence will gain you additional credit.

## Applying the Law

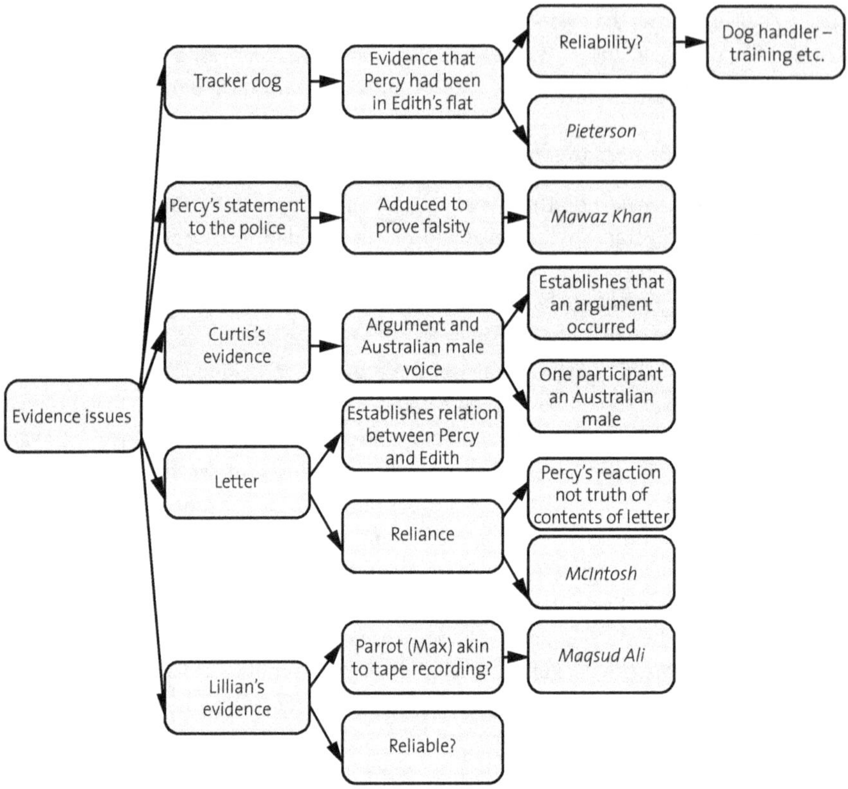


*This mind map shows the evidential issues that relate to each of the pieces of evidence which you must discuss in your answer.*

# ANSWER

The tracker dog presumably led the police to Percy's flat because the animal picked up Percy's scent in Edith's flat. There might have been a perfectly innocent explanation for this but, in view of Percy's denial that he had ever been inside the flat, the evidence is capable of supporting the prosecution case. *Pieterson* (1995) established that evidence of the activities of tracker dogs is admissible, provided a proper foundation can be laid to establish reliability. The dog's handler should give evidence about its training, and should also establish that over a period of time, it behaved reliably as a tracker during controlled tests.[19]

Evidence can be given of what Percy said to the police. The prosecution will wish to show that Percy lied about his association with Edith and will invite the jury to infer guilt from

19 *Pieterson* should be used as an example to support the admission of tracker dog evidence on the proposition that its reliability can be established. This evidence provides evidence of the falsity in Percy's denial.

this. The purpose in adducing evidence of what Percy said will be to show its falsity, not its truth. In these circumstances, the rule against hearsay does not apply (*Mawaz Khan v R* (1967)).

Curtis can give evidence of the sounds that he heard coming from Edith's flat on the evening of 14 July. A jury would be entitled to infer from this that an argument was going on at the time. Curtis could also say that he heard the accent of an Australian male to show that such a person was present on that occasion. Neither of these items of evidence infringes the rule against hearsay because the purpose of adducing the evidence is not to establish the truth of what was said, but the fact that there was an argument and that one of the participants was an Australian man.[20]

The evidential value of the letter found in Percy's desk is not that it establishes the truth about Edith's love life, but that it enables us to infer that Percy had been having some sort of relationship with a woman named Edith and that he probably had a vengeful state of mind towards her. The argument can be put thus: why should Percy have such an interest in the letter that he kept it in his desk if he did *not* have any such relationship? In other words, it is Percy's reaction to what was written that is relied on, not the truth of what was said in the letter. Evidence was admitted for a similar purpose in *McIntosh* (1992) where the defendant was charged with importing drugs. In a house where he had been living before his arrest, the police found a piece of paper that contained calculations, not in the defendant's handwriting, of the purchase and sale prices of 12 oz of an unnamed commodity. The Court of Appeal held that this evidence had been properly admitted as circumstantial real evidence tending to connect the accused with the crime charged. Though not spelled out by the court, the reason appears to have been that the person in possession of the document kept it because he was interested in the information that it contained.[21]

A similar decision in a case closer to the given facts is *R v Toussaint-Collins* (2009), where D was charged with the murder of X. The case for the prosecution was that the murder was a revenge killing, motivated by the belief that X had been responsible for the earlier murder of Y. The question arose whether a letter from another person to D, in which the writer expressed his regret that Y's death had not been avenged, was admissible to prove D's motive for murdering X. D had kept it for some months after receiving it. The Court of Appeal held that this item of evidence was not hearsay, and was admissible, because it helped to show D's vengeful state of mind towards X.

Given that there was a relationship between Percy and Edith, then, *regardless of the truth of what was said about Edith in the letter*, the fact that the allegation was read and the

20 This discussion highlights how evidence classed as hearsay can legitimately be adduced to prove something else, showing one of the ways in which the courts avoided the rule against its admission.

21 The case of *McIntosh* is used to support the admission of evidence suggesting that Percy and Edith had some 'relation'. In absence of a precedent, do not be afraid to use authorities with similar facts. When doing this you should state that the case is used in this context.

letter kept suggests that Percy took it seriously, and from that it can be inferred that he may have had vengeful feelings towards Edith.

One possible inference from the parrot's behaviour is that the bird was repeating what it heard Edith shout on the evening when she was murdered. From this it could be inferred that, because Frederick is named rather than Percy, it was not Percy who murdered her. The first point to be made is that what the parrot 'said' was not a statement. If Edith uttered those words, she did not do so for the purpose of causing another person to believe anything, as required by **s 115(3)** of the **Criminal Justice Act 2003**. As a non-statement, therefore, what Edith said is not caught by the rule against hearsay. Because some parrots tend to repeat human language that they hear, Max might be seen as a recording device. Had a tape recorder been operating at the time, the tape could well have been admissible as direct evidence of what was going on. In *Maqsud Ali* (1966), the Court of Appeal held that a tape recording is admissible in evidence provided, inter alia, the accuracy of the recording can be proved and the voices properly identified.

The real difficulty here is not one of hearsay and, by analogy with *Taylor v Chief Constable of Cheshire* (1987), Lilian should be allowed to give evidence of what she heard if Max is properly seen as a recording device. The prosecution could legitimately object, however, that as a recording device Max is most unreliable. How could the court be satisfied, even on a prima facie basis, that Max did not pick up this expression on some quite different occasion or from someone other than Edith? The truth of the matter is that Max is quite different from the sort of mechanical recording devices whose products have been admitted hitherto by the courts as real evidence. Lilian's evidence is therefore most unlikely to be admissible for the defence.[22]

22 The discussion in the last two paragraphs required some creativity. It demonstrates lateral thinking of the process of inclusion and the related issue of accuracy. Often, facts such as this may arise as they do in the practice of law, but are here to assess your application of the rules to varying scenarios.

# 5 Hearsay II

## INTRODUCTION

The scope of the rule against hearsay has been much reduced. The **Civil Evidence Act 1995** has abolished the rule completely for civil proceedings. In 1995 the Law Commission published a Consultation Paper on the subject of hearsay in criminal cases, and in 1997 published a Report. The recommendations of the Commission have been very largely incorporated in **Part 11, Chapter 2** of the **Criminal Justice Act (CJA) 2003**, which has created four principal categories of admissibility, all of which are available to both the defendant and the prosecution:

- hearsay admissible by statute;
- hearsay admissible under any preserved common law rule;
- hearsay admissible by agreement;
- hearsay admissible in the interests of justice (the 'safety-valve').

Reference has already been made in Chapter 4 to the unavailability exception in **s 116** of the **CJA 2003** and to the 'safety-valve' exception in **s 114**. It is important to note that hearsay statements under either section can be oral or written.

Under **ss 23** and **24** of the **Criminal Justice Act 1988**, documentary hearsay statements were admissible under certain conditions. However, the interpretation of **ss 23** and **24** gave rise to difficulty, and the powers to admit hearsay statements under them were the subject of a wide judicial discretion, contained in **ss 25** and **26**, that gave rise to accusations of inconsistency and uncertainty. These provisions were repealed by **Sched 37, Part 6** of the **CJA 2003** and replaced by an exception in favour of 'business and other documents' in **s 117**.

With the exception of the rules preserved by **s 118**, the common law rules governing the admissibility of hearsay evidence in criminal proceedings are abolished. As well as some minor exceptions, two major common law exceptions are preserved: *res gestae* statements and statements in furtherance of a common enterprise.

*Res gestae* statements are generally taken to include four different categories:

(i) Statements that accompany and explain an action of the person making the statement.
(ii) Spontaneous exclamations made in response to an event so dramatic as to rule out any opportunity for concoction. The leading case is *Andrews* (1987), and you should know the tests for admissibility that it establishes.

(iii) Declarations about the maker's contemporaneous state of mind or emotion. The law has developed in a haphazard and unsatisfactory way, and is consequently in a state of some uncertainty (and so is a favourite topic for examination questions). It is odd that the **CJA 2003** did not attempt to clarify it. You should pay particular attention to the cases on statements of intention.

(iv) Declarations about the maker's contemporaneous physical sensations. Note that the declarations cannot be used to prove what caused the sensations.

*Statements in furtherance of a common enterprise* made by one party to the enterprise are admissible against others, even where they have had nothing to do with making the statement and may not know that a statement has been made. This rule is not confined to conspiracy cases; it applies wherever the prosecution alleges a joint enterprise. But the statement must have been made in furtherance of the enterprise, so it will not apply to the confession of one party after his arrest: *Walters* (1979).

The law relating to confessions is also preserved, but this topic is separately considered in Chapter 7.

Do not neglect the supplementary provisions in **ss 121–125** of the **CJA 2003**. The rules about multiple hearsay are particularly important. You should always be aware that admissible hearsay can still be excluded, either at common law or by statute.

**Checklist**

**Students should be familiar with the following areas:**

- the unavailability exception (**s 116**);
- the business and other documents exception (**s 117**);
- the preserved common law exceptions (**s 118**);
- the 'safety-valve' exception (**s 114**);
- the supplementary provisions (**ss 121–125**);
- common law and statutory powers of exclusion.

## QUESTION 16

Herbert is charged with the murder of Ivan. The case for the prosecution is that the murder was the result of a street fight. The deceased was accosted by two youths, Joss and Herbert. Herbert attacked Ivan with a garden ornament and a fight ensued between them. In the course of the fight, Herbert called for Joss, who was carrying a knife, to stab Ivan. Joss did so and caused fatal wounds. Joss was arrested several days later. When interviewed under caution he admitted stabbing Ivan at the instigation of another man, whom he did not identify. In due course he pleaded guilty to murder. Before his arrest, Joss had a conversation with Karen, his girlfriend, in the course of which he admitted stabbing Ivan and said that he had done so at Herbert's instigation. After Joss had pleaded guilty to murder, Karen made a written statement to the police giving a full account of what Joss had told her about Herbert's involvement.

Karen is now resident in Australia. Originally she agreed to give evidence at Herbert's trial. The police have recently been told that she has now changed her mind. Joss has refused to cooperate with the police in their investigations concerning Herbert. He refuses to have anything to do with Karen.

- **Discuss the evidential matters arising.**

## How to Read this Question

The focus of this question is the written statement. The discussion should explore the basis of admissibility (hearsay provisions under the **CJA 2003**) in the event that she does or does not attend to give oral evidence in court.

## How to Answer this Question

The sole question is whether Karen's written statement can be used at Herbert's trial. It is unlikely that a question in the examination would be restricted to such a narrow scope, but the exercise will be useful because it shows how carefully exceptions to the rule against hearsay should be considered.

Note first that the admissibility of the evidence is assessed on the basis that Karen will attend to give oral evidence. There are obvious problems already; note the importance of the Court of Appeal's decision in *Y* (2008). Next, assume that her evidence will be admissible if she attends. What will the position be if she does not attend? In particular, can the prosecution use any of the provisions in **s 116**? Note that **s 117** is not available because of the circumstances in which Karen herself received the information. Now assume that **s 116** can be used. The result will be multiple hearsay. You will have to examine **s 121** to see, finally, if this obstacle can be overcome. Do not expect to be able to come to a firm conclusion.

## Answer Structure

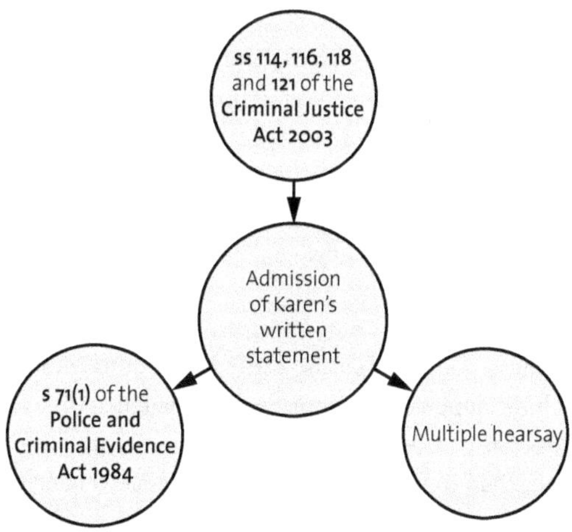


*This diagram outlines the evidential issues that exist in terms of the admission of Karen's written statement.*

## ANSWER

The availability of Karen seems very uncertain. It will be useful to consider first whether she could give evidence of what Joss told her if she were to give oral evidence at Herbert's trial. If she were to do so, it is clear that she would be repeating what Joss said to her in order to establish the part played by Herbert in Ivan's death. The basic rule, laid down by **s 114(1)** of the **CJA 2003**, is that a statement not made in oral evidence in the proceedings is admissible as evidence of any matter stated if, but only if, one of conditions (a) to (d) inclusive is satisfied. **Subsection (1)(b)** allows such statements if any rule of law preserved by **s 118** makes it admissible. By **s 118(1), para 5**, there is preserved any rule of law relating to the admissibility of confessions or mixed statements in criminal proceedings. **Subsection (1)(a)** allows hearsay evidence if provided for by the **CJA 2003** or by any other statutory provision. By **s 76(1)** of **PACE 1984** a confession made by an accused person may be given in evidence against him in so far as it is relevant to any matter in issue in the proceedings and is not excluded by the court. The difficulty with Joss's statement to Karen is that so far as the proceedings against Herbert are concerned, it is not a confession made by an accused person because Joss has already been dealt with and the only accused person is Herbert. Even if Joss and Herbert had been tried together, what Joss said to the police would have been admissible only against him. **Section 76(1)** explicitly confines admissibility to admissibility against the maker of the statement, and this reflects the pre-**PACE** common law, as expressed in *Gunewardene* (1951). Neither under **s 114(1)(a)** or **(b)** would the evidence that Karen can give be admissible against Herbert. **Subsection (1)(c)** will clearly not apply, and that leaves only **subs (1)(d)**: hearsay evidence will be admissible where the court is satisfied that it is in the interests of justice for it to be admissible. In deciding this question the court must have regard to the factors set out in **s 114(2)**. However, in *Taylor (Stuart)* (2006) the Court of Appeal said that this does not require the judge to embark on an investigation so as to reach a conclusion in relation to any one of them, let alone each one of them. What is required is the exercise of judgement after giving consideration to these factors and to any others that the judge considers relevant.[1]

A further question arises on these facts. Is **s 114(1)(d)** capable of allowing the admission of hearsay material which is contained in a confession by a person other than the defendant, or is it excluded by the presence in the Act of **s 118(1), para 5**? The argument for the defence would be that the preservation of the common law rules relating to the admissibility of confessions preserves, inter alia, the rule laid down in *Gunewardene* that a confession is admissible against its maker only.

This question was considered by the Court of Appeal in *Y* (2008). The Court observed that the aim of the Law Commission in proposing the enactment of what is now **s 114(1)(d)** was to provide a residual judicial power to admit hearsay evidence that would not otherwise be admissible. The Court also observed that **s 118** is expressly stated to be concerned with the admissibility, rather than the inadmissibility, of evidence. It concluded that hearsay in

1 This discussion demonstrates knowledge of the changes in the law introduced by the **CJA 2003**, and the fact that Joss's statement is of no use against Herbert.

the form of a confession is in law as open to admission under **subpara (d)** as any other hearsay. That provision prevails over the general common law rule that hearsay is inadmissible, and so it prevails over the particular common law rule that hearsay contained in the form of a confession is inadmissible against anyone other than the maker.

The position therefore is that Karen's evidence would in principle be admissible if she were to attend in person. The next question is whether her statement could be introduced under **s 116** if she did not attend. The condition set out in **s 116(2)(c)** appears to be the most appropriate, although the prosecution might also have to rely on **s 116(2)(d)**. There is at present no evidence that she is refusing to give evidence through fear.[2]

**Section 116(2)(c)** was considered by the Court of Appeal in *C* (2006), in which the Court of Appeal said that the expression 'reasonably practicable' has to be judged on the basis of the steps taken, or not taken, by the party who wishes to secure the witness's attendance. The court has to consider what efforts should reasonably be made to secure the attendance of the witness or, at least, to arrange a procedure whereby the contents of his statement can be tested by cross-examination. In Herbert's case, no steps appear to have been taken to discover from Karen herself whether she is willing to attend. What efforts should reasonably be made to secure her attendance? Presumably the prosecution is willing to pay her expenses, though this is not stated. What other steps, such as evidence by video link, could be taken? On the facts as they stand it seems unlikely that a judge could reach a decision to admit Karen's statement under **s 116(2)(c)**.[3]

If **s 116(2)(d)** is relied on, there must be evidence of what steps it is reasonably practicable to take to find her and whether those steps have been taken. If such steps have been taken, what have been the results?

It is possible that a court might be satisfied in due course that Karen's statement was in principle admissible, under either **s 116(2)(c)** or **(d)**. Her statement would then be put forward as hearsay evidence of what Joss said to her about Herbert's part in Ivan's death. The hearsay would be 'multiple', and by **s 121(1)** such a hearsay statement is not admissible unless one of three conditions is satisfied. The first, in **subs (1)(a)**, applies where either of the statements is admissible under **ss 117, 119** or **120**. **Sections 119** and **120** have no application. **Section 117** does not apply because although Karen's witness statement is a document received by a person in the course of police business, she herself is not a person who received the information in the course of a trade, business, etc., as required by **s 117(2)(c)**. For the statement to be admitted, reliance would therefore have to be placed on **s 121(1)(c)**. (**Section 121(1)(b)** can obviously not be relied on.) Without more knowledge of the facts of the case it is not easy to see whether a judge would be prepared to admit the evidence on

2 Highlighting the issues in relation to Karen's evidence where she does and does not attend, and in relation to the common law and statutory scheme under the **CJA 2003**, demonstrates knowledge of the rules under the common law and now statute.

3 Discuss the decision in *C* because it is a current case that highlights the factors the courts consider when deciding whether or not to admit evidence under **s 116(2)(c)**.

this basis. The potential value of the evidence is high, but it is impossible to tell, without at least reading the statement, what assessment is likely to be made of its reliability.[4]

# QUESTION 17

Adrian, Billy and Charlie are charged with possession of drugs with intent to supply. In the house where all three lived, police found a large quantity of cocaine and £28,000 in used banknotes. When interviewed, all three defendants said that the money had been the proceeds of successful gambling. They said that they had just moved into the house and had no knowledge of the presence of the cocaine, which had been discovered in the loft. The police also found a diary in Adrian's handwriting, in which there appeared inside the back cover a list containing references to first names, to various quantities of something that was unspecified and to sums of money. Below the list was written: 'Adrian to get half; Billy and Charlie a quarter each.' There were also various entries for the week before the date when all three were arrested. One of these read: 'Billy and Charlie are getting cold feet. I wish they hadn't persuaded me to let them in on the deals.' For two weeks before the arrests were made, DC Kray kept watch outside the house, which was visited by 26 people. He was able to identify 18 of these as persons with previous convictions for the possession of drugs.

- **Discuss the evidential matters arising.**

## How to Read this Question

This question requires a discussion of the following pieces of evidence; the money, the contents of the diary and the evidence of DC Kray. You should explore whether each piece of evidence is admissible and if so (or not) on what basis. Finally, you should also consider whether any judicial directions will also be required.

## How to Answer this Question

There are three items of evidence that need your consideration:

- Is evidence of finding the money admissible? If so, does the judge need to say anything about it in summing up?
- Are the contents of Adrian's diary admissible? Against whom? Don't forget that the entries should be dealt with separately. Will the judge need to give any special direction?
- Is the evidence of DC Kray admissible for the prosecution?

### Up for Debate

You can gain extra credit by mentioning the potential on conviction (not sentence) for the court to make a confiscation order in confiscation proceedings initiated under s 6 of the **Proceeds of Crime Act 2002**.

4 The conclusion should include reference to an argument for inclusion based on the value of such evidence and its reliability.

## Answer Structure

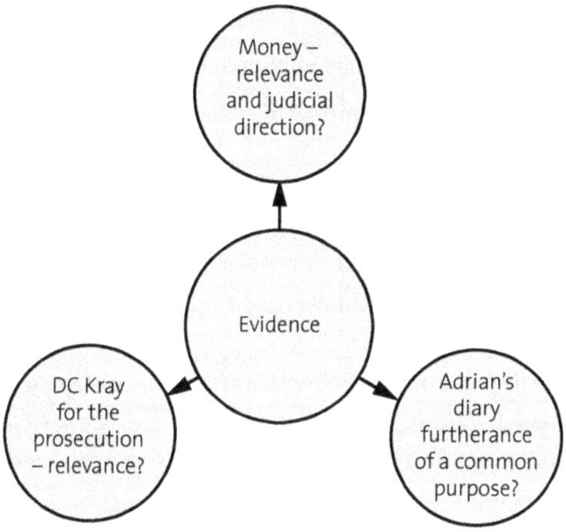


*This diagram illustrates the main factors that you must consider in terms of the evidence (the money, the diary and its entries, and that of DC Kray).*

# ANSWER

In relation to the cash, two questions arise. Is it relevant to the prosecution case? If it is, what directions should the judge give to the jury about it? In *Wright* (1994), the Court of Appeal held that the discovery of £16,000 in cash in the defendant's flat was admissible to support a charge of possessing cocaine with intent to supply, on the basis that drug dealers are known to deal in large sums of cash. However, in *Batt* (1994), the Court of Appeal held that the finding of cash (albeit in that case a much smaller sum) was inadmissible, because it was suggestive only of past dealings. As such, it was unfairly prejudicial because it showed only a disposition to commit such offences. *Batt* seems difficult to reconcile with *Wright*, but later cases have tended to prefer the reasoning in *Wright*. Therefore, the position is that the finding of the cash is likely to be admissible to support the charge, but there are two elements in the charge, both of which the defendants deny. Not only do they deny intent to supply, they also deny *possession* (their case is that they knew nothing of the presence of the cocaine). In *Guney* (1998), the Court of Appeal said that whether evidence is relevant depends on the circumstances of each case. Where possession with intent to supply is charged, there are many circumstances in which evidence of cash and lifestyle might be relevant and admissible in relation to the issue of possession itself, especially to the issue of knowledge as an ingredient of possession. Thus, the discovery of the cash may be relevant to possession as well as intent to supply.[5,6]

5 See also *Griffiths* (1998).

6 Discussion of *Wright* and *Batt* demonstrates knowledge of the preferred or likely approach of the courts where the evidence of the money is concerned.

However, a careful direction will have to be given to the jury about the use they can make of this information. In *Grant* (1996), the Court of Appeal said that before relying on such evidence, the jury must be satisfied that the money was not in the defendant's possession for any innocent reason that may have been advanced (in this case, as a result of successful gambling) and that, even if they find that it does relate to drug dealing, they must be satisfied that it relates to an ongoing course of dealing, and is not merely the proceeds of past deals. However, at the time when *Grant* was decided there were severe restrictions on adducing evidence that was relevant only to a defendant's disposition. These were substantially reduced in the **Criminal Justice Act 2003**, and it might now be enough for the cash to be taken only as evidence of past dealing.[7,8]

In *Pearce* (1979), the Court of Appeal held that wholly exculpatory statements made by suspects when confronted with incriminating evidence are admissible to show their reactions to the accusations being made, but are not evidence of the truth of their contents. Accordingly, the defendants' statements about ignorance of the presence of cocaine, and their explanations for the presence of the money, will be admissible for this limited purpose.

The entries in Adrian's diary should be separately considered. It was held in *Gray and Others* (1995) that a statement made in furtherance of a common purpose by one defendant is admissible as evidence against the others, though made in their absence. The reason for this is that a combination of persons for the purpose of committing a crime is regarded as implying an authority to each to act or speak in furtherance of the common purpose on behalf of the others. For example, in *Devonport and Pirano* (1996), where the defendants were charged with conspiracy to defraud a bank, a document drawn up by the girlfriend of one of the defendants, at the latter's dictation, showed an intended division of the proceeds of the offence between all the defendants, who were named. It was held that this was evidence against all the defendants, there being evidence in addition to the document to show that they were all parties to the conspiracy. Since the document was a record of *intended* distribution of the proceeds when the conspiracy had been fulfilled, it had been prepared in furtherance of the conspiracy, and was thus admissible. It would have been different if the document had been merely a record, made when everything was finished, of what had happened. This common law exception was preserved by **para 7** of **s 118(1)** of the **CJA 2003**.

The entries at the back of Adrian's diary show an *intended* distribution between the three defendants, and there is other evidence (the discovery of the drugs and the cash in the house where all three lived) to link Billy and Charlie to a common enterprise, even though not charged as a conspiracy. On this basis, the entry is admissible against all the defendants. But the judge will have to warn the jury that they must be satisfied that the entry

7 See also Question 3.

8 The discussion of *Grant* and the subsequent reduction in restrictions on the admission of the evidence of the money highlights the changes brought in by the **CJA 2003** and the fact that the evidence may now be admissible as evidence of past dealing.

was not only evidence of past dealing, but capable of going to intention to supply in the future. In other words, the diary entry must be treated with the same caution as the discovery of the cash: see *Lovelock* (1997). But the reservation noted in relation to *Grant* in respect of such a direction after the passing of the **CJA 2003** might be relevant here also.[9]

The second entry about Billy and Charlie getting cold feet is clearly not made in furtherance of the common enterprise. It is admissible as a confession by Adrian.[10]

The evidence of DC Kray may be relevant because it shows the sort of people frequenting the house, and tends to show that the house was being used for drug dealing. Similar evidence was admitted in *Warner* (1993), where the prosecution's case was that the pattern of visits was consistent with the method of drug dealing testified to by prosecution witnesses. The defence case was that the visitors had been making only social calls but in *Hasson* (1997), evidence that the defendants, who were charged with being concerned in the supply of cannabis resin, had associated with persons with drug-related convictions was held inadmissible. In contrast to *Warner*, it was not part of the prosecution case that the defendants were supplying drugs to those whose convictions were adduced in evidence. The question on these facts therefore appears to be whether there is a nexus between the defendants' association with these visitors and any specific allegation of dealing made by the prosecution. In the absence of such a nexus, the evidence is likely to be inadmissible.

# QUESTION 18

The admission of hearsay evidence has always been contentious. Discuss with reference to the changes made by the **Criminal Justice Act 2003**.

## How to Read this Question

Here you must explore the hearsay rule before and after the reforms brought about by the **CJA 2003**. Thus, you should cover the development of the rule, its harshness and its varied application.

## How to Answer this Question

This essay question requires you to discuss one of the most discussed principles in the law of evidence – hearsay. Start by outlining the exclusionary rule and its rationale. The essay raises issues relating to the criticisms of the original rule including the exclusion of evidence that is both credible and reliable even though it may have resulted in an acquittal of the defendant. You should highlight the historical development of the rule and the ways in which the courts avoided its application. Furthermore, mention should be made of the changes brought about by the Law Commission proposals for reform, which, adopted in

9 This discussion demonstrates knowledge through an analysis of how evidence of statements in a diary may be admissible against others where a common purpose exists and most importantly the relevance of it as evidence of past and future dealing.

10 For confessions, see Chapter 7.

the **Criminal Justice Act 2003**, had the effect of preserving the rule but extending the exceptions and allowing judicial discretion on admission of hearsay evidence. One of the main thrusts of the argument from the perspective of the defendant is on the unfairness that results from its admission.

In summary, your answer should make reference to the following:

- the exclusionary rule and its rationale;
- the harshness of excluding credible and reliable evidence;
- the historical development of the hearsay rule;
- how the courts tried to bypass it;
- the Law Commission reforms and the **CJA 2003**.

## Applying the Law

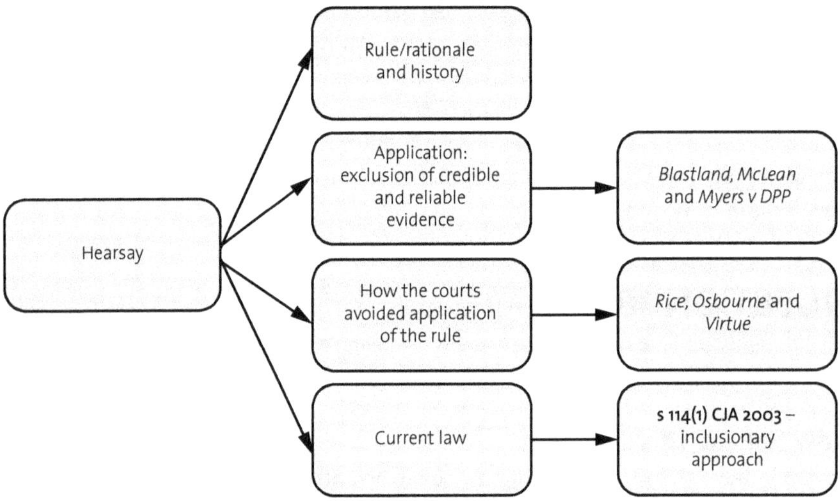


*This mind map highlights the main arguments that you should include when discussing the admission of hearsay evidence and the approach of the current law.*

## ANSWER

Hearsay is now defined in **s114(1)** of the **Criminal Justice Act 2003** as 'a statement not made in oral evidence in the proceedings that is evidence of any matter stated'. The Act preserves the rule, introduces a number of exceptions and an inclusionary judicial discretion. In this essay I shall discuss the effect of the **CJA 2003** on the discretion of judges in admitting hearsay evidence.[11]

---

11 In questions such as this it is useful to set out the law and its extent; discretion for the inclusion of hearsay evidence.

There are a number of reasons why hearsay developed as an exclusionary common law rule. The main thrust of the reasoning that supports exclusion centres on the witness having wrongfully perceived the events, concocted or distorted them, perhaps failed to accurately recall what they had seen or they may have misinterpreted the statement they heard or had written down. The problem here lies in the inability of the defence to cross-examine the witness who had made the hearsay statement. Furthermore, the comments of Lord Bridge in *R v Blastland* (1986) suggest that the jury may attribute far more weight (or probative value) to such evidence than it rightfully deserves. The application of the exclusionary rule was such that even evidence that was credible and reliable was excluded if it did not neatly fall within one of the exceptions to it as in *R v McLean* (1967) and *Myers v DPP* (1965). The rule applied to both written and oral statements, or those statements made by means of gestures (*R v Gibson* (1887)).

A brief perusal of the case law surrounding the rule substantiates the view that the rule was seen as unduly restrictive, and thus over the years judges sought to restrict the application of the rule, perhaps mainly for purposes of practicality – but so as not to exclude evidence that was credible and reliable as in *R v Rice* (1963). In *R v Osbourne; R v Virtue* (1973) the court held that the rule was not breached where a police officer testified that an eyewitness with an inaccurate recollection of the event positively identified an accused in an identification parade. The common law exceptions to the exclusionary rule included statements made by persons since deceased, *res gestae* statements and statements in public documents.[12]

The **CJA 2003** evidences the legislative trend towards the admission of such evidence. The Law Commission recognised that this was an area of the law that required reform; however, it stopped short of its complete abolition. In its report 'Evidence in Criminal Proceedings: Hearsay and Related Topics' (No. 245, Cm 3670, 1997) it recommended 'that there should be a general rule against hearsay, subject to specified exceptions, plus a limited inclusionary discretion' (p. 194 at para 6.53). The proposals were both embraced and criticised; however, the law at present does not abolish the rule but does weaken its application. In contrast the **Civil Evidence Acts of 1968 and 1972** were much earlier in their important steps that more liberally admitted hearsay evidence in civil proceedings.[13]

Other than preserving the rule and introducing new exceptions to it, the Act also introduces an inclusionary discretion. The latter creates flexibility in the admission of such evidence but, however, can also result in uncertainty. For instance it is a logical conclusion that it would be undesirable to convict a defendant on the basis of hearsay evidence alone, but this is arguably possible under the current regime. This argument weighs in favour of such discretion being exercised and thus it is likely that the courts will continue their careful approach where the admission of such evidence is concerned. In *R v Mills*

12 This paragraph demonstrates knowledge on the variety of issues that relate to the harshness of the hearsay rule, the relevance of certain forms of hearsay evidence and how judges avoided its application.

13 This paragraph highlights the change in approach by the current lawmakers, thereby weakening the application of the rule in criminal proceedings.

(2003) the Court of Appeal was swift in quashing a conviction where hearsay evidence had been wrongfully admitted.

Further arguments that centre on the admission of such evidence relate to **Art 6** of the **European Convention on Human Rights** and the right to a fair trial, something that is also promoted by the **CJA 2003** itself. The Act has not yet fallen foul of these provisions, for instance in *R v Imed-Al-Khawaja* (2006) the admission of the statement of a witness who had died prior to the trial was not a breach of the right under the **Convention**.[14]

In conclusion, case law relating to the development of the hearsay rule substantiates the fact that judges took a cautionary approach to the admission of such evidence. The preservation of the exceptions to the rule and the introduction of an inclusionary discretion serve to highlight the risks associated with such evidence. Thus, even though the **CJA 2003** introduced an inclusionary discretion it has not resulted in a carefree admission of hearsay evidence. It is likely that the admission of hearsay evidence will always remain contentious, with jurists arguing both for and against its admission.

14 This case, *R v Imed-Al-Khawaja*, highlights how the admission of hearsay evidence and the right to a fair trial are balanced by the **CJA 2003**.

# 6 Hazardous Evidence

## INTRODUCTION

It can be stated that all evidence, without exception, is hazardous and that there are several reasons for this.

The first is that all evidence emerges as the result of some sort of selection. One kind may be loosely described as 'natural selection'. Not all the evidence that is relevant to a particular inquiry will have survived. Witnesses may have died; documents may have been destroyed; the physical features of a building may have been altered. Another sort of selection is human selection. In any investigation, someone has to gather the evidence that has survived. But to gather evidence effectively, you have to be intelligent enough to recognise what may be significant, and honest enough to do the job without pre-conceived ideas of what the outcome of the investigation should be. Natural selection and human frailty between them ensure that no jury ever sees more than a part of the whole picture, and that part may indeed be a very small and misleading one.[1]

Another reason for the hazardous nature of evidence is that too much has to be taken on trust. It is not always appreciated that the only direct experience upon which a tribunal of fact can depend in a legal inquiry is its perception of witnesses testifying in the witness box, and perhaps also the perceptions that it experiences from its own examination of an item of real evidence. In relation to a testifying witness, two difficulties arise. The first comes from uncertainty as to whether the witness can trust the evidence of his own senses. He may believe that he saw the defendant stab the victim, but what guarantee has he that things were not otherwise? The second difficulty comes from the fact that the jury has to rely on the witness for an insight into what happened on the occasion under investigation. But all the jury can perceive is the witness in the box giving evidence. What is their justification for inferring from the witness's testimony that the defendant did in fact stab the victim?

A third reason for the hazardous nature of evidence is that, save for some items of real evidence, it is presented through the medium of language. But language is notoriously ambiguous. 'Words may easily be misunderstood by a dull man. They may easily be

1 This is perhaps more obviously true of a historian's work. See EH Carr, *What Is History?*, 2nd edn, 1987, Chapter 1. But a little reflection should be enough to show that the same is true of the investigation that precedes a criminal or civil trial.

misconstrued by a knave. What was spoken metaphorically may be apprehended literally. What was spoken ludicrously may be apprehended seriously. A particle, a tense, a mood, an emphasis may make the whole difference between guilt and innocence.'[2] But more than this, the very adversary system adopted in our courts tends to perpetuate ambiguity. One of the earliest lessons learned by a student of advocacy is how to avoid giving a witness whom he is cross-examining a chance to explain his testimony. Closed, leading questions that require a 'yes' or 'no' answer are recommended. These may be good trial tactics, but they are ill-designed for the discovery of the truth.[3]

Politicians and lawyers have generally turned a blind eye to these fundamental defects. Attempts to make verdicts a little more reliable have been made only erratically and on a piecemeal basis. This chapter deals with attempts that have been made to control the way in which juries think about evidence that at various times has been thought to be particularly unreliable. These attempts gave rise to law that compelled judges to warn juries in a particular way when they had to consider certain types of evidence, or evidence from certain types of witness.

## MANDATORY WARNINGS TO THE JURY

In the eighteenth century, when the beginnings of our modern law of evidence can be perceived, both prosecution and defence were often unrepresented by counsel, and the judge played a much larger part in criminal cases than he did in the nineteenth century and later. In particular, judges had a greater control over juries' deliberations. Summings up could contain much more of the judge's opinion than would now be thought proper. Where it appeared that a deliberation was likely to be short, the jury would often not leave the jury box, and this could provide an opportunity for informal dialogue with the judge about the evidence. Even if a jury returned a verdict with which the judge disagreed, he could persuade them to reconsider.

In time, this informal procedure gave way to a system more like the one we are used to today, though there was one major difference: until 1898, there was no general right for a defendant to testify in his own defence. Prosecution and defence came increasingly to be represented by counsel, possibly because of an increase in the size of the Bar, and the judge's control over the jury's deliberations slackened. But because jurors were free to weigh the evidence without judicial intervention, it became more necessary to warn them in a formal way during summing up about the weight to be attached to certain types of witness and testimony, and of the danger in convicting on the basis of such evidence without some independent support. Warnings were thought to be necessary in three main cases: those involving the evidence of children, of accomplices and of complainants in cases where a sexual crime was alleged.

2 Macaulay (Lord), *The History of England from the Accession of James the Second*, 1848–1861, reprinted 1880, Vol. 2, Chapter 5, p. 161. Even more hazardous is evidence of statements alleged to have been made on an earlier occasion by a defendant.

3 See, for example, M Stone, *Cross-Examination in Criminal Trials*, 1988, p. 107; A Boon, *Advocacy*, 2nd edn, 1999, pp. 113–114; cf. J McEwan, *Evidence and the Adversarial Process: The Modern Law*, 1992, pp. 16–19.

For a long time, the manner in which a warning was given, and even whether a warning was given at all, was a matter solely for the trial judge's discretion. But when the Court of Criminal Appeal was set up in 1907, discretionary practices tended to harden into rigid rules of law. Before long, a highly complex law of corroboration had developed. Eventually, it was thought to be so unsatisfactory that Parliament very largely abolished it in **s 34(2)** of the **Criminal Justice Act (CJA) 1988** and in **s 32** of the **Criminal Justice and Public Order Act (CJPOA) 1994**.

Alongside the strict law of corroboration, there had also developed a less formal body of law about warnings that should be given to a jury where a witness might be unreliable even though he did not fall within the limited classes to which corroboration law applied. Thus, it was held that an informal warning should be given where witnesses had a purpose of their own to serve in giving evidence, or suffered from mental disorder (*Beck* (1982); *Spencer* (1986)). In *Stone* (2005) the Court of Appeal held that this body of law had not survived the abolition of the former rules of corroboration. In *Makanjuola* (1995), the Court of Appeal emphasised the wide discretion possessed by trial judges to adapt warnings about the testimony of any particular witness to the circumstances of the case. The exercise of that discretion will only exceptionally be reviewed by the Court of Appeal. *Makanjuola* has also been helpful in killing the notion that the old law about corroboration might still somehow apply once the judge had decided to give a discretionary warning.

There remains one common type of evidence where a warning is required which is still governed by a rule-based rather than a discretionary system. Identification evidence that falls within the principles set out in *Turnbull* (1977) and subsequent cases must be the subject of a particular type of judicial warning in the summing up. A body of case law has also developed about warnings that should be given to the jury where a defendant's lies, whether told inside or outside court, could be taken to support the prosecution case. See *Lucas* (1981) and *Burge* (1996).

**Code D** of the current **(2011) Codes of Practice** made under the **Police and Criminal Evidence Act (PACE) 1984** is likely to be relevant in any problem involving identification. The whole of the Code is important, but you should pay special attention to **Annex A** (video identification), **Annex B** (identification parades) and **Annex E** (showing photographs).

If there has been a breach of the Code, you must be able to advise on the likely consequences. Remember the following:

- ❖ What allows the court to look at the provisions of the Code and what makes them relevant? See **s 67(11)** of **PACE**.
- ❖ If the quality of the identification evidence is poor and there is no other evidence to support it, the jury should be directed to acquit (*Turnbull* (1977)). Thus, the Code breach may so weaken the identification evidence that a submission of no case to answer will be successful.
- ❖ The evidence may be excluded under **s 78** of **PACE**. (See Chapter 7 for further details.)

## Checklist

**Students should be familiar with the following areas:**

- the abolition of corroboration law in the **CJA 1988** and the **CJPOA 1994**;
- the effect of this – see *Makanjuola* (1995);
- the guidelines in *Makanjuola* about discretionary warnings;
- the rules concerning identification in *Turnbull* (1977);
- **Code of Practice D**;
- **s 62(11)** of **PACE**;
- the possible effects of Code breach;
- warnings where a defendant has lied;
- **s 34** of the **CJPOA 1994**, and the directions that must be given where that section is relied on (see Chapter 7);
- **ss 41–43 Youth Justice and Criminal Evidence Act 1999** (see also Chapter 10).

# QUESTION 19

Archie is charged with the rape of Clare. Both are aged 20, live in Worcester and know each other socially. The case for the prosecution is that one evening they were at a party near Worcester given by John, a local politician. Towards the end of the evening Archie offered Clare a lift back to Worcester in his car, which she accepted. It is alleged that Archie stopped the car at some stage during the journey and dragged Clare into a nearby field, where he raped her. Clare says that she was so shocked by what happened that afterwards she returned to the car with Archie and let him drive her home.

Geoff, her elder brother, was at home when she arrived. He noticed that she had mud in her hair and on her clothes and said to her, 'Clare, what has happened? Be sure you tell me the truth, or you are no longer my sister!' Clare then told him that she had been raped by Archie. Geoff later gave a statement to the police reporting what he had seen and heard, but a few days later he was killed in a pub brawl.

When Archie was interviewed under caution by the police, he said, 'Look, let me tell you what happened. I wish I'd never offered her a lift. She'd had quite a bit to drink and could talk of nothing except the idea of having sex in the open air. When we reached a road that ran by a field she tried to stop the car; we nearly went into a ditch. I did have sex with her, but I'd never have done so if she hadn't kept on about it.'

Archie wishes to call Ethan and Fergus in support of his account. Each will say that about a month before the alleged rape he had sex with Clare at her suggestion, and that she had insisted on having sex in a park or field.

Archie has recently heard that last year Clare made an allegation of rape against Harry, but that there was no prosecution because of lack of evidence.

- **Discuss the evidential matters arising.**

## How to Read this Question

This question requires you to consider a range of admissibility issues including a hearsay statement by a witness now unavailable (Geoff), Archie's statement to the police, the potential evidence of Ethan and Fergus and the allegation made against Harry.

## How to Answer this Question

There are four principal topics for discussion. The first is whether the prosecution can make use of Geoff's statement to the police. You will appreciate from the fact that Geoff is dead that if this statement is to reach the jury at all, it will have to do so on the basis that it is hearsay evidence and that the maker is unavailable. **Section 116** of **CJA 2003** will be applicable, and because of **s116(1)(a)** you will need to ask whether Geoff could have given evidence in accordance with his statement had he been alive. The statement refers to something observed by Geoff, and clearly he could have given evidence of that. But it also contains an account of what Clare said to him. This in itself is hearsay, but it is admissible by virtue of **subs (4)** and **(7)** of **s120**. Remember, however, the warning that must be given to the jury under *Islam* (1999). Since Geoff is not available, this part of his statement will be second-hand hearsay if his witness statement is read in evidence and the multiple hearsay provisions of **s121** will apply.

The next topic for discussion is what Archie said during his interview with the police. No question of impropriety arises. You are not told about access to legal advice, but don't waste time discussing that if you are not told anything about it. Archie admits having sex but denies rape. It will be to his advantage to be able to show that his defence at trial was raised at the first possible opportunity. Is it admissible? You will need to refer to *Sharp* (1988) or *Aziz* (1995).

Is the evidence of Ethan and Fergus relevant? Clearly it is because it supports Archie's account of events by making it more likely that what he says about Clare's insistence on sex in the field is true. But will this evidence be excluded by **s41** of the **Youth Justice and Criminal Evidence Act 1999**? The issue is one of consent; **s41(3)(b)** will not apply because the events took place too long ago, but **s41(3)(c)** may well do so. There should be some discussion of what amounts to similarity for these purposes. Reference should be made to what was said on this subject in *A* (2002).

The earlier allegation against Harry did not lead to a prosecution, and this might suggest that on that occasion Clare was lying, from which it might be inferred that she is doing so again on this occasion. But this sort of information is strictly regarded by the courts; see, for example, *M* (2009) and *D* (2009).

### Up for Debate

You can gain some extra credit for stating that DNA or forensic evidence revealing 'physical trauma' can help prove rape occurred and that those who make false allegations are also subject to prosecution for the common law crime of perverting the course of justice.

## Applying the Law

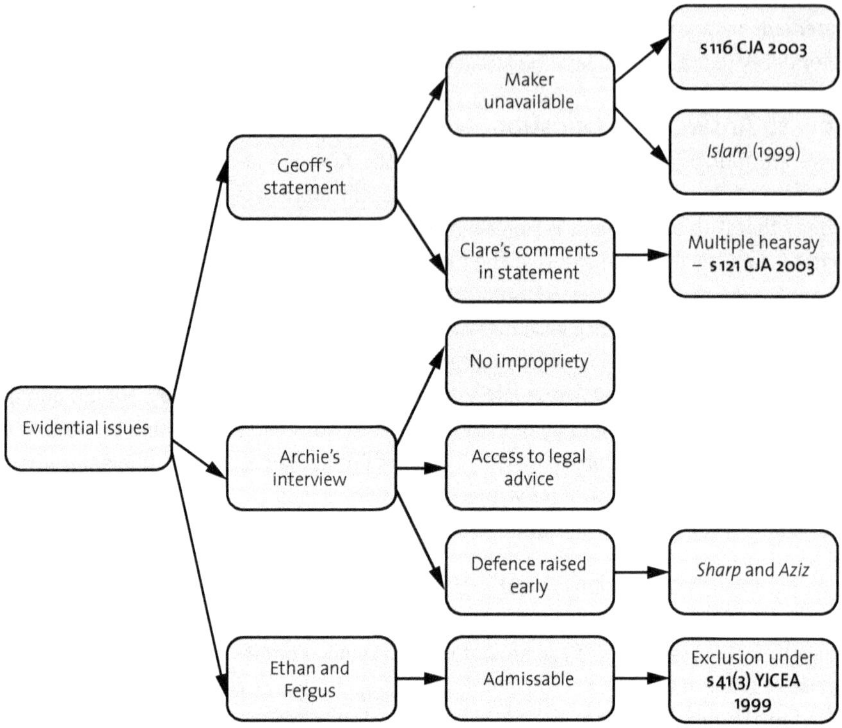


*This mind map shows the main factors around Geoff's statement, Archie's interview and the evidence of Ethan and Fergus to discuss in your answer.*

# ANSWER

The first question is whether the prosecution can make use of Geoff's statement to the police. Since Geoff is dead, there appears to be a case for admissibility of the statement under **s116(2)(a)**. To be admitted, however, the condition in **s116(1)(a)** must also be satisfied. Could Geoff have given oral evidence of what he saw when Clare returned home? Clearly, he could. But could he also give evidence of what Clare said to him? On the assumption that Clare herself testifies for the prosecution, he can if what she said amounts to an admissible previous statement under **s120(4)** and **(7)** of the **Criminal Justice Act 2003** (hereafter '**CJA 2003**'). Presumably there will be no difficulty in satisfying the **subs (4)** conditions. The only condition under **subs (7)** that might give rise to argument is **subs (7)(e)**. The words 'you are no longer my sister' could be construed as a threat. Whether they are may depend on how seriously Clare took them. Did she construe them as only an exaggeration that expressed her brother's concern? Or did she take them seriously, perhaps in the light of her brother's previous conduct towards her? If her previous statement is admitted, it will be evidence of the truth of its contents by virtue of **subs (4)**, but the judge in summing up must direct the jury that the earlier statement cannot operate as confirmation from an independent source of the evidence she gives from the witness box. The same direction must also be given in respect of Geoff's evidence about her appearance (*Islam* (1999)).[4]

There is no mention of impropriety in the interview with Archie that the police conducted. What he said amounts to a 'mixed' statement, since it contains an admission that he had sexual intercourse with Clare but also an assertion that this was with her consent. As a mixed statement, it will be admissible and is to be considered by the jury as evidence of the truth of all its contents (*Sharp* (1988); *Aziz* (1995)).

The evidence of Ethan and Fergus is clearly relevant as a matter of common sense. A woman who asks for open-air sex on two fairly recent occasions is likely to have done so again on a third. But admissibility will also depend on whether **s 41** of the **Youth Justice and Criminal Evidence Act 1999** can be satisfied. The issue at trial is one of consent, and **s 41(3)(b)** will not apply because the earlier incidents took place too long ago. The favoured meaning of 'at or about the same time' was accepted in *A* (2002) to be, broadly speaking, within the range of 24 hours on each side of the alleged incident.

But **s 41(3)(c)(i)** is likely to apply. The request made to the defendant for sex in the open air and the act of intercourse with him in the field should be seen as one event. Even if this is not done, the request is clearly 'other sexual behaviour of the complainant' which took place 'at or about the same time as' the alleged rape. The question then will be whether the incidents with Ethan and Fergus are so similar to the events described by Archie that they 'cannot reasonably be explained as a coincidence'. These words have not been precisely defined, and probably are incapable of exact definition. In *A* (2002) it was said by Lord Clyde that the requirement falls short of the earlier test of 'striking similarity', although he added that *mere* similarity would not be sufficient. In *Tahed* (2004), consensual use of the same item of equipment in a park on an earlier occasion was held, with other evidence, to be sufficiently similar to the act complained of. The location on these facts is of a more general nature, but there is at least a reasonable chance of persuading a judge that the condition is satisfied. The prosecution may argue in aid of the illustration of sex in motor cars; this would not be admissible according to Lord Williams during the debate on the Bill in the House of Lords.[5]

On the limited information given, the earlier allegation against Harry will be inadmissible. 'Sexual behaviour' within **s 41(1)** does not include false accusations of sexual offences on earlier occasions (*T; H* (2002)). However, in the same conjoined appeals the Court of Appeal stated that such evidence cannot be admitted unless there are grounds for establishing not only that the earlier allegation was made, but also that it was false. In *D* (2009) it was held that the mere fact that police had decided that there was insufficient evidence to prosecute is not evidence that the earlier allegation was false.

4 This discussion highlights how the statutory scheme under the **CJA 2003** operates to include evidence of those witnesses since deceased and the safeguards, and the importance of relevant judicial directions.

5 The use of the *A* case is authority for the way in which the courts have interpreted the terminology of **s 41 YJCEA 1999**, namely that the similarity cannot reasonably be explained as a coincidence.

# QUESTION 20

Rupert and Edward have been committed for trial, charged with burglary. The case for the prosecution is that they broke into a shop in Holborn (London) owned by Rimsky & Romanov, a firm of jewellers, and there stole a quantity of watches.

Evidence for the prosecution will be given by Tabitha, Rupert's former girlfriend. She has made a statement in which she states that on the evening when the burglary took place, she drove Rupert and Edward to a public house. While drinking there, she overheard Rupert and Edward discussing a plan to break into the premises of Rimsky & Romanov. Later, they all left the public house. Tabitha says that she then drove them in the direction of her house but that on the way Rupert asked her to stop, saying that he and Edward needed to relieve themselves. This was near the rear entrance to the shop owned by Rimsky & Romanov. Tabitha states that she waited in the car for about half an hour until Rupert and Edward returned, and that they then drove to Tabitha's house. Tabitha also states that she helped them with some luggage which they had with them, and that the men left the next day. When the police came to ask for Tabitha's help in this matter, they discovered one of the stolen watches in her bathroom.

The prosecution also have a statement from Tabitha's nephew Archie, aged 10, who says that he found the rest of the stolen goods in Edward's garden shed.

When interviewed by the police without a solicitor, Rupert refused to answer any questions. Edward when interviewed denied having any part in the offence. He said that he spent the evening and the night in question at a hotel in Manchester with a woman called Sheila.

- **Discuss the evidential matters arising.**

## How to Read this Question

This question requires you to consider a number of different issues – take these in turn and by each actor in turn. For instance what (if any) warnings are required in relation to Tabitha's evidence, have Rupert and Edward made a confession? Can an adverse inference be drawn for Rupert's failure to answer questions? Should a *Lucas* direction be given in relation to the alibi?

## How to Answer this Question

There are five topics that need to be discussed in the answer to this question:

- Should there be an informal warning about the reliability of Tabitha's evidence? Note how it is possible to use the old law to argue by analogy, but be careful to avoid any suggestion that it still has any force as binding authority.
- Look at the content of Tabitha's evidence. She is reporting what she heard other people say quite a lot. Is all this admissible? Why?
- What is the position about Archie's evidence?

- What is the significance now of Rupert's failure to answer police questions? Try to summarise what the Act says accurately. A student who simply said, for example, that Rupert's silence was evidence of his guilt would not get much credit.
- What are the problems arising from Edward's alibi? Have you read the question carefully enough to deal with this point fully?

## Up for Debate

You will gain credit by highlighting that the Crown Court Bench Book (*Directing the Jury*), published in 2010 by the Judicial Studies Board, provides guidance to judges to avoid mechanical application of non-binding specimen directions that did not directly link to the cases being tried.

## Applying the Law

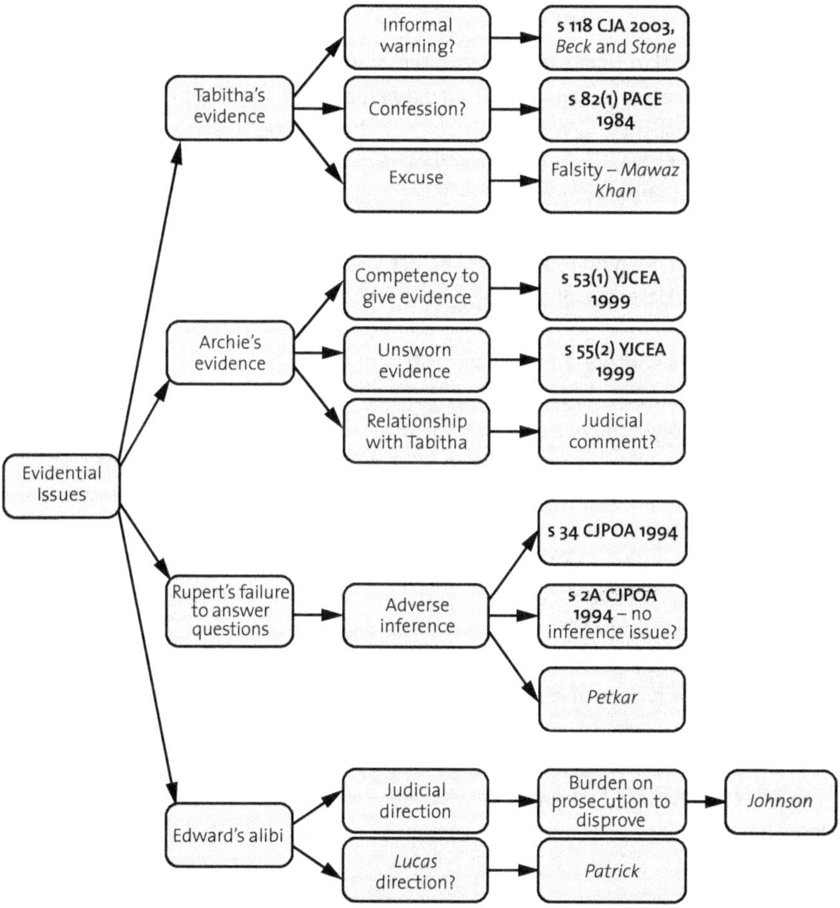


*This mind map outlines the many evidential issues and the rules of evidence that require consideration in this question.*

# ANSWER

The first question that arises is whether the judge should give an informal warning about the reliability of Tabitha's evidence when summing up to the jury. There are two reasons why such a warning might be desirable. We are told that she is Rupert's former girlfriend. Is there any evidence of antipathy towards him that would make it possible that she is implicating him from a desire for revenge? The rule in *Beck* (1982) was that where a witness might have a vested 'interest or purpose of his own to serve' in giving evidence, the judge should warn the jury about this. Earlier cases such as *Willis* (1916) and *Evans* (1965) established that where a wife gave evidence in support of an accomplice, the jury should be warned of the danger in relying on her testimony because she had an interest to serve. In earlier cases, warnings in situations analogous to those requiring corroboration had been required. In *Stone* (2005) the Court of Appeal held that this requirement had not survived the abolition of the corroboration rules. Nevertheless, it would seem sensible to warn the jury about the different but perhaps equally strong interest of someone giving evidence against a former boyfriend towards whom she felt animosity.[6]

It is worth noting that under the old law, the jury might have had to be warned that Tabitha was an accomplice and that it would be dangerous for them to convict on her uncorroborated evidence (*Davies v DPP* (1954)); this suggests another reason for an informal warning to be given about Tabitha's evidence. It is possible that, although she was never charged, she was an accomplice. She clearly knew of the plan to break into the shop. She stopped the car near the shop and it is unlikely that she believed that Rupert and Edward took half an hour to relieve themselves in its vicinity. She helped them with their 'luggage', and later one of the stolen watches was found in her bathroom.

No special difficulties are presented by the content of Tabitha's evidence. Her report of what she heard Rupert and Edward saying about their plans to break into the shop will be admissible as an exception to the rule against hearsay as showing the contemporaneous state of mind and intentions of the accused. **Section 118(1)** of the **Criminal Justice Act 2003** preserves, *inter alia*, the common law relating to *res gestae* exceptions to the rule against hearsay, including declarations about contemporaneous states of mind such as intention. In *Moghal* (1977), a statement of intention to murder made some six months before the commission of the crime was considered admissible. This particular decision was subsequently criticised by Lord Bridge in *Blastland* (1986) on the ground of relevance. However, the House of Lords emphasised in *Blastland* that such a declaration would be admissible if the state of mind evidenced by it was directly in issue at the trial, or was of direct and immediate relevance to an issue arising in the trial. Clearly, those conditions are satisfied here.

It might also be possible to argue that what was said amounted to a confession by both defendants. A confession is another exception to the rule against hearsay preserved by

6 This discussion demonstrates knowledge of the issues that arise where a witness knows the accused – here in the capacity of a former girlfriend. It also highlights, through *Willis*, *Evans* and *Stone*, how the courts have sought to protect the jury from such evidence. Make sure you use authorities appropriately.

**s118**. By **s82(1)** of the **Police and Criminal Evidence Act (PACE) 1984**, a confession includes any statement wholly or partly adverse to the person who made it, whether made to a person in authority or not. It may be, despite apparent oddity, that things said before the commission of an offence can amount to confessions if the offence is subsequently committed.[7]

Tabitha will be able to report the excuse given by Rupert for stopping the car near the shop because the prosecution will be relying on its falsity, as in *Mawaz Khan* (1967), rather than its truth.

It is just conceivable that the judge would think it appropriate to comment on the weight to be attached to Archie's evidence in view of his relationship to Tabitha if the defence makes a point of this. By **s53(1)** of the **Youth Justice and Criminal Evidence Act 1999**, at every stage in criminal proceedings all persons are (whatever their age) competent to give evidence. By **subs (3)**, a person is not competent to give evidence in criminal proceedings if it appears to the court that he is not a person who is able to understand questions put to him as a witness and give answers to them that can be understood. There is no suggestion that Archie falls into this category and he will therefore be competent to give evidence. However, his evidence will be unsworn. By **s55(2)** of the **1999 Act**, a witness may not be sworn unless he has attained the age of 14.

Rupert's failure to answer police questions is now governed by **s34** of the **Criminal Justice and Public Order Act 1994**. The failure of an accused in such circumstances to mention any fact relied on later in his defence, if it was a fact which in the circumstances existing at the time the accused could reasonably have been expected to mention, will allow the jury in determining whether the accused is guilty of the offence charged to draw such inferences as appear proper. But it is important to know if Rupert was offered a solicitor. **Subsection (2A)** of **s34** provides that where the accused was at an authorised place of detention at the time of his failure to mention any fact relied on in his defence, no inferences may be drawn unless he was allowed an opportunity to consult a solicitor before being questioned.

If it is an appropriate case for an **s34** direction, the judge should follow the guidelines set out in *Petkar* (2004). He must identify the facts on which Rupert relies and which were not mentioned on questioning. He must identify the inferences which it is suggested might be drawn from failure to mention such facts, to the extent that they may go beyond the standard inference of late fabrication. The jury should be told that, if an inference is drawn, they should not convict wholly or mainly on the strength of it. They should be told that an inference should be drawn only if they think it is fair and proper, and it should be drawn only if the only sensible explanation for failure to mention facts relied on is that Rupert had no answers, or none that would stand up to scrutiny. Moreover, an inference should be drawn only if, apart from Rupert's failure to mention facts relied on,

7 This discussion demonstrates knowledge of the current statutory scheme under the **CJA 2003** for the admission of hearsay evidence and what could be a confession as an exception to it.

the prosecution case is so strong that it clearly calls for an answer by him. The jury should be reminded of the evidence on the basis of which they are invited not to draw any inferences from Rupert's silence.[8]

The trial judge should tell the jury that it is for the prosecution to disprove the alibi beyond reasonable doubt (*Johnson* (1995)). In *Burge and Pegg* (1996), it was said that a *Lucas* (1981) direction should be given where, among other cases, the defendant relies on an alibi. However, it is clear that a *Lucas* direction does not have to be given in every case where an alibi is raised by a defendant. For example, in *Patrick* (1999) the Court of Appeal held that there is no need for a direction where the only possible basis for rejecting a defendant's alibi would be acceptance by the jury of the prosecution's identification evidence. A rather similar situation arises on these facts. In effect, the members of the jury have to be satisfied beyond reasonable doubt that Tabitha's account is reliable. If they decide that it is, Edward's alibi must be false. In *Broadhurst* (1964) (a case involving lies rather than an alibi) it was highlighted that where a jury reject an alibi because they conclude that the defendant is lying they must be directed that this does not lead to the conclusion that because he is lying he must be guilty. In *Middleton* (2000), the Court of Appeal said that a *Lucas* direction should not be given where it would only confuse the jury, and probably that would be its effect here.

# QUESTION 21

'We regard mistaken identification as by far the greatest cause of actual or possible wrong conviction.' (Criminal Law Revision Committee, 11th Report, 1972)

- **Has enough been done to reduce this risk?**

## How to Read this Question

This question requires you to consider what has been done to mitigate wrongful conviction on the basis of unreliable identification evidence. Thus, your discussion should include **PACE Code D** and *Turnbull* warnings in addition to other authorities.

## How to Answer this Question

Start by identifying the modes of protection: *Turnbull* (1977) warnings and **Code D**. Then deal with the adequacy of *Turnbull* warnings; some reference to voice identification and to 'evidence of description' would be appropriate here. The problems with the application of **Code D** should then be considered.

In summary, therefore, the essay is constructed as follows:

- outline of the two ways of protecting against mistaken identification;
- the *Turnbull* (1977) guidelines: *Thornton* (1995); *Slater* (1995); *Pattinson and Exley* (1996); *Qadir* (1998);

8 In discussing adverse inferences under the **CJPOA 1994** be sure to highlight the resultant effect, namely that the inference is not on its own evidence of the defendant's guilt.

- distinction between evidence of identity and evidence of description: *Gayle* (1999);
- voice identification: *Hersey* (1998); *Gummerson and Steadman* (1999);
- **Code D**: *Kelly* (1992); use of **s 78(1)** of the **Police and Criminal Evidence Act (PACE) 1984; Code D, para 3.12**; *Forbes* (2001).

## Up for Debate

You will gain credit for highlighting that where the trial judge exercises his discretion and allows admission of the evidence despite a breach of **Code D** then he must also give a direction to the jury explaining its effect and relevance – the jury should give the breach such weight as they hold fit (*Forbes* (2001)).

## Answer Structure

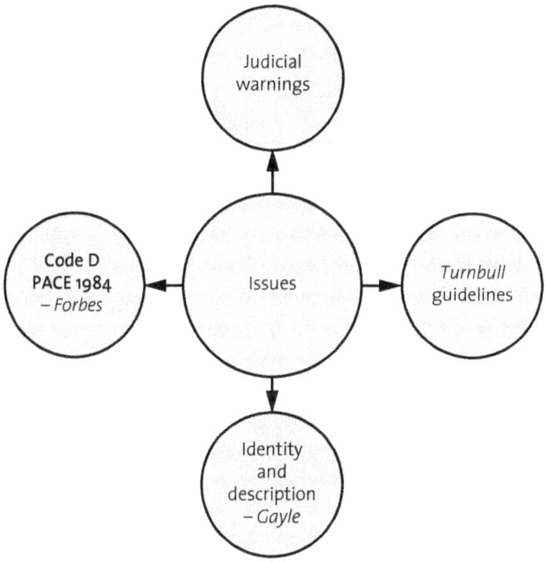


*This diagram highlights the main points to discuss in relation to the risks involved in the admission of identification evidence that you should discuss in your answer.*

# ANSWER

English law tries to protect defendants from wrongful convictions that are based on mistaken identification evidence in two ways: by a system of judicial warnings to juries, and by a Code of Practice that governs identification procedures.[9]

9 This paragraph highlights the issue raised for English law by convictions based on mistaken identification and how it has tried to deal with it.

In *Turnbull* (1977), the Court of Appeal established guidelines that were to apply where the prosecution case depended 'wholly or substantially' on the correctness of one or more identifications of the defendant. The words 'wholly or substantially' have not in practice limited the range of cases in which the guidelines have been considered appropriate. A *Turnbull* direction has to be given in cases where identification is based on recognition as well as in cases where the risk of misidentification might seem greater: for example, where identification is based on a fleeting glimpse. The need for a direction will usually arise when the defendant denies that he was present at a particular place. But the direction may also be necessary where the defendant admits being present at a relevant place but denies involvement in the criminal activity taking place there. So, for example, it was held in *Thornton* (1995), where the defendant was charged with causing grievous bodily harm at a wedding reception, that the *Turnbull* warning ought to have been given because, where others present were similarly dressed, a mistake was clearly possible. As Rose LJ emphasised in *Slater* (1995), the key question is whether there was, in the particular circumstances, the possibility of mistake. Thus, the circumstances in which the warning is required are probably adequate.

Is the nature of the warning adequate? According to *Turnbull*, several stages have to be followed. First, the judge must warn the jury of the special need for caution before convicting on the basis of identification evidence. Second, he must tell the jury why such a warning is needed. Some reference should be made to the fact that a mistaken witness can be a convincing one, and that a number of convincing witnesses can all be mistaken. Third, he must direct the jury to examine closely the circumstances in which each identification was made. In *Turnbull*, the court gave examples of topics for comment, such as the light and the length of the period of observation, but in *Pattinson and Exley* (1996), the Court of Appeal said that it was not necessary in every case for the judge to summarise all the weaknesses in the identification evidence. The court added that where the judge does summarise the identification evidence, he should point out strengths as well as weaknesses. In later cases, however, such as *Popat (No 2)* (2000), *Stanton* (2004) and *Nash* (2004), failure to mention weaknesses has given rise to a successful appeal. Fourth, the judge should direct the jury to consider whether the identification evidence is supported by any other evidence. Fifth, he should identify the evidence that is capable, and incapable, of providing such support. Not surprisingly, the Court of Appeal has deprecated rigid formulas for the fulfilment of *Turnbull* requirements. Thus, in *Qadir* (1998), it was said that the form and contents of the summing up should, even when identification is in issue, be tailored to the circumstances of the individual case. Nevertheless, the *Turnbull* procedure appears to provide a strong protection for defendants who challenge identification evidence. Further, it was said in *Turnbull* that cases should be withdrawn from the jury where the identification evidence is poor and there is no supporting evidence.[10]

*Turnbull* almost certainly does not extend to evidence from a witness who says that he would be unable to recognise the person he saw if he were to see him again, but who

10 The case of *Turnbull* shows the cautious approach taken by the courts where identification evidence is concerned. Do not be afraid to state this.

remembers some identifying features of that person. But there seems to be no reason why it should be extended in this way to such 'evidence of description'. As Henry LJ pointed out in *Gayle* (1999), the danger of an honest witness's being mistaken as to distinctive clothing, or the general description of the person he saw, are minimal.[11]

But *Turnbull* assumes that most identifications are visual ones. That is so, but sometimes identification may be by the sound of the human voice. On this topic, the law is undeveloped. In *Hersey* (1998), the Court of Appeal showed support for the equivalent of identification parades for voices, and said that juries should be directed as in cases of visual identification, with appropriate modifications. But, in *Gummerson and Steadman* (1999), the Court of Appeal disapproved of 'voice identification parades', and the content of any warning in the summing up remains unclear.[12]

The protection given by **Code D** is less satisfactory. Failure to comply with the appropriate procedure will not lead inevitably to the exclusion of identification evidence (*Kelly* (1992)). What has to be shown is that the breach is sufficiently grave to bring the evidence within the scope of **s 78(1)** of **PACE**.

**Code D, para 3.12** provides that, except in certain stated circumstances, whenever a suspect disputes, an identification procedure shall be held unless it is not practicable, or it would serve no useful purpose in proving or disproving whether the suspect was involved in committing the offence. It has been suggested that the effect is to reverse the decision of the House of Lords in *Forbes* (2001), which held that the identification procedure was mandatory save in very limited circumstances, and to revive the Court of Appeal decision in *Popat* (1998), to the effect that the provision did not apply where a suspect had previously been 'properly and adequately' identified by the witness, or where there had already been an 'actual and complete' identification by the witness. But it is unlikely that **Code D, para 3.12** has this effect. If it were otherwise, the problems perceived by the House of Lords in *Forbes* would arise again. First, the police would have to make difficult decisions about the adequacy of earlier identifications. Second, to have to make such decisions would be at odds with their primary duty to investigate and prosecute crime. Third, the *Popat* approach overlooked the fact that miscarriages of justice had resulted from identifications that were thought at the time to be satisfactory, but were later proved to be wrong.[13]

It has been argued that the new primacy of video procedures puts a suspect in a more vulnerable position than was the case when identification parades were the primary identification procedure. When a suspect agrees to take part in a parade, he can withdraw

11 This discussion highlights that the application of the *Turnbull* warning does not extend to evidence of mere description and the rationale behind that. Do not be afraid to point out that where the latter is concerned the jury would already be aware of its relative value.

12 This discussion highlights an area not currently covered by a relevant code, and the reticence of the courts to accept the 'creation' of such a procedure.

13 This substantiates the current debate and criticism surrounding the requirement to hold identification procedure where an initial identification had already taken place.

his consent if he raises a reasonable objection to its composition or to some other element of unfairness. But once an image has been provided for video procedures, he has no control over the use to which it might be put.[14]

It is too early to say whether enough has been done to reduce the risk of mistaken identification. The contents of a *Turnbull* warning remain uncertain so far as identifying weakness in the identification evidence is concerned, although current authority suggests that this is now an essential feature of the direction. The law relating to voice identification has yet to be developed. The interpretation of **Code D, para 3.12** is open to argument. Subject to this, however, much has been done to allay the fears of the Criminal Law Revision Committee.

It seems clear that the Code does not apply to identifications made only a short time after the commission of the offence. Thus, in *Kelly* (1992), the defendant was charged with attempted rape. The offence took place in a street, and the attacker was distracted before he could commit the full offence. The police arrived soon afterwards, and the victim, while talking to the police, saw the defendant, and told the police that she had seen her attacker. An officer questioned, but did not arrest, the defendant. Meanwhile, the victim was brought closer to him in a police car. She then said that she was sure the man she had seen had been her attacker, and the defendant was arrested. The Court of Appeal rejected the argument that this procedure had denied the defendant the benefit of an identification parade. It added that where a suspect is found within minutes of the crime and close to the scene, it might well be that **Code D** did not apply. Later decisions such as *Hickin and Others* (1996) and *Malashev* (1997) have confirmed this view.

14 See the commentary on *Marcus* [2005] Crim LR 384.

# 7 Confessions and Ill-Gotten Evidence

## INTRODUCTION

One of the most important of the defence counsel's objectives at trial is to ensure that as little of the prosecution evidence as possible reaches the jury – unless, of course, it happens to favour the defendant. This chapter deals with two important statutory weapons in the defence's armoury: **ss 76** and **78** of the **Police and Criminal Evidence Act (PACE) 1984**. These deal with confessions, and with a discretion to exclude for reasons of fairness evidence on which the prosecution proposes to rely. The sections are very often relied on in the alternative; it was decided in *Mason* (1988) that **s 78** applies to confessions just as much as to any other evidence.

Students of this topic need an important warning. In reading cases where evidence has been excluded under either section, but particularly under **s 78**, you are almost never reading precedents that will have to be followed in later cases. The reason for this is that no situation is ever exactly repeated, defendants are not all alike and the effect of acts or omissions by the police is likely to vary greatly from case to case. Knowledge of previous decisions cannot be a substitute for rigorous thought about the facts of your own particular case, facts that of course include the personal characteristics of the defendant. This is plain enough from looking at the basic law. **Subsection (2)(b)** of **s 76** – probably the provision in that section which is most relied on – has the effect of requiring the court to attend to the particular circumstances of the individual defendant who relies on the provision. And, in *Jelen and Katz* (1989), the Court of Appeal emphasised that the application of **s 78** was 'not an apt field for hard case law and well founded distinctions between cases'.[1]

It is, of course, in relation to a confession that an argument for exclusion will very often have to be made. When a confession appears in a set of prosecution statements or in an examination question, you need to be able to do three things. You must be able to recognise it when you see it, assess its impact on the case as a whole and work out what arguments are available to you to get it excluded.

1 See also *Roberts* (1997).

## RECOGNISING THE CONFESSION

You may think a confession would be easy to spot: 'OK guv; it's a fair cop. You've got me bang to rights.' Perhaps in real life that sort of thing is said more often than we might expect. But because examiners are interested in grey areas, you are not likely to have to deal with anything so simple in the examination. Your starting point is the partial definition contained in **s 82(1)** of **PACE**. With that in mind, you must interpret what has been said. Remember that a favourite topic for questions is the extent to which an accused person can, by something other than an oral statement, *adopt* an allegation against him. Consider some possibilities: he begins to weep; he hangs his head; he blushes violently; he runs away; he says nothing; he attacks the accuser. For a vivid example, see *Batt* (1995).

## IMPACT ON THE CASE AS A WHOLE

The obvious impact is that of something said by an accused person which inculpates the maker of the statement in relation to the offence in question. It used to be the case that an out-of-court confession implicating a co-accused, but made in the absence of that co-accused, was admissible evidence only against the maker of the confession (see e.g. *Gunewardene* (1951)). That traditional rule must now be read in the light of *Y* (2008), the effect of which is that such a confession can now, by the operation of **s 114(1)(d) CJA 2003**, be evidence not only against the person making the statement containing the confession, but also against anyone else whom the statement implicates. You should read the case and note the reservations about admitting such evidence as a matter of practice which the Court of Appeal made. These reservations might affect the practical application of the new law, but they don't alter the fact that the law has changed significantly. The result is that it is now wholly unclear in what circumstances the confession of one defendant is likely *in practice* to be admitted against another.

There is a very widespread misapprehension that wherever defendants have embarked on a joint endeavour, anything said at any time by any of them, even after arrest, will be admissible evidence against any of the other absent defendants. The case of *Blake and Tye* (1844) is often cited in this connection. This is a totally false understanding of the law, as a reading of *Blake and Tye* would show. Probably because the report is an old one and not readily available, not many students have read it. Fortunately, to understand the law on this point you do not have to read this case because the matter was dealt with more recently by the Court of Appeal in *Gray and Others* (1995). In that case, the court cited and adopted as an accurate exposition of the law a passage from the judgment of Dixon CJ in the Australian case of *Tripodi v R* (1961). In the course of his judgment, in the passage cited and adopted by the English Court of Appeal, Dixon CJ said that the reason for admitting the evidence of the acts or words of one defendant in a joint enterprise against the others was that the agreement to commit the crime was considered as implying an authority to each to act or speak *in furtherance of the common purpose* on behalf of the others. But from the nature of the case, it could seldom happen that anything said by one of the defendants which was no more than a *narrative or account of events that had already taken place* could be admissible against his companions in the common enterprise, though it might be admissible as a confession against the speaker. Usually, Dixon CJ said, the question of admissibility would relate to directions, instructions or arrangements, or to utterances accompanying acts.[2]

Another favourite topic for questions is the evidential worth of the exculpatory parts of a mixed statement.[3]

## EXCLUDING THE CONFESSION

In practice, this will involve the operation of **s 76(2)** of **PACE** and, as a subsidiary argument in case the first should fail, **s 78**. Many candidates lose marks because they fail to construct sensible *arguments* at this point in answering a question. The examiner does not want a string of cases; he wants an argument based on the facts of the particular problem. Note particularly that it is foolish to say much in relation to **s 76(2)(a)** unless there is a proper factual basis for suggesting that there may have been oppression.[4]

In very many cases, you will be relying on breaches of **Code C** (latest version adopted May 2014). Remember that even though there may have been a breach, you still need to put an argument on paper about why this is relevant to exclusion. Remember also that this is an area where decisions in other cases are of limited use.[5]

This has an advantage for you because it means that you don't have to learn lists of 'authorities'; on the other hand, you will be required to think creatively in the examination about the facts.

Particular attention should be paid to the extent to which the provisions of **Code C** apply to persons who are at a police station 'assisting the police with their inquiries' but who, technically, are there voluntarily because they have not been arrested.

2 [1995] 2 CR App R 100, pp. 128–129. But it has been said that an account of events narrated by one of the parties to another while the common enterprise was continuing, in order to bring that other up to date, might be regarded as in furtherance of the enterprise, and so admissible against all the parties referred to in it: see *Jones and Others* (1997).

3 See *Sharp* (1988); *Grayson* (1993).

4 See **s 76(8)** and look at what was said about the definition of oppression in *Fulling* (1987) and *Parker* (1995).

5 See, for example, observations to this effect in *Jelen and Katz* (1990) and in *Grannell* (1990).

**Checklist**

**Students should be familiar with the following areas:**

- the definition of 'confession';
- the adoption by an accused person of allegations made against him;
- the distinction between *Gunewardene* (1951) and *Rudd* (1948);
- the principle in *Sharp* (1988);
- **s 76** of **PACE**;
- **s 78** of **PACE**;
- the provisions of **Code C**;
- the extent to which **Code C** provisions apply to persons who have not been arrested;
- **ss 34, 35, 36, 37** and **38** of the **Criminal Justice and Public Order Act (CJPOA) 1994**.

# QUESTION 22

'The reforms made by the **Criminal Justice and Public Order Act (CJPOA) 1994** to the right of silence in the police station are more extensive and more difficult to defend than those relating to the accused's failure to testify at trial.'

- Discuss.

## How to Read this Question

This question concerns the right to silence but in two distinct situations; at the station and at trial. You should consider the position of the law in relation to each prior to the **CJPOA 1994** and after it came into force; burden, effect and justification. In short, contrast the extent of the reforms in relation to both.

## How to Answer this Question

The question itself contrasts the two different situations where a right to silence has to be considered. In each case, it is necessary to look at the old law to see how much change has been effected by the **1994 Act**. It is probably better to take the right to silence at trial first, as the change in this respect seems, in view of the way the common law was developing, far less radical than the provisions affecting the right to silence in pre-trial proceedings. A good summary of arguments for and against the changes that were being debated before the **1994 Act** can be found in S Greer, 'The right to silence: a review of the current debate' (1990) 53 MLR 709, pp. 709–730.

In summary, therefore, the essay is constructed as follows:

- comments on failure to testify at common law: *Bathurst* (1968); *Brigden* (1973); *Martinez-Tobon* (1993);
- effect of **s 35** of the **CJPOA 1994**: *Murray v DPP* (1993);
- **s 35** and the burden of proof;
- justification of **s 35**;

- effect of **s 34** of the **CJPOA 1994**;
- arguments in favour of **s 34**;
- counter-arguments;
- conclusions on **ss 34, 36** and **37**.

## Up for Debate

You will gain marks for highlighting that many commentators in the UK consider the right to silence to be a legal fiction rather than a reality now, even though the rationale for enacting the relevant provisions in the **CJPOA 1994** was to redress the imbalance that favoured an accused. You may choose to contrast the UK with other jurisdictions that still preserve the right (as at March 2015), for instance, Canada and the United States of America.

## Answer Structure

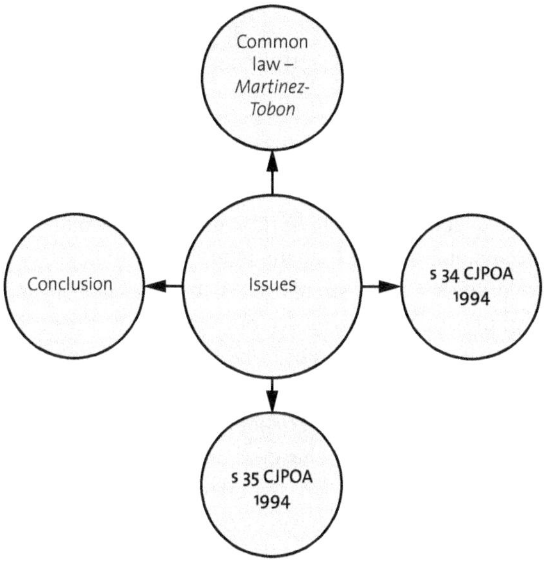


*This diagram shows the main factors that you should discuss when considering the erosion of the right to silence and adverse inferences.*

# ANSWER

At common law, the trial judge was permitted to comment on the failure of an accused person to testify at his trial, but he was required by *Bathurst* (1968) to emphasise that the jury must not assume guilt from such a failure. In certain cases, provided this basic point had been made, some criticism was regarded as acceptable. For example, in *Brigden* (1973), the accused's case, put to the appropriate witnesses in cross-examination, was that the police had planted incriminating evidence on him. The accused himself did not testify. The Court of Appeal approved the trial judge's comment to the effect that the jury had not heard from the accused, and that this might help them in deciding whether there was any truth in the allegation against the police. The same sort of criticism could be made where the accused did not testify, but relied on facts that must have been within his knowledge. Thus, in *Martinez-Tobon* (1993), the accused was charged with the illegal importation of cocaine in a packet. The defence was that he had thought the packet contained emeralds, but the accused did not testify. The trial judge commented in his summing up that if the defendant had thought the drugs were emeralds, one might have thought that he would be very anxious to say so. On appeal against conviction, it was argued that the judge's comment had gone beyond what was permissible, but the Court of Appeal disagreed. Provided the *Bathurst* essentials were complied with, a judge might think it appropriate to make a stronger comment where the defence case involved alleged facts that (a) were at variance with the Crown's evidence or additional to it and exculpatory, and (b) must, if true, be within the defendant's knowledge.[6]

By **s 35** of the **CJPOA 1994**, the court or jury, in determining whether the accused is guilty of the offence charged, may draw such inferences as appear proper from the failure of the accused to give evidence or his refusal, without good cause, to answer any question once he has chosen to testify. However, the section does not make the accused a compellable witness.

How far does this go beyond the common law? It is likely that the section involves a significant change by making it permissible to infer guilt from failure to testify. In *Murray v DPP* (1993), the House of Lords had to interpret a provision in similar terms to **s 35** in the law of Northern Ireland. It was held that the inferences that could be drawn were not limited to specific inferences from specific facts, but included an inference that the accused was guilty of the offence charged. As Lord Slynn put it, if the evidence clearly calls for an explanation that the accused ought to be in a position to give if an explanation exists, then a failure to give any explanation may as a matter of common sense allow the drawing of an inference that there is no explanation, and that the accused is guilty. This looks very much like the law as it was being developed in *Martinez-Tobon*, minus the protection afforded by the *Bathurst* direction. The effect of *Martinez-Tobon* was to create a situation only too familiar to students of evidence law, where a judge follows an approved formula to save himself from the strictures of the Court of Appeal, gives the defendant protection with one hand, promptly takes it away with the other, and thoroughly confuses any thinking members of the jury.[7]

It was sometimes argued that to change the law in this respect would shift the burden of proof. But, there is no reason why changes in evidence law to help the prosecution

6 This discussion shows the development of judicial directions relating to the jury's use of certain evidence where an accused has failed to testify. It is always useful to outline the relevant test here as set out in *Bathurst*, if you can.

7 The discussion in this paragraph shows how the courts interpreted **s 35** of the **CJPOA 1994** – the use of authorities, here *Murray* and *Martinez-Tobon*, substantiate the development of the law prior to the enactment of the **1994 Act**.

*discharge* its burden should have the effect of *shifting* it. Even before the **1994 Act**, it was not the case that the prosecution's obligation was to establish the accused's guilt beyond reasonable doubt *without any help from the accused*. If it had been so, evidence of such matters as breath tests, fingerprints and handwriting would have had to be excluded, and **s 62(10)** of the **Police and Criminal Evidence Act (PACE) 1984** provided that such inferences as appeared proper might be drawn from refusal to provide an intimate sample.

**Section 35** can be defended on the basis that it makes sense out of a confusing situation at common law and does not affect the burden of proof.[8]

The change in law affecting the right to silence at the police station is both more radical and far less easy to defend. At common law, no inference was permitted from the exercise of the right to silence in the face of questioning by the police or others charged with the investigation of offences. By **s 34** of the **1994 Act**, the failure of an accused in such circumstances to mention when questioned any fact relied on later in his defence, if it was a fact that, in the circumstances existing at the time, the accused could reasonably have been expected to mention, will allow the jury in determining whether the accused is guilty of the offence charged to draw such inferences from the failure as appear proper.

The essence of the argument in favour of this change was twofold. First, there was a gut reaction that anyone who was innocent would trust the police and would want to explain things to them as soon as possible. Second, although in the past a very few police had misbehaved, the protection given in **PACE** of access to legal advice and recorded interviews meant that no suspect who was innocent now had anything to fear.

Unfortunately, research suggests that this protection is insufficient. It has been proved that the police use a number of devices to discourage access to legal advisers, such as reading the suspect's rights too quickly or failing to mention that legal advice is free. There have been routine breaches of the **PACE Codes of Practice**, such as the holding of improper 'informal' interviews before the recorded interview. The style of questioning in at least one interview was so bullying as to be branded oppressive by the Court of Appeal. Legal advisers may be not only unqualified, but also inexperienced and passive, providing no protection at all for the suspect.[9]

Police do not have to be corrupt for the innocent suspect to fear for his safety. They need only to have made some assumptions about the guilt of their suspect and be prepared to use guile to establish what they believe to be the truth. The innocent citizen probably sees the possibility of making a false confession as remote and so, perhaps, it may be. What is

8 These last two paragraphs highlight one of the criticisms of the **1994 Act**. Do not be afraid to form a judgement where a question requires it, and here it is clearly stated 'discuss'.

9 S Greer, 'The right to silence: a review of the current debate' (1990) 53 MLR 709, pp. 721–722; A Sanders and L Bridges, 'Access to legal advice and police malpractice' [1990] Crim LR 494, pp. 494–509; J Hodgson, 'Tipping the scales of justice: the suspect's right to legal advice' [1992] Crim LR 854, pp. 854–862. For a particularly gross example of police oppression, see *Paris* (1993).

far more likely is that he will give an ambiguous answer that will add to the case against him. And how can he avoid giving ambiguous answers? Not only is language riddled by its very nature with ambiguity, but all the circumstances surrounding a police interrogation conspire to increase the risk. The suspect may be in a highly emotional state. He may feel guilty even though he has committed no offence – for example, feelings of anger or guilt are well-established reactions to bereavement. He may be ignorant of a vital fact that explains away suspicious circumstances. He may be frightened, confused or forgetful.[10]

Nor does the innocent suspect have to fear anything so horrific as a miscarriage of justice at trial, though past experience has shown that this is all too possible. A mistake or ambiguity in something said to the police can suggest that there is at least a reason for charging the suspect and a case to answer. That may mean a remand in custody. At the very least it is likely to mean months of anxiety while on bail awaiting trial. Much is made of the high standard of proof that is required before a court may convict on a criminal charge. But no such standard applies to other decisions made during the pre-trial stages. Yet these decisions may have terrible implications for an innocent suspect's liberty and for his own and his family's financial security and peace of mind.

At the pre-trial stage, a right to silence is, as things stand now in this country, an essential protection for the innocent. The innovations brought about by **ss 34, 36** and **37** of the **1994 Act** are indeed *defensible*, but only on the most short-sighted and crudely utilitarian basis, which accepts that it is expedient that innocent people should suffer for the sake of the majority.

# QUESTION 23

Nigel is arrested on suspicion of murdering Olive. At the police station, he is told of his right to a solicitor but says he does not want one because 'they cost too much and waste a lot of time'. His watch and other personal possessions are taken away from him and he is then locked in a cell for five hours. At the end of that time, he is interviewed by DS Lestrade. After three hours of questioning, Lestrade suddenly produces a photograph. 'Just look at that', he says. 'Now, will you tell me the truth, or do I have to get my box of tricks out?' The photograph, which is in colour, shows Olive's mutilated body. Nigel screams and says: 'For God's sake, my nerves can't stand it. I killed her but I never meant to. She drove me to it.' The next day, he is interviewed again by DS Lestrade, but this time in the presence of a solicitor. He again confesses to the murder.

- **Discuss the evidential issues that arise.**

## How to Read this Question

This question requires you to consider confession evidence and whether its admissibility is affected by factors at the time, for example, oppression or things said or done (**s 76 PACE 1984**) with reference to relevant authorities.

10 This demonstrates knowledge of the current debates surrounding the provisions of the **CJPOA 1994** and the potential for abuse by the police whether conscious or subconscious. Although in a question such as this it is important to highlight these, you must remain aware of how far this takes the discussion.

## How to Answer this Question

Here, we have two confessions and the admissibility of each has to be considered.

*The first confession*

- Application of **s 82(1)** of the **Police and Criminal Evidence Act (PACE) 1984**;
- The possibility of oppression;
- Causation – always vital when considering **s 76**;
- Note the use made of the information about the watch;
- Breaches of **Code C**.

*The second confession*

- The continuing effect of the first confession – *McGovern* (1991); *Neil* (1994).
- Finally, remember the point based on *Sharp* (1988).

A useful case to remember when dealing with any breach of the Codes is *Elson* (1994), where the Court of Appeal said that the **Codes of Practice** were there to protect the individual against the might of the State. The individual, the court said, was at a great disadvantage when arrested by the police, and that was so whether or not the police behaved with the utmost propriety.

### Up for Debate

You will gain credit by outlining that fairness in trial proceedings is safeguarded by **Art 6** of the **ECHR** (see also *R v Quinn* (1990)). You should also highlight that although a confession may be excluded, relevant facts discovered thereby may still be adduced.

## Applying the Law

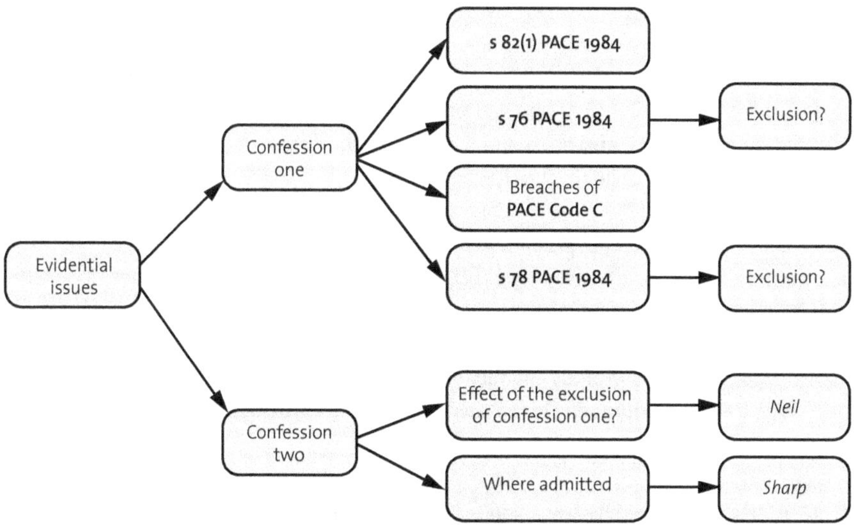


*This mind map outlines the law that you must consider in terms of the two confessions in this question.*

# ANSWER

Two main questions have to be considered: the admissibility of Nigel's first confession and that of the second confession, made in the presence of a solicitor.

In relation to the first confession, there are two problems: (a) is it likely to be excluded under **s 76** of **PACE**? And (b) if not, then is it likely to be excluded under **s 78**? Although the first confession contains exculpatory matter, it is obviously partly adverse to the maker, and so falls within the definition of 'confession' in **s 82(1)**.[11]

Might the first confession have been obtained by oppression? Once this question is raised, the burden is on the prosecution to prove beyond doubt that the confession was not so obtained. The court is likely to be interested in two matters: the reference to the 'box of tricks' and the showing of the photograph. Oppression is partly defined in **s 76(8)** of **PACE** as including 'torture, inhuman or degrading treatment, and the use or threat of violence (whether or not amounting to torture)'. It is possible that 'box of tricks' could have been understood as a reference to equipment designed for torture, or at least violence, so as to make what was said a threat of violence. However, a causative link has to be established between the threat and the confession and Nigel must be able to confirm that this threat, as well as the shock of seeing the photograph, operated on his mind at the time in question.

Showing the photograph to Nigel does not fall within the partial statutory definition of oppression. However, in *Fulling* (1987), the Court of Appeal approved the *Shorter Oxford Dictionary* definition of oppression as the 'exercise of authority or power in a burdensome, harsh or wrongful manner; unjust or cruel treatment of subjects, inferiors, etc., or the imposition of unreasonable or unjust burdens'. The court added that it would be hard to envisage any circumstances in which oppression would not entail some impropriety on the part of the interrogator. Showing the photograph appears to be on the borderline of oppression. It could be argued that it was psychologically burdensome to show it. There appears to be a good chance of persuading the court that the confession *may* have been obtained by oppression, and an even chance that the prosecution would be unable to prove beyond reasonable doubt that it was not.[12]

Even if the argument on oppression failed, the matters relied on could be used to support an argument for exclusion based on **s 76(2)(b)**. Other matters may be relevant under this head. Nigel may well have been suffering from disorientation after the time spent first in his cell and then in being questioned. His watch had been removed, and he was therefore very likely to have been without any means to measure the passing of time. It is possible that the police acted improperly in removing the watch. **Paragraph 4.2** of **Code C** says that

11 This part of the discussion highlights the provisions under which confessions can be excluded: **ss 76** and **78** of **PACE 1984**, and how a confession is defined. In terms of the latter it is important, where a statutory provision that defines exists, that you do use it – this will also demonstrate knowledge of the law.

12 The authority of *Fulling* is used to substantiate the court's approach in interpreting oppression. It also demonstrates knowledge in relation to how the law developed.

a detained person may retain clothing and personal effects unless the custody officer considers that he may use them to cause harm to himself or others, interfere with evidence, damage property or effect an escape, or they are needed as evidence. Did any of these reasons apply? The police might also try to argue that the watch was an 'item of value', and so excluded from the definition of personal effects under **para 4.3**.

The detention for five hours before the interview began may have been a breach of **para 1.1** of **Code C**, which requires that all persons in custody must be dealt with expeditiously. What was the reason for the delay? The three hours of interviewing may have been a breach of **para 12.8**, which requires breaks at recognised meal times and short breaks for refreshment at intervals of approximately two hours, subject to the interviewing officer's discretion. There may also have been a breach of **para 11.2** of **Code C**, which requires the interviewing officer to remind the suspect immediately before the interview begins of his right to *free* legal advice. One of the reasons given by Nigel for not wanting a solicitor suggests that he was not aware of this right.[13]

**Section 78** of **PACE** applies to evidence of a confession (*Mason* (1988)). Thus, all the matters referred to in connection with **s 76** could be used, if submissions under that section fail, to support a fairness argument based on **s 78** (see also *R v Quinn* (1990)). But, under this section, there is only a discretion to exclude, and, as the Court of Appeal acknowledged in *Anderson* (1993), it is not entirely clear where the burden of proof lies.[14]

If the first confession is excluded under **s 76**, the question arises whether the second confession was so tainted by the circumstances in which the first was made that it should be excluded also. In *McGovern* (1991), the defendant had confessed in two interviews. The first had been without a solicitor and, because of breaches of **s 58** of **PACE** and for other reasons, that confession was excluded. The Court of Appeal emphasised that when an accused person has made admissions at a first interview, the very fact that those admissions have been made is likely to have an effect on the person during the course of the second interview. It was therefore held that the confession in the second interview should have been excluded, as well as that in the first (see also *Ismail* (1990)). In *Neil* (1994), the Court of Appeal said that where there is a series of two or more interviews, and the court excludes one on the ground of unfairness, the question whether a later interview that itself is unobjectionable should also be excluded is a matter of fact and degree. It is likely to depend on whether the objections leading to the exclusion of the first interview were of a fundamental and continuing nature and, if so, if the arrangements for the later

13 These last two paragraphs highlight the factors from the scenario that are likely to be taken into account by the court when deciding whether the confession was obtained through oppression. When discussing such matters it is important, unless you are answering a general essay question, that you stick to relevant issues as outlined within the scenario rather than having a philosophical discussion on the types of things that may amount to oppression.

14 However, in *Stagg* (1994), very experienced prosecuting counsel accepted that it was for the prosecution to show either that there was no unfairness, or that its degree did not warrant the exclusion of the evidence.

interview gave the accused a sufficient opportunity to exercise an informed and independent choice as to whether he should repeat or retract what he said in the objectionable interview, or say nothing. There is clearly room for argument in Nigel's case. Much may depend on what he says about his state of mind in the second interview (see also *Nelson* (1998)).[15]

If the confession is admitted, the evidential value of the exculpatory part will have to be considered. This may be particularly important if Nigel chooses not to give evidence at trial. The Court of Appeal in *Duncan* (1981) held that the jury should be directed that both incriminating and exculpatory parts of a confession must be considered in deciding where the truth lies, and that it was not helpful to try to explain that the exculpatory parts were something less than evidence of the facts they stated. The judge may, however, comment on the relative weight of the two parts. This approach was approved by the House of Lords in *Sharp* (1988) and also in *Aziz* (1995).

# QUESTION 24

Earlier this year, a painting by the well-known modernist painter Bruno Hatte was stolen from a public art gallery in Barchester. Acting on information received, DS Proudie arrested two local men, Josh and Luke, in connection with the theft. When they arrived at the police station, they were placed in separate cells.

After about 10 minutes, Josh was taken to an interview room where Proudie was waiting. Josh said at once: 'I want to see a solicitor.' Proudie replied: 'Look, a valuable painting has been stolen. If there should, at present, be any chance of recovering the painting, that chance will cease to exist if we have to wait for a solicitor. Besides, you know the form. You don't need some pimpled trainee to hold your hand.'

After cautioning Josh, he questioned him for 80 minutes, but all Josh would say in answer to questions was 'No comment'. Finally, Proudie said: 'Right. We'll see what your friend Luke has to say. You won't mind waiting in a cell for a few more hours, will you? You won't be lonely; we've just pulled in a bunch of football supporters for fighting in the street.' Unknown to Proudie, Josh was terrified of football supporters because he had recently been attacked by a group of them. He said to Proudie: 'Look, don't put me with them. Luke and I did it together. But I only got involved because he made me; he's such a bully. We hid the painting in the well in Luke's garden.'

Proudie then visited Luke in his cell. Luke said at once: 'You got nowhere, did you?' Proudie laughed and said: 'In the well in your garden.' Luke shouted: 'Treacherous bastard!' He then refused to say any more.

15 This discussion demonstrates knowledge through outlining how the court deals with more than one confession. Remember that as a matter of common sense if one confession is excluded by reason of the method or process by which it was obtained then there is a very strong argument, as outlined by the Court of Appeal in *Neil*, that any subsequent confession is also tainted and should be excluded.

The painting was found in the well by the police on the following day. Josh and Luke were then offered access to free legal advice, which they both refused. They were then charged with theft of the painting and cautioned. Neither made any reply.

- **Discuss the evidential issues that arise.**

## How to Read this Question

This question requires you to consider the admissibility of confession evidence, evidence or relevant facts discovered as a result of a potentially excluded confession and any inferences that can possibly be drawn from silence.

## How to Answer this Question

*Josh*

- Definition of confession;
- Quick reference to **ss 76** and **78** – need to refer to **Code C**;
- Dispose quickly of the possibility of oppression. Don't waste time by going in detail into what is meant by oppression; there are more important things to write about in an answer to this question;
- What exactly was said about a solicitor? Anchor your argument to the facts and ask for further information, as you would in practice;
- Circumstances in which the police can refuse access to legal advice;
- The *Alladice* point;
- The 'special motive' point – *Rennie* (1982);
- The reliability point – note that the emphasis in **s 76(2)(b)** is on potentiality; it is irrelevant that evidence obtained afterwards confirms the truth of the confession;
- Old favourites: *Gunewardene* (1951) and *Sharp* (1988).

*Luke*

- Discovery of evidence via an inadmissible confession;
- Is what Luke said a confession within the definition? **Police and Criminal Evidence Act (PACE) 1984**;
- Arguments for exclusion.

*Both defendants*

- Their refusal to answer police questions or to say anything after caution when charged.

## Applying the Law

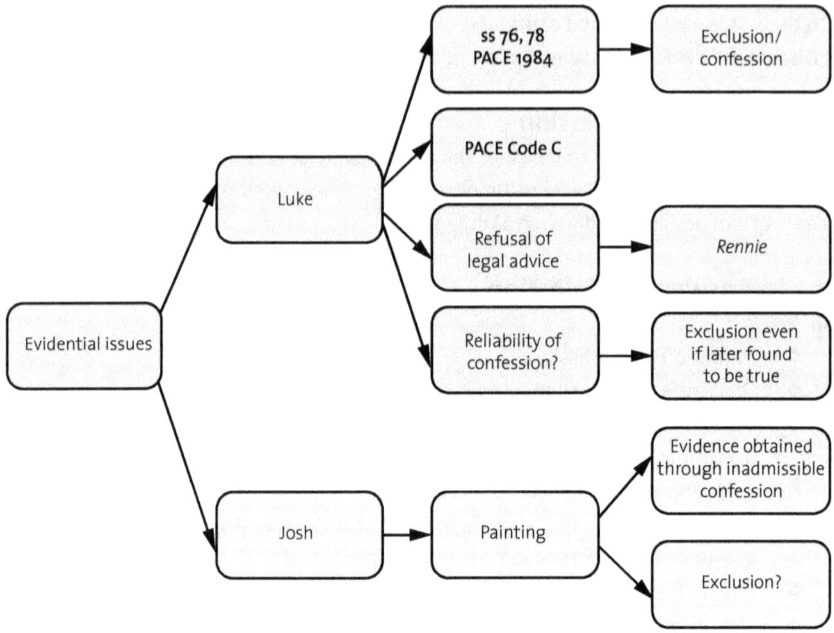


*This mind map outlines the main evidence, evidential issues and the law relating to the evidence stacked against Luke and Josh.*

# ANSWER

## THE CASE AGAINST JOSH

Josh has made a statement to the police that is partly adverse to him and is therefore a confession within the definition in **s 82(1)** of **PACE**.

The first matter that has to be considered is whether the confession is likely to be excluded under either **s 76** or **s 78**. In considering this question, it will be necessary to take into account the extent to which there may have been breaches of **Code C** of the **Codes of Practice**.

It does not appear that any question of oppression arises in relation to Josh and, accordingly, I shall consider those matters that would be relevant in arguments based on **s 76(2)(b)** and **s 78**.

The first of these is the refusal to provide an opportunity for Josh to take legal advice. (I assume from the words uttered that this was a refusal and not just discouragement, but I should like to know whether Josh said anything more about having a solicitor after Proudie's remarks.) It is relevant to ask whether Proudie would have been entitled to delay the opportunity for Josh to obtain legal advice if Josh had already been detained. Proudie would have been so entitled if, among other things, Josh had been detained for an indictable offence, and an officer of the rank of superintendent or above had reasonable grounds for believing that the exercise of his right to legal advice would, among other things, hinder the recovery of property obtained as a result of such an offence.[16]

Theft is an indictable offence. But Proudie would almost certainly not have been justified in refusing Josh access to a solicitor. **Annex B** of **Code C, para 3** provides that authority to delay a detainee's right to consult privately with a solicitor may be given only if the authorising officer has reasonable grounds to believe that the solicitor whom the detainee wants to consult will, inadvertently or otherwise, pass on a message from the detainee or act in some other way that will have any of the consequences referred to in **s58(8)**. If this is the case, the detainee must be allowed to choose another solicitor. As **Note B3** says, a decision to delay access to a specific solicitor is likely to be a rare occurrence, and on these facts Josh does not appear to have been asking for a specific solicitor. His request could have been met by allowing him access to the duty solicitor.

The question also arises whether, even if delay had not been justified, Josh suffered prejudice as a result. If Josh is experienced in being questioned by the police, the presence of a solicitor might have made no difference. Josh's replies of 'No comment' for 80 minutes suggests that this could well have been the case. In *Alladice* (1988), the appellant admitted that he could cope with being interviewed and said that he was aware of his legal rights. He had requested legal advice because he had wanted a check on the conduct of the police during the interview. The Court of Appeal held that his confession made in the absence of a solicitor was admissible, but the decision in that case was based on findings that the police had made an honest mistake about the appellant's entitlement to legal advice, and that the interview had been properly conducted. It is not clear on the facts given whether the police acted innocently or not.[17]

There is also the problem caused by the suggestion that Josh might share a cell with some football supporters. **Paragraph 8.1** of **Code C** provides that, so far as practicable, not more than one person should be detained in each cell. Was this practicable? Or was the reference to football supporters intended as a threat? If Proudie was acting in bad faith, a court would be more likely to exclude the confession, either under **s76(2)(b)** or under **s78**, than if he was not. In *Walsh* (1989), it was said that bad faith might make substantial or significant a breach that might not otherwise be so.

The position is more difficult if Proudie was acting in good faith. A confession will not be excluded under **s76(2)(b)** merely because the accused had a special motive for making it. As Lord Lane CJ said in *Rennie* (1982), very few confessions are inspired solely by remorse. But what we have here are words uttered by Proudie to Josh that trigger a particular fear,

16 The discussion so far demonstrates a good understanding of the various parts of the law that are required for consideration in terms of this confession. Be careful to deal with the issues chronologically.

17 The case of *Alladice* highlights the considerations of the court when deciding whether to exclude a confession – here whether the officers acted innocently.

which in turn leads to the confession. **Section 76(2)(b)** can be used even where there has been no police impropriety (*Fulling* (1987)) and it might therefore be applied here. The fact that the confession is in fact proved reliable by the subsequent discovery of the painting is no bar to the operation of **s 76(2)(b)**.[18]

If the confession is admitted, it will be evidence against Josh. But it is now possible to use it against Luke also. In *Y* (2008) the Court of Appeal held that an out-of-court confession was capable of being evidence against persons other than the maker by virtue of the wide scope for admitting hearsay under **s 114(1)(d) Criminal Justice Act 2003**. The court did, however, say that this should not make the police interview of one defendant routinely admissible in the case of another. It remains unclear in what circumstances such evidence, now in principle admissible, will in practice be admitted.

## THE CASE AGAINST LUKE

Even if Josh's confession is inadmissible, evidence can be given that the painting was found in the well in Luke's garden (**s 76(4)** of **PACE**).

Has Luke by his reaction to Proudie's taunt produced a confession? It could be argued that Luke's reaction amounts to a confession on the basis that his guilt could be inferred from the words uttered. They would then fall within the partial definition of a confession in **s 82(1)** of **PACE**. However, he does not appear to have been cautioned or offered legal advice, and he was not interviewed and recorded in accordance with **Code E**. For all these reasons, his confession is likely to be excluded under **s 76(2)(b)** of the **1984 Act**.

The prosecution will be unable to rely on Josh's initial refusal to answer police questions. By **s 34(2A)** of the **Criminal Justice and Public Order Act 1994**, inferences cannot be drawn if a suspect has not been allowed an opportunity to consult a solicitor before being questioned. Nor will the prosecution be able to rely on Luke's silence in the face of questions. Not only was no offer of legal advice made, but he does not appear to have been questioned under caution, as is required by **s 34**. However, the prosecution may be able to rely on the silence of both defendants when they were charged if at trial they rely on some fact that they could reasonably have been expected to mention at that stage. In *Dervish* (2002), the Court of Appeal held that the **1994 Act** does not exclude the possibility of drawing an inference from silence on being charged, even if no inferences can be drawn from a suspect's silence on being questioned. The only question would be whether, on the facts of the particular case, it would be fair to draw inferences. The Court of Appeal added that it might not be fair where the police had acted in bad faith by deliberately breaching the Code in the knowledge that an inference could be drawn from a later silence on being charged.[19]

---

18 This provision highlights the importance the courts give to the manner in which confessions are elicited; the case of *Fulling* confirms that a confession can be excluded even if it leads to the discovery of evidence. Do not be afraid to state that even if the confession is excluded the evidence obtained as a result of it may still be admissible although the prosecution would have to remain silent on how it was discovered.

19 This discussion demonstrates knowledge in relation to the statutory scheme under the **CJPOA 1994** on drawing adverse inferences and its restrictions.

If **s 34** is held to apply, the judge will have to give a careful direction to the jury based on what was said in *Petkar* (2004). He must identify the facts on which each of the defendants relies and which were not mentioned on questioning. He must identify the inferences which it is suggested might be drawn from failure to mention such facts, to the extent that they may go beyond the standard inference of late fabrication. The jury should be told that, if an inference is drawn, they should not convict wholly or mainly on the strength of it. They should be told that an inference should be drawn only if they think it is fair and proper, and it should be drawn only if the only sensible explanation for failure to mention facts relied on is that the defendant had no answers, or none that would stand up to scrutiny. Moreover, an inference should be drawn only if, apart from a defendant's failure to mention facts relied on, the prosecution case is so strong that it clearly calls for an answer by him. The jury should be reminded of the evidence on the basis of which they are invited not to draw any inferences from silence.

# QUESTION 25

Simon and Tim are jointly charged with the burglary of a valuable collection of paintings belonging to Sheetal. Simon was the first to be arrested and interviewed by the police. Vivian, a senior police officer, refused his request for a solicitor on the ground that to allow it would hinder recovery of the paintings. He then forced Simon to remain standing while he interviewed him, after cautioning him, between 11 am and 4 pm without a break. Finally, Simon said: 'I'll tell you what you want to know. I was involved in the burglary, but it was only because Tim threatened to kill me if I didn't help him. You'll find the paintings in the house where Wanda, Tim's girlfriend, lives.' Acting on this information, Vivian went to Wanda's house. When he discovered that she had gone away, he broke in unlawfully, ransacked the house and recovered the paintings.

Tim was later arrested and taken to the police station. When interviewed by the police, he refused to answer any questions. He later instructed solicitors, and told them that he had not been involved in the burglary and that he had no knowledge of the paintings that were found in Wanda's house. He said that he now believed that they had been 'planted' there by Simon, who had a grudge against him because of an affair that Tim had had during the previous year with Simon's wife.

- **Discuss the evidential issues arising.**

## How to Read this Question

This question requires you to consider the admissibility of a confession made by Simon and the status of any evidence recovered by reason of that. You should also explore the lawfulness of the process by which the evidence was discovered and what happens to this evidence if (a) the confession is excluded and (b) the process is deemed unlawful. Finally, you are required to examine the effect of Tim's silence and the accusation he levels against Simon.

## How to Answer this Question

Take the defendants separately.

*Simon*

The first thing to do is to try to get his confession excluded. Try **s 76(2)(a)** of the **Police and Criminal Evidence Act 1984**, alternatively **s 76(2)(b)**. There's no point in discussing **s 78**; you are better off with **s 76** because of the burden placed on the prosecution by that section, and because it makes exclusion mandatory rather than discretionary. On these facts, any arguments available under **s 78** can be used equally well under **s 76**. Look for breaches of **Code C** and think about how you can use them to support arguments under **s 76**. On the assumption that the confession might not be excluded, you need to say something about its evidential status. You might add something about the burden of proof where a defence of duress is raised. **Section 76(4)** will be important for the discovery of the paintings. A brief discussion of **s 78** is appropriate to cover the unlawful entry that led to their discovery.

*Tim*

You need to discuss the effect of Tim's silence at the police station. Note the importance of discovering if he was offered legal advice. On the assumption that he was, you need to describe how the judge will direct the jury in relation to **s 34** of the **Criminal Justice and Public Order Act 1994**. Another point to consider is whether Tim's theory about planting the paintings is something caught by **s 34**.

## Up for Debate

You can gain credit for discussing evidence discovered through potentially unlawful means, for example, coercive interrogation. This is also known as 'fruit from the poisonous tree'. Outline how the law balances the fair administration of justice with the prosecution of those guilty of committing offences.

## Applying the Law

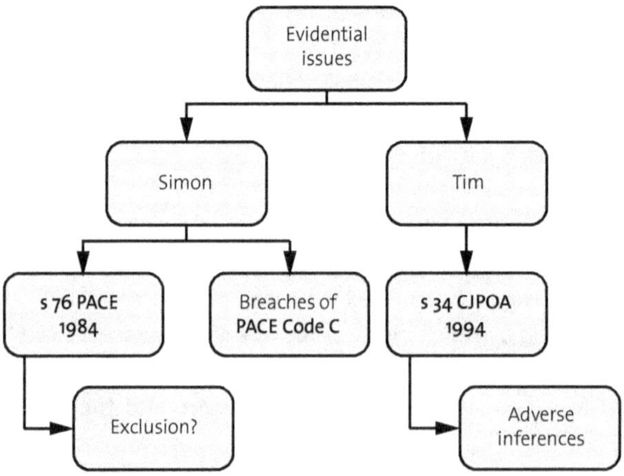


*This diagram highlights the main points you should consider in relation to the evidence, namely Simon's confession and Tim's silence.*

# ANSWER

Although what Simon said to Vivian was partly exculpatory, it was also partly adverse because he admitted taking part in the burglary. It therefore comes within the definition of a confession in **s 82(1)** of the **Police and Criminal Evidence Act (PACE) 1984**. The first question to be considered is whether it could be excluded under **s 76**. Although **s 78** is theoretically available also, all the arguments for exclusion are relevant to **s 76**, and it is better for the defence to rely on **s 76** because of the burden of proof that it imposes on the prosecution, and because exclusion under that section is mandatory if the circumstances are appropriate, whereas under **s 78(1)**, exclusion is only discretionary.[20]

By **s 76(8)**, oppression includes, among other things, 'inhuman or degrading treatment'. In *Fulling* (1987), Lord Lane CJ relied on a dictionary definition that included 'exercise of authority or power in a burdensome, harsh or wrongful manner ... the imposition of unreasonable or unjust burdens'. He also emphasised the seriousness of the conduct needed to constitute oppression. This seems to be a borderline case. No violence was involved, although *Paris* (1992) shows that this is not an essential element. It is arguable that it was oppressive to question somebody forced to stand for five hours. There was clearly bad faith; Vivian must have known that by **para 12.6** of **Code C**, persons being questioned shall not be required to stand, and that by **para 12.8**, breaks from interviewing shall be made at recognised meal times and that short breaks for refreshment shall be provided at intervals of approximately two hours. There is nothing to suggest that the exceptional conditions referred to in that paragraph apply here.[21]

If an argument under **s 76(2)(a)** fails, the same facts can be relied on under **s 76(2)(b)**. In addition, Simon could rely on the fact that he was wrongly refused access to a solicitor. Under **s 58** of **PACE**, delay is only permitted for limited reasons where someone has been arrested for an indictable offence and where the authorisation of an officer of at least the rank of superintendent has been obtained. Burglary is an indictable offence. We do not, however, know Vivian's rank. If he was not at least a superintendent, was the delay in access to legal advice authorised by someone who was? Even if the delay was authorised by an officer of appropriate rank, it is most unlikely that the **s 58(8)** condition applied. **Section 58(8)(c)** does indeed authorise delay where the exercise of the right will hinder the recovery of any property obtained as a result of the offence. But the Court of Appeal stated in *Samuel* (1988) that the right of access to legal advice was one of the most important and fundamental rights of a citizen. The court also said that where the police try to justify denial of access to a solicitor, that can be done only by reference to specific circumstances, including evidence about the person detained or the actual solicitor involved. The effect of this decision was summarised in **Annex B** of **Code C, para 3**. It follows that on these facts the authorised officer would have to have reasonable grounds

20 This part of the answer demonstrates knowledge of what can amount to a confession and its admission or exclusion under the statutory scheme provided by **PACE 1984**.

21 This provision highlights the importance the courts give to the manner in which confessions are elicited; the cases of *Fulling* and *Paris* support this.

to believe that Simon's solicitor would deliberately hinder the recovery of the stolen goods if he were allowed to have access to his client. There is no evidence whatsoever to support such a belief by Vivian. Provided causation can be shown, there is no reason why an argument based on **s 76(2)(b)**, relying on the denial of access to a solicitor as well as the matters relied on under **s 76(2)(a)**, should not succeed.[22]

If, by a remote chance, the confession is not excluded, its evidential status will have to be considered. Contrary to the traditional rule, it has been possible, at least since *Y* (2008), for a confession by one defendant to be evidence against any co-defendant whom it implicates. It was said in that case that such confessions should not be allowed as evidence against a co-accused as a matter of routine. But if a judge decides in a co-defendant's favour on this point, the former law will still apply, so that references to the co-accused will not be automatically excluded. Following *Lobban v R* (1995), the references to Tim will not be edited out unless Simon agrees. He is unlikely to do so because he will want to show that he raised his defence of duress at an early stage. He does not have the legal burden of proving this defence, but he has an evidential burden in respect of it (*Gill* (1963)).[23,24]

Even if the confession is inadmissible, the discovery of the paintings will be admissible under **s 76(4)** of **PACE**. It would be possible to argue that this evidence should be excluded under **s 78** because of the unlawful way in which the paintings were discovered. But although **s 78** is probably in principle available to protect process values regardless of reliability, in practice, where the reliability of evidence has not been affected by the impropriety of the way in which it was obtained, it is unlikely to be excluded. For example, in *Cooke* (1995), a case where rape and kidnapping were alleged, the question arose whether **s 78(1)** should be used to exclude evidence of a sample of hair that might have been improperly taken from the defendant. The Court of Appeal agreed with the trial judge's decision to admit the evidence, regardless of any possible assault. The fact of an assault on the defendant would have cast no doubt on the accuracy or strength of the evidence.

Tim faces the possibility of a direction to the jury under **s 34** of the **Criminal Justice and Public Order Act 1994** in respect of his silence at the police station. However, if he was not offered legal advice before being questioned no inferences from silence can be made: see **s 34(2A)**. If he was offered legal advice, and he relies at trial on facts that he did not mention to the police, it is possible that a direction would be given. His lack of involvement in the burglary and ignorance of the paintings are facts that might be caught. The defence could argue, following *Mountford* (1999) and *Gill* (2001), that the truth of these facts was the central issue in his trial, and that accordingly, an **s 34** direction should not be given. In *Gowland-Wynn* (2002), however, another division of the Court of Appeal rejected

22 See also **Code C, Annex B**.

23 As a result of **s 114 CJA 2003** it seems that a confession may now be admissible in some circumstances as evidence against a person other than the maker. See *Y* [2008] EWCA Crim 10.

24 This part of the answer highlights how the courts have dealt with the use of a confession against a co-defendant. The authority of *Y* and *Lobban* provide supporting examples of the approach that is taken.

this approach and the law is therefore uncertain.[25] Tim's suggestion that Simon planted the paintings is a theory and not a fact and, as such, following *Nickolson* (1999), would not be caught by **s 34** unless he could reasonably have been expected to tell the police about the fact of Simon's grudge. If an **s 34** direction is given, the judge would have to follow the guidelines based on *Petkar* (2004). He must identify the facts on which Tim relies and which were not mentioned on questioning. He must identify the inferences which it is suggested might be drawn from failure to mention such facts, to the extent that they may go beyond the standard inference of late fabrication. The jury should be told that, if an inference is drawn, they should not convict wholly or mainly on the strength of it. They should be told that an inference should be drawn only if they think it is fair and proper, and it should be drawn only if the only sensible explanation for failure to mention facts relied on is that the defendant had no answers, or none that would stand up to scrutiny. Moreover, an inference should be drawn only if, apart from a defendant's failure to mention facts relied on, the prosecution case is so strong that it clearly calls for an answer by him. The jury should be reminded of the evidence on the basis of which they are invited not to draw any inferences from silence.[26]

## QUESTION 26

The police suspected that George and Harry were dealing in drugs. Without a warrant, they broke into a house occupied by the two men solely in order to look for evidence while George and Harry were away. They discovered a large quantity of cocaine. As a result of their discovery, George and Harry were arrested several days later and taken to the police station for questioning. Both men refused to answer any questions until they had received legal advice. When their solicitor arrived, she advised them to remain silent and accordingly they continued to refuse to answer any police questions. The police later placed them together in a cell in which a listening device had been installed in breach of the relevant regulations, and which recorded their conversation. At one stage, George was overheard saying to Harry: 'One thing's for sure, they can never prove we didn't have the stuff for our own use.' Harry replied: 'I wish I'd made as much out of it as you. I'd be in the south of France by now.' Then came the sound of two men laughing. Nothing further of significance was overheard.

- **Discuss the evidential issues arising.**

### How to Read this Question

This question requires you to consider the admissibility of evidence that was obtained improperly and the circumstances in which that may be excluded, inferences from silence including judicial direction and the admissibility of a potential 'confession'.

25 See also *Chenia* (2003).

26 This discussion shows knowledge in relation to the statutory scheme under the **CJPOA 1994** on adverse inferences and the relevant judicial directions that are given. Here the argument focuses on the technicality of what is caught by the provisions and thus it is important that you are clear on how the law functions and that you demonstrate this.

## How to Answer this Question

The first point should be a familiar one – improperly obtained evidence and the use of **s 78(1)** of the **Police and Criminal Evidence Act (PACE) 1984**.

You need to consider the exercise of the right to silence on legal advice, and the special direction that has to be given to the jury in such cases. Then we come to evidence obtained by bugging. You ought to be able to deal with this if you've studied the law relating to **s 78** efficiently. Finally, some thought is needed about the content of the conversation. Are there any confessions there? If so, how many? And, who made them? Note yet again that the examiner is looking to see if you can *analyse* the information you are given.

### Up for Debate

You can gain credit for highlighting authorities such as *A and Others* (2005) that there are clear circumstances in which admissible evidence should be excluded because of the method by which it is obtained. For a good overview of the issues, read: A Ashworth, 'Excluding Evidence as Protecting Rights' [1977] Crim LR, pp. 723–735.

## Answer Structure

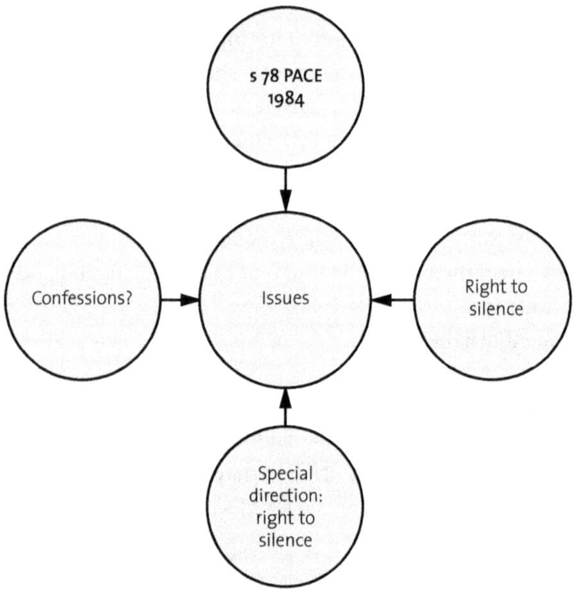


*This diagram outlines the main factors that require consideration where issues concern silence and potentially improperly obtained evidence.*

# ANSWER

The first question that arises is whether the cocaine discovered during the unlawful search will be admissible. The trial judge will have to consider whether, in view of the circumstances in which this evidence was obtained, he should exercise the discretion that he has under **s 78** of **PACE** to exclude evidence of what was found on the ground that its admission would so adversely affect the fairness of the proceedings that it ought not to be admitted.

It is implicit in **s 78(1)** that it is possible for the way in which evidence is obtained to result in its exclusion. This is particularly likely where the police have acted in bad faith. In *Matto v Wolverhampton Crown Court* (1987), the defendant was convicted of driving with excess alcohol. Police officers had requested a specimen of breath when they were on the defendant's property. This was unlawful and they knew it to be so. The specimen proved positive. The defendant was then arrested. At the police station, he provided another positive specimen. The appeal was allowed on the ground that because the police had acted in bad faith and oppressively, the Crown Court could have decided to exclude the evidence under **s 78** if it had directed itself properly.[27]

However, in cases where improperly obtained real evidence has been considered by the Crown Court in an **s 78** application, it is usually admitted because any impropriety in obtaining it is far less likely to have affected its reliability than evidence of an improperly obtained confession. Thus, in *Cooke* (1995), the Court of Appeal pointed out that the vast majority of cases under **s 78** had concerned alleged confessions obtained in breach of the Codes. In that case, where a sample of hair had been obtained from the defendant in circumstances that may have been improper, the court held that the trial judge had properly decided to admit the evidence, despite the possibility that there might have been a technical assault on the defendant. This did not cast doubt on the accuracy or strength of the evidence.

Two features might make an application to exclude slightly more likely to succeed in this case. It seems very likely that the police were acting in bad faith, and it is clear that their entry was unlawful. But the offence is regarded as such a serious one that the discretion is still not likely to be exercised in the defendants' favour.[28]

By **s 34** of the **Criminal Justice and Public Order Act 1994**, if either George or Harry failed to mention when questioned by the police any fact relied on as his defence in subsequent proceedings, and that fact was one that in the circumstances existing at the time he could reasonably have been expected to mention, the jury may draw such inferences from the failure as appear proper.

---

27 The discussion so far highlights the importance courts give to the method by which evidence is obtained, the enforcement of which is also designed to prevent potential abuses by the police.

28 This paragraph demonstrates knowledge and shows what factors, from the scenario, the court will take into account when deciding to exclude evidence.

In *Argent* (1997), the Court of Appeal said that when considering whether a fact was one that a defendant could reasonably have been expected to mention, the court must take into account all relevant circumstances at the time of questioning, including the personal characteristics of the defendant. It was also said that legal advice is something the court might have to consider as one of those circumstances. Its significance was more fully considered in *Condron* (1997). In giving guidance, the Court of Appeal said that where a defendant says he failed to answer questions on legal advice, that bare assertion is unlikely to be regarded as a sufficient reason for failure to mention matters relevant to the defence. In practice, a defendant will have to go further and provide, either through his own testimony or that of his solicitor, the reasons for the advice.

If a direction is given under **s 34**, the judge should follow the guidelines based on *Petkar* (2004). He must identify the facts on which each of the defendants relies and which were not mentioned on questioning. He must identify the inferences which it is suggested might be drawn from failure to mention such facts, to the extent that they may go beyond the standard inference of late fabrication. The jury should be told that, if an inference is drawn, they should not convict wholly or mainly on the strength of it. They should be told that an inference should be drawn only if they think it is fair and proper, and it should be drawn only if the only sensible explanation for failure to mention facts relied on is that the defendant had no answers, or none that would stand up to scrutiny. Moreover, an inference should be drawn only if, apart from a defendant's failure to mention facts relied on, the prosecution case is so strong that it clearly calls for an answer by him. The jury should be reminded of the evidence on the basis of which they are invited not to draw any inferences from silence.[29]

A special direction must be given, because the defendants' silence was on legal advice. In *Betts and Hall* (2001) the Court of Appeal held that adverse inferences could not be drawn from silence where the defendant had honestly relied on legal advice in his refusal to answer questions, and was not simply using the advice as a cloak behind which to hide. But in *Howell* (2003) the Court of Appeal held that genuine reliance on legal advice was not of itself enough to avoid the application of **s 34**. The court said that what was reasonable depended on all the circumstances. Even where silence was advised, there must always be soundly based objective reasons for that advice. In *Knight* (2003) the Court of Appeal observed, *obiter*, that if there was any conflict between *Betts and Hall* and *Howell*, *Howell* was to be preferred. Although in *Robinson* (2003) another division of the Court of Appeal seemed to prefer the approach taken in *Betts and Hall*, it was later confirmed in *Hoare* (2004) and *Beckles* (2004) that *reasonable* reliance on legal advice is necessary to prevent the drawing of adverse inferences, and this is reflected in the amended Judicial Studies Board specimen direction on **s 34**.

In theory, the admissibility of evidence obtained by a trick can be challenged under **s 78(1)** of **PACE** but, for a long time, evidence obtained by eavesdropping has been admitted, but

29 The authority of *Petkar* outlines what a direction under **s 34 CJPOA 1994** must contain. Do not be afraid to state the requirements as they are relevant here.

note the decision of the House of Lords in *A and Others v Secretary of State for the Home Department* (2005) which accepted that in some circumstances the manner in which evidence is obtained may render it inadmissible (statements that had been obtained from torture outside the UK). In *Maqsud Ali* (1966) a tape recorder was used to eavesdrop on a conversation between two suspects, and the evidence obtained was admitted. More recently, in *Bailey and Smith* (1993), the judge admitted evidence of confessions made by the two defendants and tape recorded during conversations between them while they were sharing a bugged cell at a police station after being arrested, charged and remanded in custody. The Court of Appeal upheld the decision to admit the evidence but said that this was a device to be used only in grave cases. Drug dealing for commercial gain is regarded as a grave offence, as was shown recently in *Khan* (1996) where the decision to admit evidence of drug dealing obtained by bugging private property was upheld by the House of Lords.

The exchange between Harry and George is ambiguous. Does it amount to a confession by either defendant? 'They can never prove we didn't have the stuff for our own use' is an observation that is at least partly adverse to both defendants in that it is capable of being interpreted as an admission that the drugs were in the possession of both Harry and George. Harry did not dissociate himself in any way from George's remark and may therefore be taken to have adopted it. On similar principles, a confession was admitted against both defendants in *Batt* (1995). Ashley and Kerry were convicted of robbery. One of them had appeared to be holding a gun that was partly concealed by material. While on remand in custody, they were sharing a cell. A police officer gave evidence that on one occasion Kerry had said to Ashley: 'They'll fuck themselves if they show that gun in court. It's not the one used.' The Court of Appeal held that this was evidence against Ashley as well as Kerry. Ashley had said nothing, but he had not dissociated himself from his companion's remark.

Harry's remark to George, 'I wish I'd made as much out of it as you', is capable of being interpreted as a confession to dealing and, on the principle just outlined, George's failure to dissociate himself from what was said is capable of being interpreted as an adoption of it.

## QUESTION 27

**Section 78** of the **Police and Criminal Evidence Act 1984** provides judges with a broad discretion to exclude evidence.

- **Discuss this with reference to case law.**

### How to Read this Question

This question requires you to discuss the discretion to exclude under **s78** of **PACE 1984**. You should contrast this with the common law discretion and whether the statutory provision exceeded that, discuss its application and highlight what is required for exclusion.

## How to Answer this Question

This essay question requires you to discuss one of the most assessed areas of the law of evidence – the exclusion of evidence under **s 78** of **PACE 1984**. You should start by outlining the law scope of the provision. You should highlight that the application of this provision is not just to evidence obtained unfairly, but to any evidence that the trial judge considers would have 'such an adverse effect on the fairness of the proceedings' that it should be excluded. The topics for common discussion include entrapment. In questions of this sort you should discuss a range of cases including *R v Sang* (1980).

In summary, your answer should make reference to the following:

- the scope of **s 78 PACE 1984**;
- how it differs from **82(3)**;
- authorities in support of the argument, i.e. *Matto v Wolverhampton Crown Court* and *R v Sang* (1980).

## Up for Debate

Mentioning the theory that underpins the exclusion of improperly obtained evidence, for example reliability, the protective principle (rights) or deterrence (disciplining the police), will gain you credit as it shows wider reading. Be sure to highlight the balance that needs to be struck.

## Answer Structure

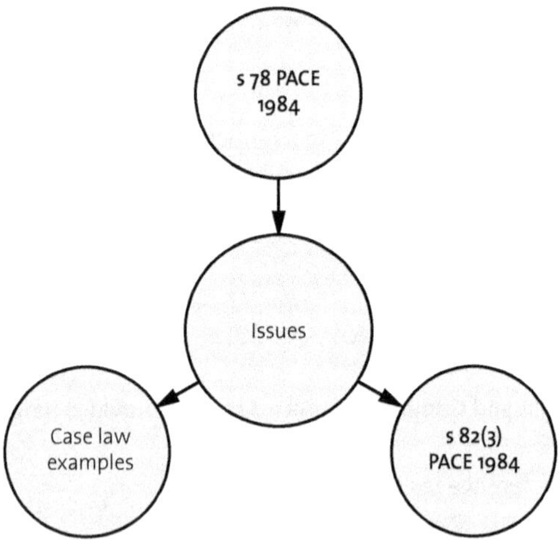


*This diagram illustrates the main topics that you must include in an answer on the discretion to exclude evidence under* **s 78 PACE 1984.**

# ANSWER

The **Police and Criminal Evidence Act 1984** and its accompanying **Codes of Practice** were enacted to regulate the powers and duties of the police, those in detention, criminal evidence and discipline. The Act was the result of years of hard work and dissatisfaction with the rules of criminal process. Judicial discretion to exclude evidence lies in both the common law (preserved under **s 82(3)**) and in **s 78** of the Act. This discussion will focus on the power to exclude in the latter provision, namely where the court may exclude the evidence because in its opinion, having regard to all the circumstances including how it was obtained, it would have an adverse effect on the fairness of the proceedings. It is salient to note that the power to exclude under **s 78** has not affected the common law discretion to exclude evidence, although both raise issues in terms of **Art 6** of the **European Convention of Human Rights** and the right to a fair trial.[30]

It is often argued that **s 78** extended the judicial common law discretion to exclude; for instance in *Matto v Wolverhampton Crown Court* (1987) the court stated that the provision would almost certainly exclude that which could be 'properly excluded at common law' and in *Khan* (1997) the court stated that the discretion to exclude under **s 78** was 'at least as wide as that conferred by the common law'. One of the main differences between the common law discretion to exclude and **s 78** is that the provision includes the exclusion of evidence based on the *manner in which it was obtained*, whereas in the common law this only applies to confessions and evidence obtained from the accused after the commission of the offence (*Sang* (1980)) – in other respects the judge has no discretion to exclude evidence on the basis of the manner in which it was obtained.[31]

What is clear is that the relationship between the discretion under **s 78** and the common law discretion preserved under **s 82(3)** of **PACE 1984** is open to a number of definitions. *Murphy on Evidence* (2008) suggests that **s 78** changed the common law position, as set out in *Sang* (1980), by introducing a specific test for whether the evidence after consideration of the manner in which it was obtained would have an adverse effect on the fairness of the proceedings. In *Chalkley* (1998) Lord Justice Auld took an alternative view of **s 78**, suggesting that the court had the discretion to admit inadmissible evidence. It was quickly argued that the extent of the discretion was to exclude otherwise admissible evidence. Further criticism of the reasoning included that the provision itself is unclear how the admission of such evidence would cause unfairness because the judge's exercise of this discretion itself involves the subjective.[32]

---

30 This is a short and clear introduction that not only demonstrates knowledge (historical) but also identifies the main thrust of the argument. It sets the course of the argument presented by outlining what the current law provides and what the focus of the essay is on.

31 This part of the discussion highlights how the power to exclude under **s 78** is greater than that conferred by the common law. It demonstrates knowledge of how the law has developed because of how the provision is of much broader application.

32 This paragraph shows a good level of knowledge and depth in understanding of the relevant issues surrounding this provision – where there are contentious issues these should be highlighted but be careful as to the extent to which you discuss them as often you will be constrained by time or a conservative word count.

Much of the case law that surrounds **s78** concerns the exclusion of improperly obtained evidence. In *Hardwicke* (2000) the court held that on an application to exclude evidence under this provision in cases of alleged entrapment a court's focus will be on procedural fairness. However, it will also take into account, as the provision allows it to, the accused's opportunity to question the reliability of the evidence presented by the prosecution. Essentially, the court confirmed that where the credibility of an agent provocateur could not be resolved through the course of the proceedings using admissible evidence the judge should exclude it. However, simply obtaining evidence by a particular method, i.e. in breach of the **Codes of Practice**, would not necessarily be sufficient in itself to merit exercise of the discretion under this provision. A number of authorities support this contention (*Loosely* (2001)).[33]

In conclusion, the courts would look to see whether the conduct of those gathering the evidence has been so seriously improper that it is likely to affect the fairness of those proceedings and bring them into disrepute. This is why the court will, when applying the test in this provision, have regard to all the circumstances.

33 This paragraph highlights how the courts have interpreted the provision and its actual application. Remember to use *Hardwicke* as an example to support this.

# 8 Character Evidence I

## INTRODUCTION

Character evidence is relevant mainly in criminal trials. Before the **Criminal Justice Act (CJA) 2003**, the common law recognised two ways in which such evidence could be relevant. It could be relevant to any witness's credibility, and it could also be relevant to the likelihood of a defendant's guilt. Whether an item of character evidence was relevant to one or both of these matters depended on the circumstances. Broadly speaking, evidence of a defendant's good character was relevant to both matters, and under *Vye* (1993) a direction to this effect became compulsory. The question whether a good character direction should be given or not, or given only in a qualified way, can arise either where the defendant has one or more previous convictions that can be regarded as not amounting to serious criminal behaviour, or where he has no convictions, but his evidence at trial discloses some criminal behaviour, though not that alleged by the prosecution. Students should note particularly the decisions in *Gray* (2004), *Goss* (2005), *Teeluck and John* (2005) and *Payton* (2006). Evidence of bad character was primarily relevant to guilt, where the prosecution was allowed to introduce it as part of its case against a defendant under the rules relating to similar fact evidence. Where such evidence was admitted only because of the way in which the defence was conducted, under rules contained in the **Criminal Evidence Act 1898**, it was generally meant to be relevant only to credibility. This distinction was not always easy to maintain in practice, and the **CJA 2003** did not preserve it. In former editions of this book it was easy to deal with these topics separately, because the sources of law for each were quite distinct. This is no longer the case, as the law relating to evidence of bad character is now governed by the provisions of **Part 11, Chapter 1** of the **CJA 2003**. To some extent, therefore, there is overlapping of the subject matter of Chapters 8 and 9 in this book, although the emphasis in Chapter 8 is on what used to be called similar fact evidence, and the emphasis in Chapter 9 is on evidence of bad character that becomes admissible by virtue of the way in which the defence is conducted. The information in this part of the chapter should be treated as an introduction to both chapters.

The relevant provisions where the prosecution wishes to adduce evidence of bad character as part of its case against a defendant are **s101(1)(c)** and **(d). Subsection (1)(c)** has to be read with **s102**. Very broadly speaking, it covers the sort of evidence that was admissible before the **CJA 2003** as 'background' evidence. Examples can be found in *Fulcher* (1995) and *M(T) and Others* (2000). **Section 101(1)(d)** has to be read in conjunction with **s103**.

The provisions that can be used to admit evidence of bad character by virtue of the way in which the defence is conducted are **s 101(1)(e), (f)** and **(g)**. These provisions must be read with **ss 104, 105** and **106** respectively.

Where evidence of a defendant's bad character is not admitted by agreement under **s 101(1)(a)** or elicited on behalf of the defendant himself under **s 101(1)(b)**, it is necessary to consider arguments that may be available to exclude it. You should note particularly **s 101(3)** and **(4)**, and **s 103(3)** and **(4)**. You should also consider the possibility of using the common law discretion, confirmed by *Sang* (1980), to exclude prosecution evidence where its prejudicial effect exceeds its probative value. This discretion appears to have been unaffected by the **CJA 2003**. Save in relation to **s 101(1)(d)** and **(g)**, which are covered by **subs (3)**, it may also be useful to consider the application of **s 78(1)** of the **Police and Criminal Evidence Act (PACE) 1984**, but it should be remembered that this provision applies only to evidence on which the prosecution proposes to rely.

The Court of Appeal has considered the new legislation on evidence of bad character on frequent occasions. Guidelines have been given in some cases to help trial judges to apply the statutory rules. Those laid down in *Hanson* (2005) are particularly important. There are several consolidated appeals where application of the legislation in particular cases can be studied: for example, *Edwards* (2006), *Renda* (2006) and *Weir* (2006). These are useful to read in order to get the 'feel' of the way in which the legislation is being applied, but it must be remembered that cases are likely to be decided very much on their own facts. It would be a mistake to regard these decisions as precedents in the strict sense.

One of the most important of the guidelines in *Hanson* concerns the direction that a judge should give to a jury where evidence of previous convictions has been admitted. For reasons of space, and to avoid too much repetition, I have not included this in all the model answers. However, in your examination you should remember to set it out in full if there is any possibility that previous convictions will be admitted. It will show the examiners that you have at least some familiarity with the *Hanson* guidelines, and that you recognise the growing importance in evidence law of the content of judicial directions in a summing-up. The judge in summing up should make these points to the jury:

(i) They should not place undue reliance on previous convictions. In particular, they should not conclude that the defendant has been untruthful or has committed the offence with which he has been charged merely because he has these convictions.
(ii) Whether the convictions do in fact show propensity is for them to decide.
(iii) If they do find propensity, they are entitled to take this into account when determining guilt. But it is only one relevant factor, and they must assess its significance in the light of all the other evidence in the case.

## Checklist

**Students should be familiar with the following areas:**

- relevance;
- **Part 11, Chapter 1** of the **CJA 2003**;
- *Sang* (1980);
- **s 78(1)** of **PACE**;
- **s 27(3)** of the **Theft Act 1968**;
- evidence of good character; note particularly the guidelines set out in *Gray* (2004) for cases where a defendant does not have an absolutely good character;
- the guidelines in *Hanson* (2005).

# QUESTION 28

James is charged with indecently assaulting Kate in a large department store during the January sales. The case for the prosecution is that he approached her from behind and whispered in her ear, 'You look sexy. What about a drink?' It is alleged that he then fondled one of her breasts. James denies that he said anything to Kate, whom he had never met before. He admits that he might have touched her breast, but says that if he did, it was an accident. A crowd of shoppers had suddenly pushed him forward, and he had instinctively clutched at the person standing in front of him to ensure that he did not lose his balance and fall to the ground. James was carrying a briefcase at the time. When this was lawfully searched by the police after his arrest it was found to contain several magazines devoted to heterosexual pornography. James was convicted three months ago of a public order offence in connection with a political demonstration and was fined £50.

- **Discuss the evidential issues arising.**

## How to Read this Question

This question requires you to consider whether the possession of the magazines and the previous conviction are admissible as bad character evidence under the **Criminal Justice Act (CJA) 2003**, and whether any directions should be given to the jury if not.

## How to Answer this Question

This appears to be a relatively simple set of facts, but in order to answer the question well you must analyse them carefully. There are two potential problems to be considered: the discovery of the magazines, and the significance of the previous conviction.

*The magazines*

The first question to consider is relevance. Remember how to construct an argument for relevance by finding an appropriate generalisation. Why is relevance so important? Note the *dictum* of Lawton LJ in *Turner* (1975). Take into account the possibility that, while logically relevant, the evidence may not be weighty enough to be legally relevant. Don't be satisfied with reaching the conclusion that the evidence is irrelevant and leaving the matter there. What if the judge decides it *is* relevant? What law will be applicable?

It might be the common law, because the **CJA 2003** applies only to evidence of 'bad character' within the meaning of **s 98** and **s 112**. Look at those sections. Do you think the discovery of the magazines might count as evidence of bad character for the purposes of the **2003 Act**? Can you get any guidance from some of the principles in *Hanson* (2005)? (You should memorise a summary of these.) The distinction drawn in *Weir* may be helpful. What opportunities for exclusion are there: (a) assuming the Act does not apply; (b) assuming that it does?

*The previous conviction*

Note the missing information that may well determine what happens at trial. Can the defence argue that James should be treated effectively as a man of good character? If so, what is the position about a *Vye* direction? (Don't forget to spell out for the examiner the contents of such a direction.) Could the prosecution make use of the previous conviction? Obviously it wasn't for a similar offence. How, then, could they use it? Have you studied the **2003 Act** sufficiently well to remember **s 103(1)(b)**?

## Up for Debate

You will gain credit by mentioning that when lawyers refer to bad character they meant previous convictions; the new law allows a much broader set of behaviour to be included – as Roderick Munday states, '[possibly] envok[ing] defendants' entire discreditable past and not simply their previous convictions'.

## Applying the Law

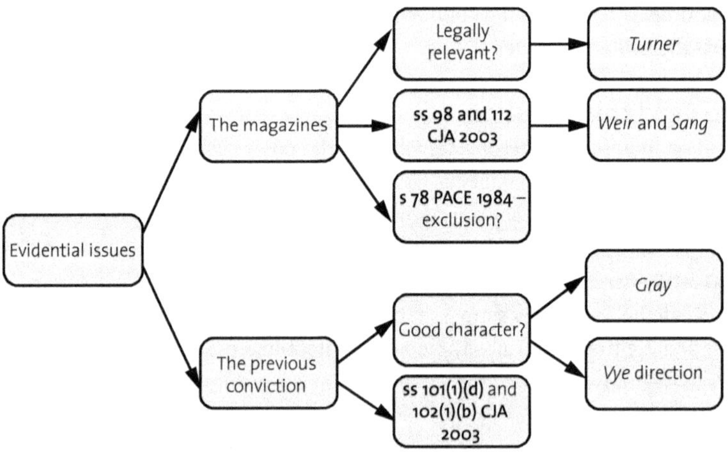


*This mind map outlines the main evidential issues that arise in terms of relevant and admissible evidence, here magazines and James's previous conviction for a public order offence.*

# ANSWER

The first question is whether the prosecution can rely on the magazines to support the case against James. Are they relevant at all? If they are, does their discovery amount to evidence of bad character within **s 98** of the **CJA 2003**?

It could be argued that they are relevant on the basis that a man with an interest in heterosexual pornography is more likely than a man without such an interest to commit an indecent assault on a woman. But the success of such an argument must be doubtful. Obviously, if a judge is not persuaded of the truth of the generalisation that would make the magazines relevant, they will be excluded. Relevance, as Lawton LJ said in *Turner* (1975), is a condition precedent to admissibility. A judge might decide that the evidence was logically relevant, but of insufficient weight to give it legal relevance. In those circumstances also it would be excluded. If a judge decides that it has both logical and legal relevance, it will have to be decided if it is evidence of 'bad character' within **s 98** of the **CJA 2003**.[1]

By **s 98**, evidence of a person's 'bad character' is evidence of, or of a disposition towards, misconduct on his part. (It does not appear that the evidence has anything to do with the alleged facts of the offence, or that it is evidence of misconduct in connection with the investigation or prosecution of the offence.) 'Misconduct' is defined in **s 112** as 'the commission of an offence or other reprehensible behaviour'. Possession of the magazines presumably does not constitute an offence in itself. Might it count as reprehensible behaviour? In *Weir* (2006) a contrast was drawn between behaviour that was 'reprehensible' and that which was merely 'unattractive'. The distinction might well be drawn here. If possession of the magazines does not count as reprehensible behaviour, it will not amount to evidence of bad character within the meaning of **s 98**. In that case, the **2003 Act** will have no application and admissibility will be decided on ordinary principles. (It is assumed that a judge has decided it to be relevant.) The first of these is the common law principle, established in *Sang* (1980), which allows a judge to exclude prosecution evidence where its probative value is exceeded by its prejudicial effect. Reliance could also be placed on the discretion contained in **s 78** of the **Police and Criminal Evidence Act 1984**.[2]

If it is thought that possession of the magazines does amount to reprehensible behaviour, the prosecution will argue that it is evidence of bad character that is admissible under **s 101(1)(d)** of the **CJA 2003**, on the basis that it is relevant to an important matter in issue between the defendant and the prosecution, because it shows a propensity in the defendant to commit offences of the kind with which he is charged (see **s 103(1)(a)**). At this stage

1 It is important, as done here, to highlight how relevance and admissibility are connected; the authority of *Turner* is correctly used to support this contention. Remember that relevance is always considered first; to consider admissibility before relevance would be an inefficient exercise.

2 This part of the discussion demonstrates knowledge of the statutory scheme for the admission of bad character evidence under the **CJA 2003**. You should highlight the distinction the law seeks to draw in relation to conduct that may be considered by many to be 'wrong' but that does not fall into that which the law prohibits.

it will be important for the court to consider some of the principles laid down by the Court of Appeal in *Hanson* (2005).

The starting point should be to bear in mind that Parliament's purpose in the legislation was 'to assist in the evidence-based conviction of the guilty, without putting those who are not guilty at risk of conviction by prejudice'. Where propensity to commit the offence is relied on as the basis for admitting evidence of bad character under **s101(1)(d)**, it has to be considered whether the proceedings will be unfair if the evidence is admitted. The court has a duty, not merely a discretion, under **s101(3)** to exclude evidence that is in principle admissible under **s101(1)(d)** if it appears to the court that the admission of the evidence would have such an adverse effect on the fairness of the proceedings that the court ought not to admit it. If the evidence is admitted, the judge when summing up should tell the jury that whether possession of the magazines does show propensity is for them to decide. If they do find propensity, they are entitled to take this into account when determining guilt. But it is only one relevant factor, and they must assess its significance in the light of all the other evidence in the case.[3]

The next consideration is James's previous conviction. There may be a persuasive argument for treating him as a person of good character for the purposes of this trial. In *Gray* (2004) the Court of Appeal discussed what should be done where a defendant does not have an absolutely good character. Among guidelines laid down was one stating that if a defendant has a previous conviction which, because of its age *or nature*, may entitle him to be treated as being effectively of good character, the trial judge has a discretion to treat him in this way. Another guideline stated that where the previous conviction is irrelevant in relation to the offence charged, the judge's discretion ought to be exercised in favour of the defendant. The conviction for the public order offence clearly falls into this category. If a defendant is treated as being effectively of good character, the judge must then give a full direction in accordance with the rules laid down in *Vye* (1993). That is to say, he must tell the jury that good character is relevant to a defendant's credibility and also to the likelihood of his having behaved as alleged by the prosecution. In James's case there may be a slight difficulty if it is decided that evidence of the magazines should be admitted as evidence of disposition. A judge might decide to qualify the *Vye* direction in some way. On the other hand, he might choose to refer to the evidence of the magazines but balance that reference by giving a full *Vye* direction.[4]

If the defendant pleaded not guilty at the earlier trial, and gave evidence in his own defence, the prosecution might wish to rely on his conviction as evidence of a propensity to be untruthful because his evidence had been disbelieved. But the defence would rely

3 Do not be afraid to state that the prosecution trying to establish a link between the lawful possession of pornographic material and an automatic assumption relating to the likelihood of the commission of an assault is rather tenuous.

4 This part of the discussion demonstrates knowledge of the way in which the courts treat a defendant's old or irrelevant conviction(s) when dealing with his or her character. You should use the authority of *Vye* which sets out the rules in terms of a judicial direction on this matter.

on *Campbell* (2007), where the Court of Appeal said that the question whether the defendant has a propensity for being untruthful will not normally be capable of being described as an *important* matter in issue between the defendant and the prosecution so as to fall within **s101(1)(d)**, because a propensity for untruthfulness will not, by itself, go very far towards establishing the guilt of the defendant. The only circumstances in which there is likely to be an *important* issue as to whether a defendant has a propensity to tell lies is when telling lies is an element of the offence charged. The prosecution, however, could argue that the Court of Appeal in other decisions, such as *Alobaydi* (2007), has been less forthright, and that the approach taken in *Campbell* makes a 'dead letter' of **s103(1)(b)**.[5]

# QUESTION 29

Louis is charged with sexually assaulting Mary on a train journey between London and Plymouth. The case for the prosecution is that they had not met before, but were sitting next to each other, and that after a while Louis began a conversation by commenting on the fine weather. It is alleged that Louis touched Mary's breast during the conversation that followed. Louis denies the charge. He says that he might have touched Mary's breast, but says that if he did, it was only an accident when the train slowed suddenly and he lost his balance in his seat. Last year Louis was convicted of sexually assaulting Nellie, who had been sitting next to him on a coach journey between Bournemouth and London. On that occasion Louis had begun a conversation with Nellie, whom he had not previously met, and a little later had fondled her thigh. His defence, in support of which he gave evidence, was that he had not touched Nellie and that she had invented the whole incident.

- **Discuss the evidential matters arising.**

## How to Read this Question

This question requires you to consider whether the prosecution can adduce evidence of the previous conviction and how it came about, for instance, the similarities.

## How to Answer this Question

You have to consider the relevance and admissibility of the earlier conviction and of the circumstances leading to it. Note the two possible arguments for admissibility under **s101(1)(c)** and **(d)** of **CJA 2003**. You should consider arguments for exclusion and how use can be made of the *Hanson* guidelines. When dealing with propensity under **s101(1)(d)**, note the two possibilities under **s103(1)(a)** and **(b)**, but in connection with the latter you will need to consider the effect of *Campbell* (2007).

5 Mirfield, 'Character, credibility and truthfulness' [2008] LQR 1.

## Answer Structure

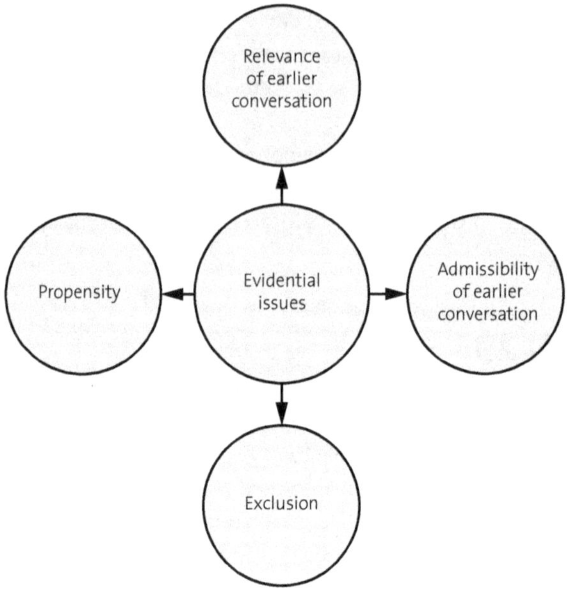


*This diagram highlights the points that you should discuss in terms of the admissibility and exclusion of such evidence, and issues relating to propensity under the statutory scheme.*

# ANSWER

The question is whether the prosecution case can be supported by evidence of Louis's previous conviction and the circumstances that led to it. It can plausibly be argued that a man with a recent conviction for sexually assaulting a woman is more likely to be guilty of a further sexual assault on a woman than someone without such a conviction. It can also be argued that where features of the current allegations resemble features of the earlier offence, the likelihood of the defendant's guilt is increased. The previous conviction is obviously 'misconduct' within **s 112(1) CJA 2003**. It is therefore evidence of bad character within **s 98**, and **Part 11, Chapter 1** of the Act will govern its admissibility.[6]

There are two possible arguments for admissibility. The first is that the evidence is admissible under **s 101(1)(c)** on the basis that it is important explanatory evidence as defined by **s 102**. It would have to be argued that without this evidence the court would find it impossible or difficult to understand other evidence in the case, *and* that its value for understanding the case as a whole is substantial. On these facts, the prosecution might argue that the court would find it difficult to assess properly the defendant's evidence of accident without knowing about the earlier offence, and that its value for understanding

6 This discussion effectively demonstrates knowledge of how the statutory scheme for the admission of bad character evidence works.

the case as a whole was for that reason substantial. But this assumes that assessing the weight of evidence is at least part of the process of understanding it. A judge might consider this questionable, and a safer course for the prosecution would be reliance on **s101(1)(d)**.

Under this subsection the prosecution would say that evidence of the earlier conviction is relevant to an important matter in issue between the defendant and the prosecution, namely, that Louis touched Mary's breast without her consent and that his touching was sexual and not accidental. The prosecution will argue that Louis has a propensity to assault women sexually, and that in giving expression to that propensity he follows a similar course of action. Such evidence would rebut Louis's defence of accident and would fall within **s103(1)(a) CJA 2003**. It might also be argued that the evidence shows a propensity to be untruthful, because on the earlier occasion Louis gave evidence in his defence and was disbelieved. However, this argument is unlikely to be put forward, or if put forward to succeed, because in *Campbell* (2007) the Court of Appeal said that the question whether the defendant had a propensity to be untruthful will not normally be an *important* matter in issue between the defendant and prosecution so as to fall within **s101(1)(d)**. And in *Foster* (2009) the Court of Appeal approved an observation in *Campbell* to the effect that in general it is unhelpful to tell a jury that they can take bad character into account when deciding whether a defendant's evidence is truthful.[7]

In considering whether to admit evidence of the previous conviction or to exclude it under **s101(3)**, or under the statutory and common law preserved by **s126(2)**, the judge will take into account the guidelines laid down in *Hanson* (2005), where the Court of Appeal said that there are three questions to be considered in circumstances like these. First, does the history of the convictions establish a propensity to commit offences of the kind charged? Second, does that propensity make it more likely that the defendant committed the offence charged? Third, is it unjust to rely on the convictions, and would this result in the proceedings being unfair if they are admitted? Importantly for this case, the court said in *Hanson* that although there was no minimum number of events necessary to demonstrate propensity, a single previous conviction for an offence of the same description or category would often not be enough. But the court also said that it might be enough if it showed a tendency to unusual behaviour, or where its circumstances demonstrated probative force in relation to the offence charged. Those circumstances were not to be confined to those showing striking similarity.[8]

It could be argued on the facts given that both these conditions are satisfied. The previous conviction, it could be said, by itself shows a tendency to unusual behaviour. Even if

7 These last two paragraphs evidence how the court has balanced 'propensity' and 'truthfulness' so that the jury do not conflate the two issues, for an increased propensity to commit an offence does not lead to the assumption that the accused is also more likely to be untruthful. Be sure to use case examples to substantiate your points, here *Campbell* and *Foster*.

8 The case of *Hanson* highlights the considerations of the court when considering evidence related to the accused's propensity to commit an offence of the type with which they stand charged.

sexual assault by itself is insufficient to show this, it could be argued that sexual assault on a woman previously unknown to the defendant shows such a tendency, especially since the circumstances were unlike those where relations between strangers are more relaxed and where sexual tension may be heightened, as for example at a party or in a nightclub. The mode of commission of the previous offence, including starting a conversation with a stranger during a journey and taking advantage of the proximity afforded by public transport, tend to rebut the defendant's defence on the current charge. On the other hand, it would be pointed out on his behalf that the classic situation in which reliance is placed on a previous conviction is where the defence raised then was the same as that raised in answer to the current charge. That is not the case here. On the earlier occasion the defence was that the complainant had fabricated the whole story; the current defence is accident. The prosecution might then reply that the defence of accident has traditionally been one where the courts have been readier to admit evidence of similar facts, as can be seen from *Makin v Attorney General for New South Wales* (1894) and similar cases. On balance, it seems likely that the conviction will be held admissible.

## QUESTION 30

Edgar is charged with indecently assaulting Fergus. Fergus, aged 15, was flying his kite at dusk in a public park when he was approached by a man who said that he had a collection of kites and invited Fergus to his house, which he said was nearby, to see them. Fergus agreed to go with him, but while they were walking together the man made suggestions of a sexual nature and then sexually assaulted him by placing his hand under Fergus's trousers. Fergus, somewhat hesitantly, picked out Edgar in an identification parade. Garry, aged 17, has made a statement to the police in which he says that he was in another public park in the same town shortly before the date of the assault on Edgar. He said that he was flying his kite when he was approached by a man who said that he had a collection of kites and invited him to his house to see them. Garry agreed to go with him, but while they were walking together the man made suggestions of a sexual nature to him. At this, Garry knocked him down and then ran away. Garry identified Edgar in an identification parade as the man who had approached him. Garry and Fergus attend the same school and know each other slightly. Rumours have been circulating at the school about a man who sexually assaults local boys. When Edgar's house is lawfully searched, no kites are found, but the police find a collection of homosexual videos, some leather masks and several pairs of handcuffs.

Edgar denies meeting Fergus and Garry and claims to have been mistakenly identified by them.

- **Advise the prosecution on the evidential issues arising.**

### How to Read this Question

This question requires you to consider the identification evidence of two witnesses, its admission and possible exclusion (collusion) under **PACE 1984, s 78**. It also requires you to consider whether the items found in Edgar's home are admissible as evidence.

## How to Answer this Question

First, you need to determine the relevance of Garry's evidence, i.e. the probative job that it is intended to do. It is clearly evidence of the defendant's bad character; what argument for admissibility does the **Criminal Justice Act (CJA) 2003** provide? What are the possibilities for exclusion? Don't forget to deal with the possibility of some form of collusion, and with the problems of relevance arising from the search.

### Up for Debate

You will gain extra marks for highlighting that the **CJA 2003** was an attempt to move more towards greater evidence-based convictions, i.e. the inclusion of bad character and to rebalance the criminal justice process in favour of the victims.

## Answer Structure

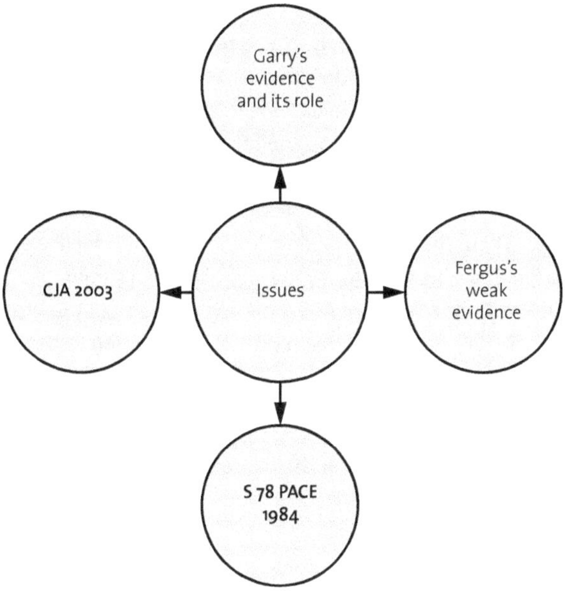


*This diagram illustrates the points that you should discuss in terms of the evidence discovered at Edgar's home and that of the two witnesses Garry and Fergus.*

# ANSWER

The primary question is whether the evidence of Garry can support the rather weak evidence that Fergus is able to give. It is important that it should be supported because of the special danger that attaches to evidence of identification, and the consequent need for directions to be given to the jury in accordance with *Turnbull* (1977). According to the decision of the Court of Appeal in that case, a judge must warn the jury of the special need for caution before convicting on identification evidence. He must tell the jury the reason for having to give such a warning. Some reference should be made to the possibility that a mistaken witness can be a convincing one, and that a number of convincing witnesses can all be mistaken. He should direct the jury to examine the circumstances in which each of the identifications was made. Although the Court of Appeal has not always been consistent, recent decisions such as *Donald* (2004) suggest that another essential ingredient of a *Turnbull* direction is that the judge should point out to the jury the weaknesses in any identification evidence. The judge should also direct the jury to consider whether the identification evidence is supported by any other evidence, and should identify for them the evidence that is capable of providing such support.[9]

Garry's evidence is clearly evidence of Edgar's bad character within **ss 98** and **112(1)** of the **CJA 2003**. Although the events narrated by Garry were close in time, place and in some circumstances to those narrated by Fergus, it seems unlikely that it will qualify as important explanatory evidence under **s 101(1)(c)**; it can hardly be said that without it the jury would find Fergus's evidence impossible or difficult to understand properly, as required by **s 102**.

But Garry's evidence could be relevant to an important matter in issue between the defendant and the prosecution – namely, the identity of the assailant – and therefore admissible under **s 101(1)(d)**. By **s 101(3)** the court must not admit evidence under **s 101(1)(d)** if, on an application by the defendant to exclude it, it appears to the court that its admission would have such an adverse effect on the fairness of the proceedings that the court ought not to admit it. This test is the same as that contained in **s 78(1)** of the **Police and Criminal Evidence Act (PACE) 1984**, and the decisions under that subsection show that the test can be satisfied where the prejudicial effect of an item of evidence exceeds its probative value. For example, in *Boyson* (1991) and *Lee* (1996) this argument led to the exclusion of convictions tendered under **s 74** of **PACE**. Either under **s 101(3)**, therefore, or under the common law discretion confirmed by *Sang* (1980), it will be open to the defence to argue that Garry's evidence ought to be excluded.[10]

So far as the weight of Garry's evidence is concerned, everything depends on the extent to which collusion is a likely danger, and on the improbability of similar features in the incidents being due merely to coincidence.

The relevant similarities are as follows:

(i) both the victims were teenage boys;
(ii) both were in public parks in the same town;
(iii) both events took place at dusk;
(iv) both events took place within a short time of each other;
(v) both boys were flying kites when they were approached;

9 This discussion highlights the issues relating to the admission of identification evidence. You should use the authority of *Turnbull* to outline the requirements for a judicial direction on this matter.

10 These last two paragraphs demonstrate knowledge of the statutory scheme for the admission of bad character evidence under the **CJA 2003**, but also its potential exclusion. When discussing exclusion under **s 101** of the **CJA 2003** do not be afraid to also mention the judicial discretion for a judge to exclude evidence under **s 78** of **PACE 1984**.

(vi) both boys were told of a collection of kites and invited to view them;
(vii) both boys were subjected to indecent suggestions.

However, only Fergus was indecently assaulted. This may have some significance. In cases decided under the former law of similar fact evidence, such as *Johnson* (1995), the Court of Appeal said that a judge who has to decide whether each incident bears the signature of the accused should look at the nature and quality of any disparities that exist. But it was also said that the presence of some dissimilarities will not lead inevitably to exclusion. Item (vii) would be significant if the suggestions were sufficiently unusual.

It should be observed, though, that in *Somanathan* (2005) the Court of Appeal held that evidence admitted under **s101(1)(d)** does not have to satisfy the former test for admissibility of similar fact evidence, which is now to be regarded as obsolete. Dissimilarities may therefore be less significant under the new law. The guidelines laid down by the Court of Appeal in *Hanson* (2005) included one to the effect that a single conviction will often not show propensity, but that it may do so where it shows a tendency to commit unusual behaviour, or where its circumstances demonstrate probative force in relation to the offence charged. Although the incident in relation to Garry did not result in a conviction, the same principle is likely to be applied, with the court taking the view that it does show a tendency to unusual behaviour on the part of the defendant. Further, the earlier incident has probative value in relation to the offence charged because it is evidence that tends to support the complainant's identification of the defendant. On the other hand, it was also said in *Hanson* that the judge must consider the strength of the prosecution case. If there is no, or very little, other evidence against a defendant, it is unlikely to be just to admit a defendant's previous convictions. Presumably the same principle applies where an earlier incident did not give rise to criminal proceedings.[11]

There seems to be little risk of collusion in the ordinary sense because although the boys attend the same school, they know each other only slightly. However, in *DPP v Boardman* (1975), Lord Wilberforce referred also to a risk of falsity arising from 'a process of infection from media or publicity or simply from fashion', and in *Ryder* (1993) the Court of Appeal recognised the possibility of collusion in the sense of a witness being unconsciously influenced by another. What is present on these facts is a common source of rumour that might have tainted the accounts of both boys and increased their similarity. However, by **s109** of the **CJA 2003**, in the assessment of the probative value of evidence, the assumption must be made that it is true, unless it appears on the basis of any material before the court that no court or jury could reasonably find it to be true. It is very likely that the assumption of truth will be made in this case and that the possibility of even indirect collusion will be disregarded.

The absence of kites when Edgar's house was searched is ambiguous. It may show that the police have got the wrong man; on the other hand, the account of a kite collection may have been no more than a ploy to entice the defendant's victims to his house. Unless

11 The discussion thus far highlights the departure from the admission of similar fact evidence and the changes brought about by the **CJA 2003**. Importantly, remember to state that evidence of propensity can be shown from the admission of a single conviction but only where its commission was unusual in some way.

the leather masks and handcuffs can be connected with the indecent suggestions, their discovery will be irrelevant, and so inadmissible. The discovery of the videos is more difficult. If they are in Edgar's possession, they are capable of showing that he has a homosexual inclination. The probative value of this is that that it tends to confirm the identification by Fergus. It would be more than a coincidence if the man *misidentified* by Fergus also had a homosexual inclination. A case that may support this argument is *Thompson v R* (1918), where a defence of mistaken identity was rebutted by proof of facts tending to show that the defendant was a homosexual with a preference for boys. For the defence, it could be argued that the possibility of coincidence is greater than was realised in 1918, since homosexuality is recognised as a natural and frequent phenomenon just like heterosexuality. It might also be argued that proof of a general homosexual tendency has little or no probative worth where a sexual assault on a boy under the age of 16 is alleged. The interesting question arises whether possession of pornographic videos (here homosexual ones) counts as evidence of bad character under **ss 98** and **112(1)** of the **CJA 2003**; see also *R v Weir & Others* [2005] EWCA Crim 2866. If it does, the prosecution would have to establish that this evidence is admissible under **s101(1)** of the Act.[12]

# QUESTION 31

Steven, aged 18, has been charged with murder. The case for the prosecution is that on 3 May he raped and strangled Lynne, a classmate, after taking her in his car to an area known as Coppett's Wood where her body was afterwards found. Steven told the police that at Lynne's request he had given her a lift to a nearby railway station, had left her there, and had never seen her again. The prosecution have a statement from Jocelyne, another classmate of the accused. She said that she and Steven had made an arrangement to go birdwatching on 3 May in Coppett's Wood. Jocelyne said that Steven had asked her to keep the arrangement secret. On the day in question, Jocelyne had changed her mind and had decided to go shopping with some other classmates instead. There is also police evidence that when they searched Steven's locker at school they found a collection of heterosexual pornographic magazines. Two weeks before the murder, Steven had been arrested for indecently exposing himself to two women in Coppett's Wood.

- **Advise the prosecution on the evidential issues that arise.**

## How to Read this Question

This question requires you to consider the evidence of Jocelyne, the pornographic magazines and the arrest for indecent exposure. You will need to explore the relevance of each of these pieces of evidence and then whether it would be admitted.

## How to Answer this Question

This question requires consideration of three items of evidence:

- Jocelyne's statement. You need to discuss its relevance. Remember the need to determine what probative job the disputed evidence is expected to do. Note the

12 Do not be afraid to state that the prosecution trying to establish a link between the lawful possession of pornographic video material and an automatic assumption relating to the likelihood of the commission of an offence is rather tenuous, but as yet somewhat uncharted territory.

discussion of the generalisation on which the prosecution would need to rely. *Rodley* (1913) is a useful case to bring in by way of illustration. Don't forget to reach a conclusion, with reasons, for admissibility or inadmissibility.

- The magazines. Note the importance of the initial assumption that they had no special bearing on what had been done to Lynne. In practice, you would need to know the exact nature of these magazines, and you should indicate this to the examiner. Again, relevance is all important, and finding an appropriate generalisation that would establish this forms a significant part of the discussion.
- Indecent exposure. You will have to consider the relevance of these events in relation to **ss 101(1)(d)** and **103(3)** of the **Criminal Justice Act (CJA) 2003**, and also in relation to the relevant guidelines in *Hanson* (2005).

The final paragraph is an important one. Thinking in general is 'not to be conceived to "form a chain which is no stronger than its weakest link"', but as 'a cable whose fibres may be ever so slender provided they are sufficiently numerous and intimately connected' (CS Peirce, *Collected Papers*, 5, p. 265). Much defence advocacy works on the assumption that this is *not* the case.

## Up for Debate

You will gain credit for outlining that the **CJA 2003** moves towards greater evidence-based convictions in an attempt to rebalance the criminal justice process in favour of the victims.

## Answer Structure

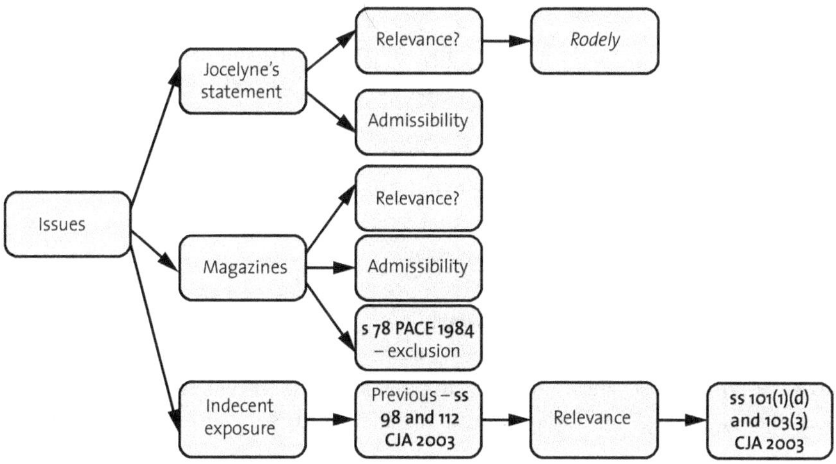


*This mind map highlights the issues that you must consider in terms of the evidence presented in this question.*

# ANSWER

With regard to Jocelyne's statement, the main problem is one of relevance. Does the arrangement with Jocelyne tend to show that the accused was not telling the truth to the police about his encounter with Lynne? It might do so if it indicated that Steven had determined to take *some* girl, regardless of who it was, to Coppett's Wood that day for the purpose of sexual intercourse, to be obtained by force if necessary. It would then appear that when Jocelyne dropped out, Lynne was substituted as the victim.

It is useful to consider whether Jocelyne's statement would be thought to have significance if she had said nothing about a request for secrecy. Almost certainly it would not. But a person who asks another to keep an assignation secret usually does so because he does not wish others to know about it. One reason, but only one, why he might wish this is because he intends to do something unlawful, or at least improper, with his companion. But there might be innocent reasons for not wanting to be disturbed by others. Thus, if a birdwatching exercise were planned, stillness and silence would be wanted.

On the assumption that Steven said nothing else to throw light on his request, the position would be that if Jocelyne were to testify, the jury would have before them a piece of evidence with very little probative value but which might easily mislead because of its tendency to invite speculation. Perhaps a similar problem arose in *Rodley* (1913). The appellant was charged with housebreaking with intent to rape. The prosecution called evidence to show that he had entered a house by climbing down the chimney and had been met by the father of his supposed victim. The appellant said that he had indeed intended to have intercourse with the daughter, but only with her consent. The prosecution also called evidence to show that later that night he had climbed down the chimney of another house and had had consensual intercourse with a woman living there. It was held that this evidence should have been excluded. It proved nothing at all about the real issue of the appellant's willingness to commit rape. On the other hand, it certainly showed a lustful disposition, which may well have prejudiced the appellant in the eyes of the jury.

So here, Jocelyne's testimony would prove nothing about Steven's willingness to commit rape and murder, but it might prejudice him because it would leave the jury guessing and without the means to advance beyond that stage to a reasoned conclusion. It is likely, therefore, that her evidence would be excluded.[13,14]

In considering the pornographic magazines, it is assumed that the pornography has no marked resemblance to what was done to Lynne. Apart from this, the finding of these magazines will be relevant if, and only if, an appropriate generalisation can be found about the way things are in the world that makes them so. We must discard at once

13 Cf. the Canadian case *Reference re R v Truscott* (1967); I Le Bordais, *The Trial of Steven Truscott*, 1966.

14 You should specifically state the problem of evidence that invites speculation; it has a low probative value which would result in it being heavily outweighed by its prejudicial effect and thus rendered inadmissible.

contentions like 'most persons who rape and murder girls take an interest in pornography'. (This generalisation will be referred to as 'G1'.) While it might be the case that most persons who rape and murder girls do in fact take an interest in pornography, it is not the case that most persons who take an interest in pornography rape and murder girls. If G1 is used to establish relevance, you attain it only by assuming the truth of the very thing that the pornography is meant to prove – that Steven is a rapist and murderer.

Might a more useful generalisation be that people who take an interest in pornography are more likely to rape and murder girls than those who do not ('G2')? In the first place, although this *may* be true, it is not obviously so, and if the prosecution is going to rely on its truth to establish guilt they must be prepared to adduce expert evidence on the matter, for it would almost certainly be challenged by the defence.[15]

But, supposing that G2 can be established, what is the probative value of the discovery? It must be almost nothing. The police evidence will have put Steven in a class of persons who are more likely to rape and murder girls than those not in that class. However, that class will certainly be a large one, and the question in relation to any individual in it will be how much greater his membership makes the likelihood of his having raped and murdered a particular victim. The possession of pornography is unlikely to increase significantly the probability that Steven committed this crime. Unless there is a resemblance between what appears in the magazines and what was done to Lynne, its discovery, even if relevant, is likely to be far more prejudicial than probative, and it will be excluded, either under *Sang* (1980) or under **s 78(1)** of the **Police and Criminal Evidence Act (PACE) 1984**.

The prosecution might wish to adduce evidence of the earlier incidents of indecent exposure. Again, relevance would seem to present difficulties. Is it the case that a man who indecently exposes himself to women is more likely than someone who does not do so to rape and murder a woman? It is far from obvious that this is so. If this evidence is regarded as relevant, it will certainly be evidence of Steven's bad character within **ss 98** and **112(1)** of the **CJA 2003**. But the guidelines in *Hanson* (2005) suggest that the evidence is unlikely to be admitted under **s 101(1)(d)**. If they are held to be relevant, the judge will have decided that they tend to establish a propensity to commit offences of the kind charged, and circumstances demonstrating probative force are not confined to those sharing striking similarity with the incident that is the subject of the charge. But there is little, if any, similarity between the current offences and the earlier incidents, and this is something that a judge may take into consideration when considering the fairness of the proceedings and **s 103(3)**. He may also take into account the respective gravity of the past and present offences. Further, it was said in *Hanson* that a judge must always consider the strength of the prosecution case. If there is no, or very little, other evidence against a defendant, which is the case here, it is unlikely to be just to admit previous convictions.

15 Do not be afraid to state that the prosecution trying to establish a link between the lawful possession of pornographic material and an automatic assumption relating to the likelihood of the commission of an offence is a rather tenuous (and costly) exercise that will almost certainly be challenged.

On these facts, of course, there are as yet no convictions in respect of the earlier incidents, which Steven may well deny on the basis of mistaken identity.[16]

In relation to all three items of evidence – Jocelyne's statement, the pornographic magazines, and whatever may be the evidence of indecent exposure – the prosecution might argue that all are items of circumstantial evidence and that they operate cumulatively. Like the strands in a cord, one might be insufficient to sustain the weight of the prosecution case, but three woven together may be of sufficient strength.[17] The answer to this is that circumstantial evidence must be evidence of relevant facts, and the objection in all three cases has been that the evidence in question is of irrelevant facts. Something that you have already decided to be irrelevant will not be made relevant by being added to something else that is irrelevant, although it is sometimes the case that what initially appears to be irrelevant may later be seen to be relevant in the light of some later discovery of relevant matter. Suppose, for example, that the magazines, contrary to the supposition in this answer, contained material that resembled what had been done to Lynne. They would then acquire more significance and would stand a greater chance of being considered relevant, and so admissible. The position would also change if it were discovered that Steven had no interest in birdwatching, so that he would appear to have been lying to Jocelyne and to have had some hidden purpose in persuading her to accompany him to Coppett's Wood.

16 You should include the case of *Hanson* to highlight the considerations of the court when considering evidence related to the accused's propensity to commit an offence of the type with which they stand charged – here rape and murder.

17 Cf. CB Pollock in *Exall* (1866).

# 9 Character Evidence II

## INTRODUCTION

This chapter continues the topic begun in Chapter 8, and you are referred to the introduction to that chapter for the background to the new law on this subject. This chapter concentrates, though not exclusively, on the ways in which a defendant's bad character can emerge as a result of the way in which the defence is conducted.

**Checklist**

**Students should be familiar with the following areas:**

- relevance;
- spent convictions;
- **Part 11, Chapter 1** of the **Criminal Justice Act 2003**;
- *Sang* (1980).

## QUESTION 32

Edna and Mavis are being tried in the Crown Court for theft. The case for the prosecution is that they are both guilty of shoplifting in the Ealing branch of Bromides, the well-known chain of chemists. A store detective gives evidence and states that Edna and Mavis were together in the store. She says that Mavis was carrying a holdall and that she opened it to allow Edna to conceal in it a bottle of shampoo and a tin of talcum powder, the property of Bromides, for which neither defendant paid. Edna gives no evidence, but her counsel cross-examines the manager of the store, who is one of the prosecution witnesses, about a conviction that he had for indecent exposure when he was a student at university. Mavis gives evidence in her own defence and states that she was with Edna in the store, but was not herself involved in any shoplifting. She admits that when stopped outside the store she was carrying the holdall, but says that it belonged to Edna, who alone had been carrying it in the store. She said that Edna had given it to her to hold outside the store so that she, Edna, could more easily look for her season ticket, which she thought she had lost. Edna has a number of recent convictions for theft and for offences involving prostitution. Mavis has several recent convictions for theft. They all involved similar items stolen from other branches of Bromides.

- **Edna and Mavis are separately represented. Discuss the evidential issues that arise.**

## How to Read this Question

This question involves a number of issues. It requires the consideration of the prosecution evidence against Edna and Mavis, the proper cross-examination of a prosecution witness, Edna's failure to give evidence and Mavis's defence. You will also need to explore what is the effect where one accused gives evidence that incriminates another.

## How to Answer this Question

The following points need to be considered:

- the effect of Edna's failure to give evidence;
- the legitimacy of the cross-examination of the manager;
- the effect of the cross-examination of the manager on Edna;
- the possible prosecution argument about Edna's previous convictions;
- the effect of Mavis's denial of the store detective's evidence about the holdall;
- the effect of Mavis's evidence on Edna;
- the possible prosecution argument about Mavis's previous convictions.

### Up for Debate

You will gain extra credit if you state that if bad character evidence that is adduced cannot be fairly taken to demonstrate propensity or to prove some other matter in issue then the jury will be given a warning, quote *Lafayette* [2008] EWCA Crim 3238.

## Applying the Law

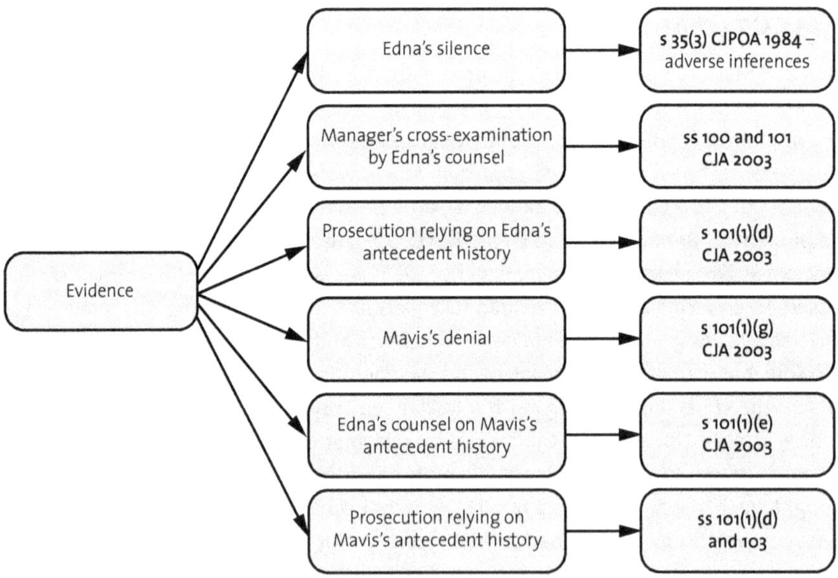


*This mind map outlines the main evidential issues that you should discuss in relation to Edna's and Mavis's charge for theft.*

## ANSWER

Edna has chosen not to give evidence and the first question that arises concerns the extent to which comment can be made on this. By **s 35(3)** of the **Criminal Justice and Public Order Act 1994 (CJPOA)**, the court or jury, in determining whether the accused is guilty of the offence charged, may draw such inferences as appear proper from the failure of the accused to give evidence. Further, under the pre-1994 law, counsel for a co-defendant always had a right to comment on a defendant's failure to give evidence, and the judge had no discretion to prevent this (*Wickham* (1971)). The **1994 Act** has not altered this. Thus, Edna's failure to testify is likely to be the subject of comment by both the judge and counsel for Mavis.

The Court of Appeal emphasised in *Napper* (1996) the general rule that it should be open to a jury to draw adverse inferences when a defendant fails to testify, and said that attempts to marginalise the section are contrary to the spirit of its provisions. The judge, in any direction under the section, must tell the jury that: (1) the defendant is entitled to remain silent; (2) an inference from silence cannot prove guilt on its own; and (3) they must be satisfied that there is a case to answer before drawing any inferences from silence. (The judge must have thought there was, or the case would have already been stopped. But the jury may not believe the witnesses whose evidence was considered by the judge to raise a prima facie case.) The judge must also tell the jury that if they conclude that the silence can only sensibly be attributed to the defendant's having no answer, or none that would stand up to cross-examination, they may draw an adverse inference. The effect of this appears to be that the jury must not draw such an inference unless sure that there is no other explanation, consistent with innocence, to account for it. However, the defence will not be able to suggest innocent reasons for the defendant's silence that are unsupported by evidence at trial (*Cowan* (1996)).[1]

The cross-examination of the manager by Edna's counsel may well have been improper. If the conviction was spent, it should not have been referred to without leave of the judge, who should not have given leave unless he was satisfied that the interests of justice required that this matter be put. Further, cross-examination of the manager is now governed by provisions relating to the bad character of non-defendants in **s 100** of the **Criminal Justice Act (CJA) 2003**. By **subs (1)**, such evidence is admissible, if not agreed, if, and only if, it is important explanatory evidence, or has substantial probative value in relation to a matter which is in issue in the proceedings and is of substantial importance in the context of the case as a whole. Even then, the leave of the court is required by **subs (4)**. On the facts, the conditions in **s 100(1)** are not satisfied, and the question should not have been put. Having put it, however, Edna is in the position of having made an attack on another person's character. Accordingly, evidence of her bad character is in principle admissible under **s 101(1)(g)** of the **CJA 2003**. The Court of Appeal held in *Highton* (2006) that wherever evidence of bad character is admitted, it is admissible for any

1 In discussing adverse inferences under the **CJPOA 1994** it is important to highlight the resultant effect, namely that the inference is not on its own evidence of the defendant's guilt.

purpose that is relevant in the case; the particular 'gateway' that allows admission does not affect this.[2]

However, by **s101(3)**, such evidence must be excluded if it appears to the court that its admission would have such an adverse effect on the fairness of the proceedings that it ought not to be admitted. The onus is on the defendant to raise the issue. In determining whether evidence of Edna's previous convictions should be admitted, the court will take into account the prejudice likely to follow from disclosure of the convictions for prostitution, and these may be excluded. The recent convictions for theft are in a different category. It might be objected that these convictions are likely to prejudice Edna because the jury will jump to the conclusion that if she has committed theft before, she is likely to have done so again. However, even under the pre-2003 law the fact that a defendant's previous convictions were for the same or similar offences to that being currently tried was not inevitably a bar to adducing them. And under the new law it would have been possible for the prosecution to argue that Edna's convictions for theft were admissible under **s101(1)(d)**, though it is difficult to predict the likelihood of success in such an application.

Mavis's evidence that she was carrying the holdall only outside the store contradicts the store detective's evidence, but this is not likely to be construed as an attack on the store detective's character under **s101(1)(g)** because it is probably a matter about which the store detective could have made an honest mistake. However, Mavis's evidence is likely to have substantial probative value in relation to an important matter in issue between her and her co-defendant, Edna. It is not wholly clear what Edna's defence is, because she does not give evidence. But the evidence of Mavis clearly has the effect of placing the blame for any theft that took place on Edna. Edna will therefore be able to cross-examine Mavis about her previous convictions under **s101(1)(e)** of the **CJA 2003**. There is no judicial discretion to exclude such cross-examination either under the Act or by virtue of the common law. The discretion confirmed in *Sang* (1980) applies only to prosecution evidence. Cross-examination of Mavis in these circumstances is very likely to be held relevant to guilt, not merely to credibility, and could therefore extend to the circumstances in which the earlier offences were committed.[3]

It would have been open to the prosecution to rely on Mavis's previous convictions under **s101(1)(d)**. **Section 103** expressly states that for the purposes of this provision, the matters in issue between the defendant and the prosecution include the question whether the defendant has a propensity to commit offences of the kind with which he is charged. Had the prosecution done so, it is unlikely, in view of the substantial similarity of the previous offences and the fact that they were recent, that a court, bearing in mind the guidelines in *Hanson* (2005), would have excluded them under **s101(3)** or **103(3)**.

2 This discussion demonstrates knowledge and the admission of evidence under the changes brought in by the **CJA 2003**, particularly the result where evidence of bad character is adduced without following the necessary procedures.

3 This paragraph evidences how a single piece of evidence can raise a number of issues that require careful consideration. Authority, here *Sang*, is used to support the argument that there is no judicial discretion to exclude such cross-examination.

If the court had disallowed a prosecution application to adduce evidence of Mavis's convictions, the question would then arise whether the jury would be entitled to consider them in relation to the prosecution case against Mavis as well as in relation to Edna's defence. The Court of Appeal is at present divided on problems of this kind. In *Price* (2005) and *B(C)* (2004) it was held that there was no need to warn a jury not to consider, when dealing with the prosecution case against D1, evidence of D1's bad character adduced by D2 rather than by the prosecution. But the contrary was held in *Mertens* (2005) and in *Murrell* (2005). In *Robinson (Dennis)* (2006), which was concerned with a similar situation, the Court of Appeal said that a direction should not needlessly perplex the jury. The result appears to be that a trial judge has a good deal of discretion in the matter. If he decides that the sort of direction given in *Mertens* and in *Murrell* will encourage confusing mental gymnastics, he can safely follow the course approved in *Price* and *B(C)*; the Court of Appeal is unlikely to upset his decision.

# QUESTION 33

Ian and Jason are both aged 26 and are charged with outraging public decency, the case for the prosecution being that they were seen engaging in oral sex in Sloane Square by PC Plod. Both plead not guilty. Ian wishes to call Katie as a defence witness. She is prepared to say that she has known Ian since they were at university together seven years ago, and that during that period she and Ian have had regular, normal sexual intercourse. Ian plays football most weekends and he also wishes to call Larry, a fellow member of his football club, to say that Ian is well known among members for his dislike of homosexuals. Ian has a letter from his local vicar which states that Ian has sung in the church choir for the last five years. The vicar also writes that from his knowledge of Ian he is sure the allegation must be false. Ian has no previous convictions of any kind, but Jason has two recent convictions for soliciting in a public place for the purpose of prostitution.

(a) Discuss the evidential issues that arise in relation to admissibility.
(b) On the assumption that Ian and Jason both testify in their own defence, how should the judge direct the jury about their characters?

## How to Read this Question

This question requires you to think about what, if any, good character evidence can be admitted in criminal trials – do the rules apply where there is more than one defendant and one defendant is of good character and another is not? Furthermore, what amounts to good character evidence? It also requires you to explore whether Jason's previous convictions are admissible as bad character evidence.

## How to Answer this Question

The first part of this question requires you to consider what is admissible as evidence of good character. You should refer to the restriction imposed by *Rowton* (1865) and point out that the sort of evidence permitted in *Redgrave* (1982) is heard because of a concession only.

You should then consider generally the impact of Jason's previous convictions and conclude by referring to the ruling of the Court of Appeal in the case of *Vye* (1993).

## Up for Debate

You will gain credit for discussing why the admission of good character has been limited (*Redgrave*), how it affects credibility (*Vye*) and its effect on the entire proceedings.

## Applying the Law

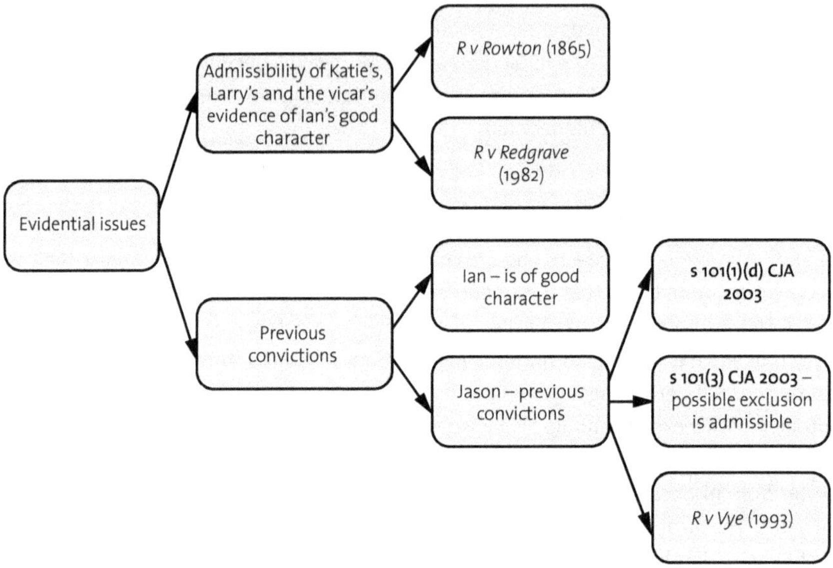


*This mind map illustrates those factors that you should consider in terms of the evidence of Ian's good character and Jason's previous convictions for soliciting in a public place.*

# ANSWER

The defence may call witnesses to testify as to the accused's good character. However, the right to adduce such evidence is restricted by the rule in *R v Rowton* (1865) that evidence of specific acts, or of the opinions of specific persons, is inadmissible to establish either good or bad character. In strictness, the only way in which character evidence can be given is by getting a witness to speak of the reputation of the accused among those who know him. In practice, this rule tends to be loosely applied.[4]

However, so far as Katie's evidence is concerned, the court would have to consider first whether it was relevant at all. Assuming it is relevant, perhaps on the basis that a man in a regular heterosexual relationship is less likely than a man not in such a relationship to

4 The case of *Rowton* impacts on the question because it restricts Ian's ability to adduce evidence of his acts and the opinions of people who know him to establish his good character.

engage in homosexual activity, the court would then have to take into account the decision of the Court of Appeal in *Redgrave* (1981). In that case, the appellant had been charged with persistently importuning for immoral purposes in a public lavatory. The trial judge refused to allow him to call evidence of his relationships with a number of girlfriends which would, the defence hoped, establish that the accused had heterosexual rather than homosexual inclinations. The Court of Appeal acknowledged that in that sort of case, indulgence was sometimes shown to accused persons, but said that it was only an indulgence and not a right. Failure to extend it to any particular defendant could not form the basis of a successful appeal.

Lawton LJ said that the court was not trying to stop defence counsel from putting questions designed to show that the accused was happily married and had a normal sexual relationship with his wife. He went on to suggest that evidence of a sexual relationship with one woman, even though she was not married to the defendant, might be unobjectionable. But he emphasised that questions on such matters could be asked only with the indulgence of the court. Katie's evidence will not, therefore, be heard as of right, but only with the goodwill of the judge. It should be added that it is not clear on the facts that the relationship with Katie has the substantial quality that Lawton LJ seems to presuppose. If, when the facts were more fully investigated, it turned out, for example, that she was merely one regular sexual partner among several and that Ian had no special emotional ties to her, it is doubtful whether her evidence would be admitted.

By contrast, Larry's evidence does appear to be evidence of reputation and so is admissible under the rule in *Rowton*. Again, however, there may be an objection based on relevance. An overt dislike of homosexuals might have been adopted, consciously or unconsciously, to try to hide a man's own homosexual tendencies. So if the jury had this information it might lead to no more than inconclusive speculation of the sort that led to the rejection of evidence in *Blastland* (1986).[5]

It seems clear that the evidence of the vicar, even if he were willing to attend court and give oral testimony, would be inadmissible under *Rowton* (1865). The fact that Ian sings in the church choir is today likely to be thought irrelevant to any question of character. In any case, testimony to this effect would not be testimony of Ian's reputation. The vicar's own opinion of Ian's innocence would certainly not be admitted.

Ian's counsel will, of course, be able to bring out the fact that his client is of previous good character in the sense of having no previous convictions recorded against him.

A zealous prosecutor might argue that Jason's previous convictions are admissible under **s101(1)(d)** of the **Criminal Justice Act 2003** and in the light of the guidelines in *Hanson* (2005). It could be argued that the evidence is relevant because a man with such convictions is more likely to have a sexual encounter with another man in a public place than a

5 Larry's evidence falls outside the rule in *Rowton* but still raises issues of relevance, which should be highlighted here.

man without such convictions. In reply, it could be argued that even if the evidence is admissible, it ought to be excluded under **s101(3)** because of the prejudice that would be caused to Ian; his guilt could be seen as more likely if his co-defendant's history is revealed. If Jason pleaded not guilty and gave evidence in his defence on the earlier occasions, the prosecution could also argue that his convictions are admissible as being relevant to the question whether he has a propensity to be untruthful. They would, however, encounter a difficulty in *Campbell* (2007), where the Court of Appeal held that a defendant's propensity for untruthfulness will not normally be an *important* matter in issue between defendant and prosecution as required by **s101(1)(d)**. Even if this objection could be overcome, the same argument for exclusion of the convictions under **s101(3)** would apply.[6]

Rules for the proper direction of the jury where good character is relevant were laid down by Lord Taylor CJ in the judgment of the Court of Appeal in the case of *Vye* (1993). They are as follows:

- A direction as to the relevance of good character to a defendant's credibility should be given where he has testified or made pre-trial answers or statements. Such a direction will clearly be appropriate in Ian's case, assuming that he testifies or has at least made some admissible pre-trial statement.
- A direction as to the relevance of good character to the likelihood of the defendant's having committed the offence charged is to be given, regardless of whether he has testified or made any pre-trial answers or statements. Again, such a direction will obviously be appropriate in Ian's case.

Where there are two defendants, one of good character and the other not, these principles still apply. The trial judge should either say nothing at all about the character of the defendant with previous convictions, or he should direct the jury that they have heard nothing about this and should not speculate.

Ian's position is therefore unaffected by the fact that Jason has previous convictions.

# QUESTION 34

Alex and Bess are charged with the robbery of Philip. Philip testifies that he was attacked in a car park one evening by Alex and Bess, one of whom grabbed a gold watch from his wrist. Alex, wearing the uniform of a security company, testifies in his defence that Philip attacked him and Bess without warning, and that he hit back to defend himself and Bess. He says that the strap of Philip's watch probably broke in the struggle and denies stealing it. Bess gives no evidence. Alex has one recent conviction for robbery of a man whom he attacked in a car park. Bess has no previous convictions.

- **Discuss the evidential issues arising.**

6 This discussion evidences changes in the law brought about by the **CJA 2003**, particularly in relation to the admission and exclusion of evidence adduced to show the propensity of an individual to commit certain offences.

## How to Read this Question

This question requires you to consider the evidence relating to Alex and Bess including bad character evidence and what happens when an accused fails to testify.

## How to Answer this Question

You should deal with the defendants separately. In relation to Alex, you need to consider whether evidence of his previous conviction can be given, either under **s 101(1)(f)** or **101(1)(g)**. You should also mention the possibility of an application under **s 101(1)(d)**. Don't forget to deal with arguments for exclusion as well, and remember that you may have to consider how far the evidence of the previous conviction can go. In this connection you have to consider the evidential value of the conviction. Is it relevant to credibility and to guilt, or only to credibility?

When you deal with Bess's failure to testify, remember to set out at least the most important directions, based on *Cowan* (1996), that have to be given. How much of the *Vye* direction will it be proper to give?

## Applying the Law

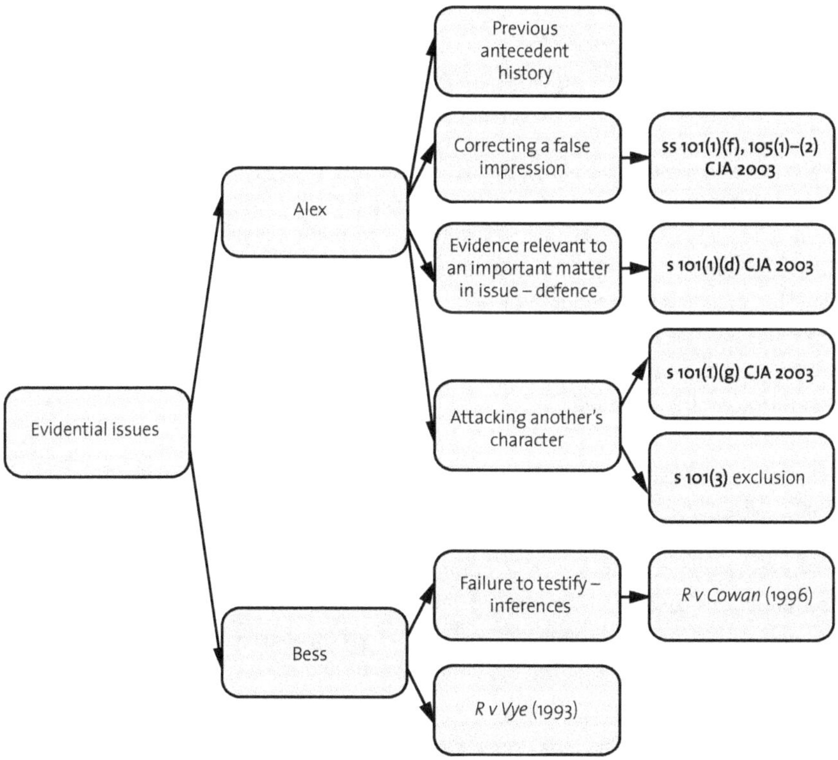


*This mind map highlights the main factors around the evidence stacked against Alex and Bess's failure to testify.*

## ANSWER

There appear to be several opportunities for cross-examination of Alex under **Part 11, Chapter 1** of the **Criminal Justice Act (CJA) 2003**. First, it may be argued that he has given evidence of his own good character, either by his testimony that he hit back to defend himself *and Bess*, or by appearing in the witness box in the uniform of a security company.[7]

On this basis the prosecution could submit that evidence of his bad character (the recent conviction for robbery) should be given under **s101(1)(f)** to correct a false impression given by Alex. By **s105(1)**, a defendant gives a false impression if he is responsible for the making of an express or implied assertion, which is apt to give the court or jury a false or misleading impression about the defendant. **Section 105(2)** lists the circumstances in which a defendant is to be treated as being responsible for an assertion. An obvious instance is where the assertion is made by the defendant while giving evidence in the proceedings: see **s105(2)(a)**.

A problem may occur where a defendant gives evidence as a necessary part of his defence that incidentally has the effect of showing good character. The same problem arose under **s1(f)(ii)** of the **Criminal Evidence Act 1898**, which allowed cross-examination of a defendant about previous convictions where he had given evidence of his good character. The provision was held to apply only where the defendant went beyond what was necessary to meet the prosecution case about the facts in issue.[8]

For example, in *Malindi v R* (1967), the defendant was charged with conspiracy involving the use of violence against property. He gave evidence that at a meeting in his house at which violence was discussed, and which the prosecution relied on as part of its case, he had disapproved of violent action and advised against it. It was held by the Privy Council that this should not have brought **s1(f)(ii)** into play: the defendant had restricted his evidence to his own account of an incident relied on by the prosecution. He had not asserted his own good character as an independent reason for making it unlikely that he had done what the prosecution alleged.

On this basis, Alex's evidence that he hit back to defend Bess, as well as himself, will not amount to giving evidence of his own good character. However, it may be that his wearing the security company's uniform would be so regarded, because it suggests that his employers regard him as a person of integrity. **Section 101(1)(f)** makes it clear that an assertion in this context can be implied, and this is confirmed by **s105(4)**, which includes false impressions given by conduct other than the giving of evidence. By **subs (5)** 'conduct' includes appearance or dress. The legitimacy of the conduct need not be challenged. It is

7 This discussion demonstrates knowledge of the changes brought about by the **CJA 2003**, in main the inclusion and exclusion of bad character evidence.

8 This demonstrates knowledge of the position of law prior to the **CJA 2003** law. It also highlights how the courts faced the problem of what amounted to an accused going beyond that, which was necessary to meet the allegation levied against them.

the claim to good character associated, rightly or not, with certain occupations at which **subss (4)** and **(5)** are aimed.

By **s 105(3)** a defendant may withdraw an assertion, but this may not be easy on the facts. If he does not, the defence might argue that the judge should exercise his discretion to exclude evidence of the previous conviction, either under **s 78(1)** of the **Police and Criminal Evidence Act (PACE) 1984** or under the common law confirmed in *Sang*.

If the judge allows cross-examination about the conviction, can questions extend to the similarities with the present charge? Cross-examination under **s 1(f)(ii)** of the **1898 Act** was relevant only to credibility, not to guilt. But this distinction was condemned by the Law Commission as unworkable in many cases. It was held by the Court of Appeal in *Highton* (2006) that whenever evidence of bad character is admitted, it is admitted for any purpose that is relevant to the case. The particular 'gateway' that allows the evidence to be admitted does not affect the use made of it. Once admitted under **s 101(1)(f)** of **CJA 2003**, the evidence of Alex's previous conviction for robbery can be used to assess his guilt as well as his credibility.[9]

In *Hanson* (2005) the Court of Appeal said that there is no minimum number of events necessary to demonstrate propensity, but that a single previous conviction for an offence of the same description or category will often not show propensity. It may do so, however, where it shows a tendency to unusual behaviour, or where its circumstances demonstrate probative force in relation to the offence charged. Circumstances demonstrating probative force are not confined to those showing striking similarity. It is possible, therefore, that an application under **s 101(1)(d)** would be successful, bearing in mind the recent date of the previous conviction, and the fact that the robbery to which that related also took place in a car park. It could also be argued that evidence of the conviction was admissible under **subs (1)(d)** to rebut the defence that Alex was defending himself and Bess from an attack by Philip.[10]

Alex's suggestion that the watch-strap broke in the struggle does not, in itself, suggest that Philip was lying, as opposed to merely being mistaken in his testimony, and alone would not bring **s 101(1)(g)** into play. But the evidence that Philip was the aggressor clearly amounts to an attack on his character and would let in Alex's previous conviction, unless excluded by **s 101(3)** or the common law discretion.

As Bess gives no evidence, the judge will instruct the jury that they may, in determining whether the prosecution has proved its case, draw such inferences as appear proper from her failure to testify. However, the directions based on *Cowan* (1996) will have to be given. In particular, the judge must tell the jury that the defendant is entitled to remain silent;

9 The case of *Highton* highlights another change brought about by the **CJA 2003**; removal of the restrictive approach advocated by the **Criminal Evidence Act 1898**.

10 The case of *Hanson* highlights the approach by the courts when assessing evidence adduced to show propensity.

that an inference from silence cannot be the sole or main basis for convicting; and that the jury must be satisfied that there is a prima facie case to answer before drawing any inferences.

Assuming that Bess said nothing outside court that was evidence of the truth of its contents, the only limb of the *Vye* direction required (on the significance of her good character) will be that relating to the likelihood of her guilt.

## QUESTION 35

Callum and Daniel are charged with the robbery of Ethan. Ethan testifies that he was attacked in a public park one afternoon by three men, two of whom were Callum and Daniel. The third man got away and was never caught. He says that one of the three men stole his wallet. Callum gives evidence in his defence to the effect that he and Daniel had been joined in the park that day by a third man, whom they did not know. He says that Ethan, who was drunk, attacked all three of them, and that he hit back to defend himself and Daniel. He denies stealing Ethan's wallet, and says that it probably fell from Ethan's pocket in the struggle. Daniel subsequently testifies in his defence that he had stopped to rest some distance behind Callum and the third man and did not see what happened when they met Ethan. When Daniel was interviewed by the police he said that he alone had robbed Ethan. But the trial judge refused to allow the prosecution to adduce this in evidence because it had been made in response to a promise by the police that Daniel would get bail if he confessed. Callum has several previous convictions for robbery. Daniel has a previous conviction for sexual assault and another for outraging public decency.

- **Discuss the evidential issues arising.**

### How to Read this Question

This question requires you to consider the use of bad character evidence both by the prosecution and by each accused against the other.

### How to Answer this Question

The best approach is to take each defendant separately and consider the arguments that the prosecution and the co-defendant might wish to use to reveal his previous convictions. These can be summarised as follows:

| *Callum* | *Daniel* |
|---|---|
| Prosecution: **s101(1)(d), (g)** | Prosecution: **s101(1)(d), (g)** |
| Callum: **s101(1)(e)** | Daniel: **s101(1)(e)** |

In addition, you need to consider whether Callum can adduce evidence of Daniel's confession even though it is not open to the prosecution to do so.

## Answer Structure

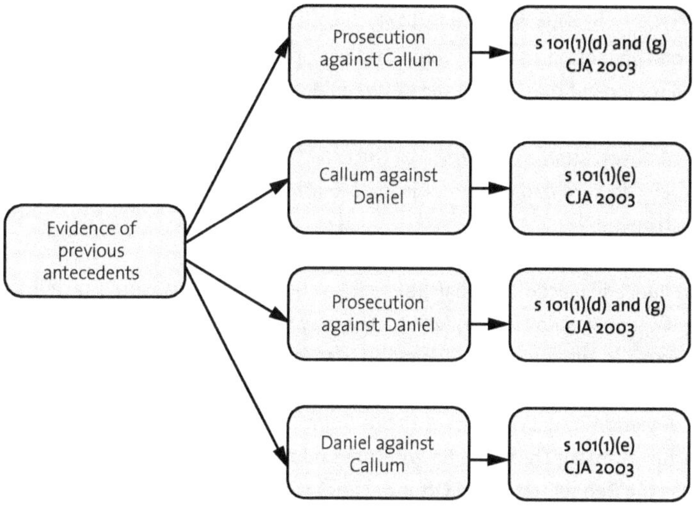


*This diagram outlines the issues that you must consider in terms of the evidence presented and its potential use by the prosecution and each defendant.*

# ANSWER

The first question is whether the prosecution can adduce evidence under **s 101(1)(d)** of the **Criminal Justice Act (CJA) 2003** of Callum's previous convictions as part of the case against him. By **s 103(1)(a)**, the matters in issue between defendant and prosecution include the question whether the defendant has a propensity to commit offences of the kind with which he is charged, except where having such a propensity makes it no more likely that he is guilty of the offence. By **s 103(2)**, the propensity can be established by evidence that the defendant has been convicted of an offence of the same description as the one with which he is charged. There are no details of idiosyncratic features of Callum's previous robberies, and the question therefore arises whether propensity to commit a commonplace offence in a commonplace way makes it more likely that Callum is guilty on this particular occasion. On one view it does, because the propensity adds weight to Ethan's evidence against him. If this submission is upheld, the defence could argue that evidence of the convictions ought nevertheless to be excluded, either under **s 101(3)** or under the common law discretion, which *Sang* (1980) confirmed, to exclude prosecution evidence where the probative worth is outweighed by prejudicial effect. An important factor might be whether his convictions are recent or are spent under the **Rehabilitation of Offenders Act 1974**.[11]

11 This discussion highlights the current law under the **CJA 2003** and the circumstances under which such evidence can be excluded.

The previous convictions might also be relevant to Callum's propensity to be untruthful, which, by **s103(1)(b)**, is capable of being a matter in issue between prosecution and defendant. However, this seems less likely since the decision in *Campbell* (2007), where the Court of Appeal said that the defendant's propensity for untruthfulness will not normally be an *important* matter in issue between defendant and prosecution as required by **s101(1)(d)**. This approach was reaffirmed in *Foster* (2009), where the Court of Appeal approved an observation in *Campbell* to the effect that in general it is unhelpful to tell a jury that they can take bad character into account when deciding whether a defendant's evidence is truthful.[12]

Whether reliance is placed on **s103(1)(a)** or **(b)** or both, the court would take into account the relevant guidelines in *Hanson* (2005). These would include the 'starting point': Parliament's purpose in the legislation was 'to assist evidence-based conviction of the guilty, without putting those who are not guilty at risk of conviction by prejudice'. The age of a previous conviction may be a relevant consideration in deciding whether to admit it. An important factor might therefore be whether Callum's previous convictions are recent, or spent under the **Rehabilitation of Offenders Act 1974**. If evidence of Callum's bad character is given, the judge in summing up should make these points to the jury:

(i) they should not place undue reliance on previous convictions. In particular, they should not conclude that the defendant has been untruthful or has committed the offence with which he has been charged merely because he has these convictions;
(ii) whether the convictions do in fact show propensity is for them to decide;
(iii) if they do find propensity, they are entitled to take this into account when determining guilt. But it is only one relevant factor, and they assess its significance in the light of all the other evidence in the case.

Another prosecution argument would be that Callum has made an attack on Ethan's character by saying that he was drunk and attacked Callum and his companions. The fact that this is a necessary part of his defence is unlikely to prevent the operation of **s101(1)(g)**. Even under the **Criminal Evidence Act 1898** that would not have been a reason for excluding cross-examination under **s1(f)(ii)**, as the House of Lords decided in *Selvey v DPP* (1970). If **s101(1)(g)** is held to apply in principle, the defence arguments for exclusion will be the same as those available in relation to **s101(1)(d)**. In *Hanson* (2005) it was said that pre-2003 authorities on what constitutes an attack on another person's character will apply to the extent that they are not incompatible with **s106**, which contains provisions supplementing **s101(1)(g)**.[13]

Daniel may be able to cross-examine Callum about his previous convictions on the strength of **s101(1)(e)**, on the basis that Callum's bad character has substantial probative

12 The cases of *Foster* and *Campbell* demonstrate knowledge of the way in which the courts interpret the law under the **CJA 2003**.

13 This discussion is a good example of how the old and new schemes have some commonalities; do not be afraid of highlighting this.

value in relation to an important matter in issue between co-defendants. If this test is satisfied, the court has no power to exclude the evidence. Daniel would argue that **s101(1)(e)** applies because Callum's evidence contradicts Daniel's case that he was some distance from the incident with Ethan and did not see what happened. On one view, Callum has simply provided the jury with another reason to acquit Daniel, so the matter in issue between the two defendants is not important. But under the former law, a line of authority based on *Crawford* (1998) supported the view that one defendant could give evidence against another for the purposes of **s1(f)(iii)** where his testimony varied from that of his co-defendant so as to undermine the co-defendant's credibility, thus making the prosecution case against him more likely to be true. **Section 104** of the **CJA 2003**, which supplements **s101(1)(e)**, says that evidence of bad character is admissible only if the nature or conduct of the defence is such as to undermine a co-defendant's defence. It is certainly possible that in interpreting **s101(1)(e)** the court will follow the *Crawford* approach. If evidence of Callum's bad character is admitted only under **s101(1)(e)**, and not under **s101(1)(d)**, it is unclear whether the jury should be told to take it into account only when considering Daniel's defence, and not when considering the prosecution case against Callum. The Court of Appeal is at present divided on problems of this kind. In *Price* (2005) and *B(C)* (2004) it was held that there was no need to warn a jury not to consider, when dealing with the prosecution case against D1, evidence of D1's bad character adduced by D2 rather than by the prosecution. But the contrary was held in *Mertens* (2005) and in *Murrell* (2005). In *Robinson (Dennis)* (2006), which was concerned with a similar situation, the Court of Appeal said that a direction should not needlessly perplex the jury.

Daniel's previous convictions show no propensity to commit robbery, and their admissibility under **s101(1)(d)** could be justified only on the basis that they might show a propensity to untruthfulness. Even this is not very likely; someone who has been untruthful about his sexual activity could be entirely reliable where other matters are concerned. If the condition in **s101(1)(d)** were found to be satisfied, the likelihood of exclusion under **s101(3)** or under the common law discretion would be substantial in view of the possible moral prejudice against Daniel when the nature of his previous convictions is revealed.

Callum might wish to adduce evidence of Daniel's previous convictions under **s101(1)(e)** on the basis of the discrepancy between Daniel's evidence and his own. But Daniel's convictions could be relevant only to his credibility. Although at common law any kind of offence was relevant to credibility, the common law rules governing admissibility have been abolished by **s99(1)** of the **CJA 2003**, and the nature of Daniel's convictions is unlikely to be considered to have any bearing on his credibility. The point has already been made that even if he pleaded not guilty and gave evidence at the earlier trials, this is unlikely to have any bearing on his credibility in very different circumstances. While a judge has no *discretion* to exclude evidence of bad character that is admissible under **s101(1)(e)**, he would have a *duty* to exclude it if he was not satisfied of its relevance.[14]

14 Cf. *Gadsby* (2006).

The final question that arises is whether Callum can adduce evidence of Daniel's confession. The relevant law is contained in **s76A(1)** of the **Police and Criminal Evidence Act 1984**, which provides in effect that where one defendant proposes to adduce evidence of a co-defendant's confession, the rules about admissibility are the same as those applying to the prosecution, save for the standard of proof. Callum is unlikely to be able to prove on the balance of probabilities that Daniel's confession was not obtained in consequence of anything said or done which was likely, in the circumstances existing at the time, to render unreliable any confession that might be made by him in consequence thereof. Accordingly, he will not be able to adduce evidence of Daniel's confession.[15]

# QUESTION 36

Liza, Mabel and Nellie are charged with committing burglary in a block of flats. Liza chooses not to give evidence in her own defence, but her counsel in cross-examination puts to one of the prosecution witnesses that her evidence against Liza is concocted out of spite because Liza has been having an affair with the witness's husband. Liza has three recent convictions for burglary.

Mabel gives evidence in her own defence and claims to have been elsewhere at the time the burglary was committed. When prosecuting counsel puts it to her in cross-examination that this is a lie, Mabel bursts into tears and shouts, 'I'm an honest woman! I've never told a lie in my life!' Mabel was convicted two years ago of fraud and of assisting in the management of a brothel.

Nellie gives evidence in her own defence. She admits having entered the building and climbed the stairs, but says that she did so because she loves animals and wanted to rescue a kitten which she had seen stranded on a window ledge. Nellie has two spent convictions for burglary.

- **Discuss the evidential issues that arise.**

## How to Read this Question

In this question there is more than one accused but it is straightforward. You are required to consider whether bad character evidence is relevant and admissible against Liza, Mabel and Nellie. It also requires you to discuss what happens when an accused fails to testify.

## How to Answer this Question

It does not appear that any of the defendants has undermined another's defence. So, each defendant should be dealt with separately.

15 Burdens of proof placed on an accused is a hot topic; often this can crop up in questions such as this. Here this discussion also impliedly acknowledges potential human rights issues.

> **Up for Debate**
>
> You will gain credit for mentioning that the right to silence was eroded by the **CJPOA 1994** – the rationale was to prevent an accused evading justice by simply remaining silent. Mention: Royal Commission on Criminal Justice 1993, Cmnd. 2263.

## Applying the Law

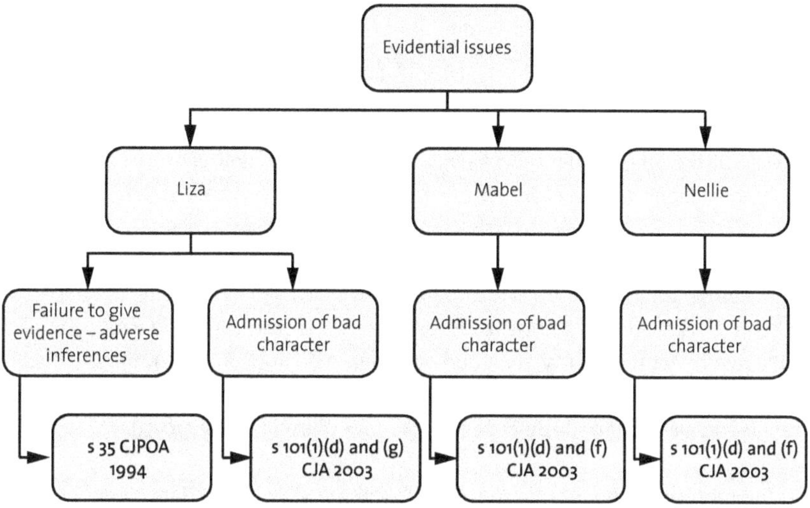


*This mind map highlights the main issues relating to the admission of Liza, Mabel and Nellie's bad character under the statutory scheme provided by the* **CJA 2003**.

# ANSWER

Liza's failure to give evidence is likely to bring into operation **s 35(3)** of the **Criminal Justice and Public Order Act 1994**. Under this provision the court or jury, in determining whether the accused is guilty of the offence charged, may draw such inferences as appear proper from the failure of the accused to give evidence. In any direction under **s 35** the judge must follow the guidelines based on *Cowan* (1996). He must tell the jury that the defendant is entitled to remain silent; an inference from silence cannot be the sole or main basis for a conviction; and the jury must be satisfied that there is a case to answer before drawing any inferences from silence. The judge must also tell the jury that they may draw an adverse inference only if they conclude that silence can only sensibly be attributed to the defendant's having no answer to the charge, or none that would stand up to cross-examination. However, the defence cannot suggest reasons for silence that are unsupported by evidence.[16]

16 In discussing adverse inferences under the **CJPOA 1994** it is important to highlight the effect that they have; the inference is not evidence of the defendant's guilt when taken on its own.

The prosecution could argue that evidence of Liza's previous convictions should be admitted under **s 101(1)(d)** as showing a propensity to commit burglary, and perhaps also a propensity to be untruthful if in any of the earlier cases she pleaded not guilty and gave evidence in her own defence. Although Liza gave no evidence on this occasion, a propensity for untruthfulness could still be relevant in light of the allegation made on her behalf against a prosecution witness. It would be open to the defence to argue, under **s 101(3)**, that the admission of this evidence would have such an adverse effect on the fairness of the proceedings that the court ought not to admit it. Alternatively, reliance might be placed on **s 103(3)**. However, such arguments would be likely to fail, as it is a recent history of convictions for the same offence, and, presumably, the prosecution has other cogent evidence to support its case against Liza. In the absence of other evidence, or if there were only weak evidence, the defence, relying on the *Hanson* (2005) guidelines, could argue that the judge has a duty to consider the strength of the prosecution case and, if there is no, or very little, other evidence against a defendant, it is unlikely to be just to admit previous convictions, whatever they are.[17]

Through her counsel, Liza has made an attack on another person's character by suggesting that a prosecution witness's evidence has been concocted out of spite. Evidence of her bad character is therefore admissible in principle under **s 101(1)(g)** and **s 106(1)(b)** of the **Criminal Justice Act (CJA) 2003**. The Court of Appeal held in *Highton* (2006) that, if admitted through this 'gateway', the evidence would be relevant to propensity as well as credibility. It would be open to the defence to argue for exclusion under **s 101(3)**.

Could the prosecution adduce evidence of Mabel's previous convictions under **s 101(1)(d)**? Neither offence is of the same kind as the current offence. The offence of fraud almost certainly involved the telling of lies, so this would be admissible in principle to show a propensity to be untruthful, regardless of her plea or whether she gave evidence on that occasion. If she pleaded not guilty to the other offence and gave evidence in her defence that the jury must have disbelieved, those facts also would show a propensity to be untruthful. But in view of the availability of the conviction for fraud, and the moral prejudice that might attach to a conviction for assisting in the management of a brothel, a defence argument that this conviction should be excluded, either under **s 101(3)** or **s 103(3)**, might be successful.

In Mabel's case the question also arises whether evidence of her convictions can be adduced under **s 101(1)(f)** in order to correct the false impression given when she said that she was an honest woman who had never told a lie. Her best course would be to withdraw the claim, which appears to have been made in the heat of the moment. If she does so, by **s 105(3)** she will not be treated as responsible for the assertion. If she fails to withdraw, it would be open to her counsel to argue that the evidence of her convictions should be excluded on the basis of the common law discretion confirmed in *Sang* (1980).

17 The case of *Hanson* highlights the approach of the courts when assessing evidence adduced to show propensity.

At this stage the judge might distinguish between the two convictions and exclude the one for assisting in the management of a brothel because of the moral prejudice to which it might give rise. Arguably, **s 78(1)** of the **Police and Criminal Evidence Act (PACE) 1984** would also be available, but a doubt is created by **s 101(3)**, which confines the **s 78** test built into **s 101(3)** to **subss (1)(d)** and **(1)(g)**. Further, by **s 105(6)**, evidence is admissible under **s 101(1)(f)** only if it goes no further than is necessary to correct the false impression. Almost certainly, the conviction for obtaining property by deception would be regarded as sufficient for this purpose. As with 'gateway' **s 101(1)(g)**, evidence of bad character admitted under **s 101(1)(f)** can be relevant to both credibility and propensity (*Highton* (2006)).[18]

Can Nellie's spent convictions for burglary be admitted under **s 101(1)(d)**? Depending on whether she gave evidence in her own defence on those occasions, the evidence could fall within **s 103(1)(a)** and **(b)**. True, both the convictions are spent, and this would invite argument for exclusion under **s 101(3)** or **s 103(3)**. It was said in *Hanson* (2005) that the age of a previous conviction may be a relevant consideration in deciding whether to admit it, but, as one of the consolidated appeals in *Hanson* showed, this will not be a conclusive argument. So far as **s 103(1)(b)** is concerned, *Campbell* (2007) suggests that the evidence is unlikely to be admitted: a propensity for being untruthful will not normally be an *important* matter in issue between defendant and prosecution as required by **s 101(1)(d)**.

It is unlikely that evidence of Nellie's spent convictions can be given under **s 101(1)(f)**. She has almost certainly not created a false impression by saying that she is an animal lover, for there is no reason why an animal lover should not be criminally inclined. Her explanation that she wanted to rescue the kitten is necessary to account for her presence on the premises. Even if that shows her character in a good light, it does so only incidentally and should not bring **s 101(1)(f)** into operation if the reasoning adopted under the **Criminal Evidence Act 1898** is followed. In *Malindi v R* (1967), the defendant, charged with conspiracy to use violence against property, testified that he had been present at a meeting during which violence had been discussed, but had disapproved and had advised against it. The Privy Council held that this had not brought **s 1(f)(ii)** of the **1898 Act** into operation because it did not amount to an independent assertion of good character.

## QUESTION 37

Oscar is charged with burglary of Penelope's flat. He gives evidence in his defence and admits being in the flat on the day when the burglary took place. But he says he was there because Penelope had given him a key as they were lovers, and he had called in that evening on his way home in the hope of having sexual intercourse with her. In cross-examination, it is put to him by the prosecution that he entered by a window, not the door. Oscar replies: 'Anyone who says that is a liar.' Oscar has three previous convictions for fraud.

- **Discuss the evidential issues that arise.**

18 This demonstrates knowledge of the law as per the **CJA 2003** and the discretion to exclude under **PACE 1984**. It is a good example of the application of a number of provisions to a single piece of evidence.

## How to Read this Question

In this question you will need to think about the use of bad character evidence. You will need to explore whether Oscar's previous convictions can be used to show that he has a propensity to be untruthful and to counter an attack made on a witness's character.

## How to Answer this Question

You have to consider the various arguments that could be put forward to admit or exclude evidence of Oscar's previous convictions. Note that the facts do not reveal whether or not they are spent. Take arguments under **s101(1)(d)** first, remembering **s103(1)(b)**. Then consider **s101(1)(g)**. Note that there are two aspects to this: whether Oscar has attacked Penelope's character, and the significance, if any, of what Oscar has said during cross-examination.

## Answer Structure

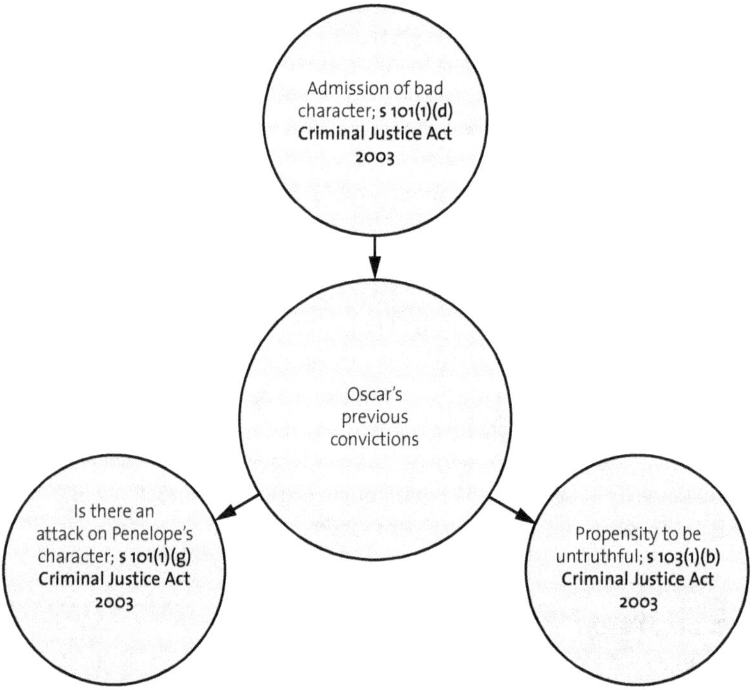


*This diagram outlines the main issues that you must discuss in your answer in relation to the admission of Oscar's previous convictions for fraud.*

# ANSWER

On what basis, if any, can the prosecution adduce evidence of Oscar's previous convictions? One approach would be to rely on **s101(1)(d)** of the **Criminal Justice Act (CJA) 2003**, arguing that evidence of the convictions is relevant to two important matters in issue between the defendant and the prosecution: first, the question whether the defendant has a propensity to commit offences of the kind with which he is charged; second, whether he has a propensity to be untruthful.[19]

By **s103(2)**, a defendant's propensity to commit offences of the kind with which he is charged may be established by evidence that he has been convicted of an offence of the same category as the one with which he is charged. Categories of offences can be prescribed by order of the Secretary of State under **s103(4)(b)**. But by **subs (5)**, a category prescribed by order must consist of offences of the same type. Fraud is not in the theft category prescribed by the **Criminal Justice Act 2003 (Categories of Offences) Order 2004**.[20]

However, the defendant has given evidence, and the prosecution may wish to establish a propensity to be untruthful under **s103(1)(b)**. Convictions for fraud could be used for this purpose, but the view taken in *Campbell* (2007), that a propensity for being untruthful will not normally be an *important* matter in issue between the defendant and the prosecution, would militate against admissibility. Nor do we know if the convictions are spent. The defence might want to rely on **s103(3)** to argue that because of the length of time that has passed, it would be unjust to rely on them. Curiously, **subs (3)** applies only to evidence of a defendant's propensity to commit offences of the kind with which he is charged. But the defence could still rely on **s101(3)** and on the common law discretion, confirmed by *Sang* (1980), to exclude prosecution evidence where the probative worth is outweighed by prejudicial effect.[21]

Another argument for admitting the convictions could be based on **s101(1)(g)**, relying on the fact that the defendant has made an attack on another person's character. By **s106(2)**, evidence attacking another person's character includes evidence to the effect that the other person has behaved in a reprehensible way. Potentially this creates a problem on these facts. Is it reprehensible for a woman to have a sexual relationship with a person to whom she is not married? Do the personal circumstances and beliefs of Penelope have to be taken into account when deciding if Oscar's allegation is one of reprehensible behaviour? Probably these awkward questions can be avoided by arguing, if Penelope denies the relationship, that the allegation necessarily implies that Penelope's evidence is deliberately false. It was established in *Britzman* (1983), for the purposes of the **1898 Act**, that a defendant could make an imputation on a prosecution witness, and so expose himself to cross-examination about his own previous convictions, if what was alleged amounted in effect to an allegation of perjury. It is inconceivable that Penelope could have made an honest mistake by denying her affair with Oscar. His allegation would therefore amount to one of perjury, and so be an attack on Penelope for the purposes of **s101(1)(g)**. Again, the defence could argue for exclusion under **s101(3)**. Following the

19 This part of the answer demonstrates knowledge of the position of law in relation to propensity and truthfulness under the **CJA 2003**. Do not be afraid to state this where a question specifically requires this.

20 **SI 3346, Sched Pt 1.**

21 The case of *Campbell* demonstrates knowledge of the way in which the courts interpret the law under the **CJA 2003**, and its common law discretion as confirmed by the decision in *Sang*.

*Hanson* guidelines, as in all cases where evidence of previous convictions is admitted, the judge in summing up should make these points to the jury:

(i) they should not place undue reliance on previous convictions. In particular, they should not conclude that the defendant has been untruthful or has committed the offence with which he has been charged merely because he has these convictions;
(ii) whether the convictions do in fact show propensity is for them to decide;
(iii) if they do find propensity, they are entitled to take this into account when determining guilt. But it is only one relevant factor, and they assess its significance in the light of all the other evidence in the case.

The prosecution might also rely on Oscar's answer in cross-examination to the effect that anyone who says he entered Penelope's flat by a window is a liar. However, it is not clear that in saying this he has attacked another person's character. Unless there is a witness who has given evidence to this effect, the expression seems to amount to no more than a strong denial. Certainly under the **1898 Act** a distinction was drawn between using words such as 'lying' or 'liar' simply as strong denials, and using the words to allege perjury. For example, in *Desmond* (1999) a prosecution witness gave an account of events that differed significantly from that in his witness statement and, in doing so, implicated the defendant further. Defence counsel in cross-examination suggested to him that he was lying under oath, but the Court of Appeal held this to be no more than an emphatic denial of the charge.[22]

# QUESTION 38

To what extent has the **Criminal Justice Act 2003** dealt with the deficiencies in the law on witness credibility?

- **Discuss with examples.**

## How to Read this Question

This question requires you to explore the differences in the law on character evidence (and its uses) in accordance with the **Criminal Evidence Act 1898** and the regime under the **Criminal Justice Act 2003**.

## How to Answer this Question

This essay question requires you to discuss one of the most notorious principles in the law of evidence – character evidence. Start by outlining the law on character evidence prior to the enactment of the **Criminal Justice Act (CJA) 2003** and then analyse the statutory regime along with contemporary case law, for instance, the decisions in *R v Hanson* (2005), *R v Gilmore* (2005). The essay raises issues relating to the distinction between credibility and propensity. For the purposes of analysis you will require detailed knowledge of the **Criminal Evidence Act (CEA) 1898** and the **CJA 2003**. Your answer should highlight the fact that the

22 These types of questions require a good understanding of the old and new regime, but also of the other possibilities in terms of admissibility or exclusion.

enactment of the **CJA 2003** has resulted in an increase in the extent to which the previous convictions of a defendant are admitted as evidence of character.

In summary, your answer should make reference to the following:

- the law prior to the **CJA 2003** and its weaknesses with case law, for instance, *R v Butterwasser* (1948);
- the differences between the **CJA 2003** and the **CEA 1898**;
- the regime post the **CJA 2003** and contemporary case law, i.e. *R v Campbell* (2007).

## Up for Debate

You will gain extra marks for highlighting that greater evidence-based convictions, i.e. the inclusion of bad character and to rebalance the criminal justice process in favour of the victims, was one of the premises of the **CJA 2003**. You should also mention that what amounts to bad character is broader under the new regime.

## Answer Structure

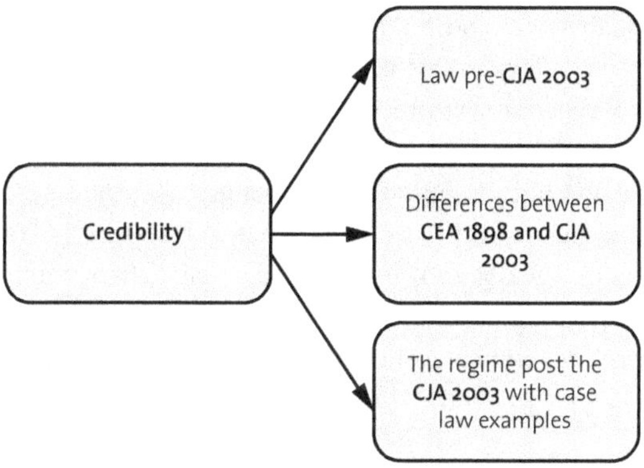


*This diagram shows how the* **CJA 2003** *has tried to deal with some of the deficiencies in the previous law on credibility – you should discuss these in your answer.*

# ANSWER

The **Criminal Justice Act (CJA) 2003** has restructured the law on evidence of bad character. The statute defines bad character and abolishes, with one exception, the common law rules on the admissibility of such evidence; it also repeals the residue of the **Criminal Evidence Act (CEA) 1898**. In this essay I shall discuss the extent to which the **CJA 2003** has tackled the deficiencies in the law on witness credibility.[23]

23 This introductory paragraph highlights that the old law relating to the admission of bad character evidence was deficient and that the current law under the **CJA 2003** has restructured the regime to try to deal with this. In essay questions this is important because it focuses the proceeding discussion.

The **CEA 1898** had as its focus the distinction between character evidence relating to propensity and credibility. The Act allowed the admission of evidence relating to the testifying defendant's bad character so that the jury may, if they chose to do so, draw the conclusion that the defendant's account may not be worthy of belief. In terms of propensity, i.e. evidence supporting the likely guilt of the defendant, there existed a set of common law rules governing admissibility, this evidence was referred to as similar fact evidence. This evidential common law rule stated that evidence that the defendant has been guilty of misconduct on previous occasions is generally inadmissible unless it is similar fact evidence relevant to an issue in the case where its probative force outweighs its prejudicial effect. If evidence of bad character was admitted as similar fact evidence then it went to support guilt and not just credibility – an important distinction between the common law rules and the **CEA 1898** where such evidence was only relevant for purposes of credibility. The **CJA 2003** abolished the residue of the **CEA 1898** and the common law rules on the admission of similar fact evidence, replacing them with a statutory scheme.[24]

There were a number of issues with the law prior to the **CJA 2003**. The law did not statutorily protect non-defendants from having their credibility called into question and thus the position of the defendant was far more protected than that of the non-defendant. Furthermore, defendants that chose not to testify did not risk having evidence of their bad character revealed. Finally, where evidence of bad character was admitted then the jury would receive a direction from the trial judge informing them that such evidence (previous convictions) was relevant for them when deciding whether the defendant's testimony was credible and not for purposes of proving propensity to commit the offence, and that a lack of previous convictions was evidence that supported credibility and a lack of the defendant's guilt. The **CJA 2003** represented a major change to the criminal justice process; the Act itself was a product of the White Paper, *Justice for All Cm 5563* (2003). The aim was to rebalance the criminal justice process to be more in favour of the victims of crime.[25]

The **CEA 1898** provided the defendant with a shield preventing them from being cross-examined on their previous convictions. This shield was lost in a number of ways including questioning the good character of prosecution witnesses with a view to establishing their own good character. In *R v Selvey* (1970) the defendant's cross-examination was limited to offences of a type similar to that with which he was charged. The main issue lay in what some have described as a fiction between evidence that undermines credibility and that which questioned propensity (or guilt). The **CJA 2003** attempts a reconciliation of this issue by allowing the admission of bad character evidence if it is relevant to an important matter between the prosecution and the defence – this includes the defendant's propensity to be untruthful. The court of appeal confirmed in *R v Campbell*

24 This paragraph shows a good level of knowledge and depth in understanding of the law prior to the **CJA 2003**.

25 This paragraph highlights the deficiencies in the law and wider understanding of the issues prior to the enactment of the **CJA 2003**.

(2007) that such an important issue between the parties is only likely to arise where telling lies is an element of the offence with which the defendant is charged.

The extensive protection provided by the **CEA 1898** to a non-testifying defendant, namely not risking having evidence of their bad character revealed by not testifying, is now covered by the **CJA 2003**. The authority for the proposition that a defendant will not lose his shield if he does not give evidence, *R v Butterwasser* (1948), was overruled. Contemporary case law such as *R v Chung* (2007) suggests that this approach has been welcomed, thus redressing the balance between the defendant's rights against those of the prosecution witness.[26]

In conclusion, the **CJA 2003** was a major move away from the law that existed in terms of the admission of bad character evidence. The Act sought to redress the balance in favour of the victims of crime and the successful prosecution of it and has to an extent achieved this goal; bad character evidence is now admissible more than it has ever been. The courts, in accepting the changes, have remained cautious – the dissipation of the unduly confusing distinction between evidence that goes to credibility and that which goes to propensity is a positive step forward.

26 This paragraph highlights another one of the deficiencies in the law and the fact of the purpose behind the **CJA 2003** directly dealing with this issue.

# 10 The Course of Testimony

## INTRODUCTION

You are likely to find the sort of problems in this chapter inserted as part of questions dealing with more central topics such as hearsay or character evidence. Another favourite of examiners is a question about a charge of rape, where points on recent complaints can arise as well as on the complexities of **ss 41–43** of the **Youth Justice and Criminal Evidence Act 1999**. It is well worth studying these sections carefully, together with the cases that have been decided about the restrictions they impose on the conduct of the defence.

Most topics concerning the course of testimony are well explained in textbooks, but a warning is needed about the finality of answers to collateral questions. The rule is sometimes expressed in this way, and sometimes by saying that when a witness in cross-examination answers questions on collateral matters, his answers are conclusive. There is quite a common misunderstanding that the effect of this is that once counsel in cross-examination gets a denial of the collateral matter that is being put, he may ask no further questions about it. This is not the case. Counsel may continue to question the witness about the collateral matter if he thinks he is likely to obtain any advantage in doing so. What he cannot do is call evidence in rebuttal if the witness persists in his denial. It is only in this sense that the witness's answers are 'final' or 'conclusive'.

You should note that, by **ss 119** and **120** of the **Criminal Justice Act (CJA) 2003**, where evidence of a witness's previous consistent or inconsistent statement is admitted, it is evidence of any matter stated of which oral evidence by the witness would be admissible. It is no longer relevant to credibility alone, as used to be the case. Note also the circumstances, set out in **s120**, in which evidence of previous consistent statements is now admissible. An important change in the law extends the 'recent complaint' exception, formerly applicable only where the charge related to a sexual offence, to all offences where the person making the complaint is a person against whom the offence has been committed. Further, it is now irrelevant, so far as admissibility is concerned, that the recent complaint was elicited, for example, by a leading question, unless a threat or a promise was involved: see **s120(8)**. The **Coroners and Justice Act 2009** has amended **s120(7)** by removing the requirement in **subs (7)(d)** that the complaint should have been made as soon as could reasonably be expected after the alleged offence. The effect of this seems to be to leave it to the judge to decide whether a particular complaint was made too late to be of assistance to the jury, and thus irrelevant and inadmissible. It has already been held in

*O* (2006) that **s 120(4)** and **(7)** allows evidence of multiple complaints to be admitted. But you should read that case for the reservations made on this subject. Clearly, evidence of complaint after complaint could be irrelevant, time-wasting and unfair.

### Checklist

**Students should be familiar with the following areas:**

- refreshing memory;
- unfavourable and hostile witnesses;
- previous consistent statements;
- cross-examination of the parties as to credit;
- *Edwards* (1991) and subsequent decisions;
- **ss 41–43** of the **Youth Justice and Criminal Evidence Act 1999** and *A* (2001);
- previous inconsistent statements;
- finality of answers to collateral questions.

# QUESTION 39

Len is being prosecuted for assaulting Mick, who had identified Len to the police in a nearby street shortly after the attack and subsequently during an identification procedure. At his trial, Len claims that he has been wrongly identified. Mick has a recent conviction for handling stolen goods.

(a) Mick identifies Len in court as the person who attacked him. May he also give evidence of his previous identifications of Len in the street and in the identification parade?

(b) Len tells his counsel that Mick is a heavy drinker and that he can produce a witness, Olive, who will support this and who can say that she saw Mick drinking whisky in a public house on the evening when Mick alleged that he was assaulted by Len, but at a time before the alleged attack took place. In cross-examination, Mick denies being a heavy drinker and says that he had nothing at all to drink that evening. May Len's counsel call Olive to rebut these denials?

(c) Len also tells his counsel that a month before the alleged assault, he had quarrelled with Mick about a woman and Mick had threatened that he would 'get even' with Len some day. Len says that his cousin Percy was present at the time and can confirm this. What use, if any, can Len's counsel make of this information?

(d) Should Len's counsel put Mick's previous conviction to him? If he does so, and Mick denies it, what is likely to happen?

## How to Read this Question

This question has a number of issues that you will need to deal with: the previous identification; whether Mick's answer regarding his drinking can be rebutted by adducing Olive as a witness; the quarrel; and Mick's previous conviction.

## How to Answer this Question

The question raises the following points:

- evidence of previous identification;
- whether the evidence about Mick's drinking is collateral to the main issue;
- the rule concerning the finality of answers on collateral matters and the exceptions to it;
- cross-examination of prosecution witnesses as to character.

### Up for Debate

You will gain credit by highlighting that the rationale that underpins the rule on the finality of answers on collateral matters is to avoid wasting valuable court time on issues that are not directly relevant to a fact in issue and that in any regard the tribunal of fact is under no obligation to accept that as being true.

## Applying the Law

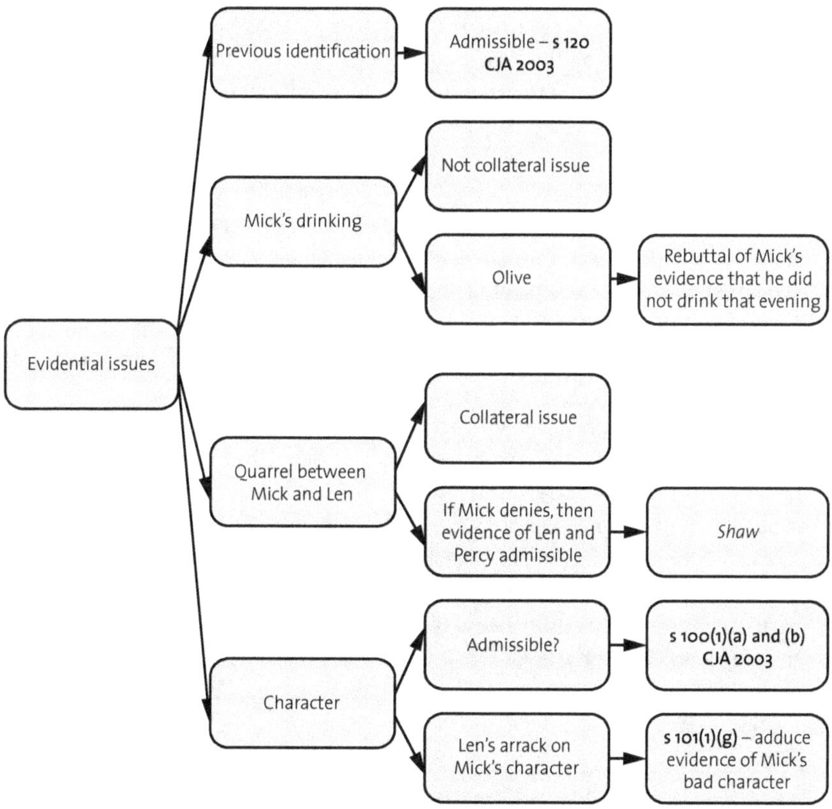


*This mind map outlines the main arguments relating to each of the evidential issues, including identification and character, which you should discuss in your answer.*

# ANSWER

(a) Despite the general rule that excludes evidence of previous consistent statements (see *Roberts* (1942)), evidence of an earlier identification was admissible at common law to show that the witness was able to identify the accused at the time and to exclude the idea that any later identification in court was an afterthought or a mistake (*Christie* (1914)). The current law is contained in **s120(4)** and **(5)** of the **Criminal Justice Act (CJA) 2003**. Mick can give evidence of his earlier identifications of Len, provided he indicates that to the best of his belief he made the earlier statements establishing identification, and that to the best of his belief they stated the truth.[1]

(b The purpose of establishing that Mick is a heavy drinker and that he had been drinking before the attack is to suggest that his identification of Len could well have been wrong as his faculties were impaired, at least to some extent, by the alcohol that he had consumed. The identification is the central issue in the case and questions designed to show that it might have been impaired by alcohol will therefore not be regarded as dealing with collateral matters. Olive can be called to rebut Mick's denial that he had had anything to drink that evening. She may also give evidence of his heavy drinking if that is a matter within her own knowledge, or of his reputation as a heavy drinker under the rule in *Rowton* (1865). The question whether Mick is a heavy drinker is probably not a collateral matter. If true, it tends to make it more probable that he was drinking on the evening in question, and also that he drank enough to impair his ordinary powers to make an accurate identification.

(c) The quarrel with Mick is a collateral matter, but if Mick denies that it took place or that he threatened Len on that occasion, evidence may nevertheless be called in rebuttal because the effect of such evidence will be to show bias on the part of Mick against Len. Facts showing that a witness is biased against a party may be elicited in cross-examination and if they are denied, rebutting evidence can be called. Thus, in *Shaw* (1888), evidence was held admissible to show that on a previous occasion a witness had threatened the defendant (see also *Phillips* (1936)). Both Len and Percy can therefore be called to give an account of the incident during which Mick threatened Len.[2]

(d) Two matters have to be taken into account when deciding whether to put this conviction to Mick. The first is whether evidence of Mick's bad character is admissible under **s100** of the **CJA 2003**, which relates to the bad character of non-defendants. It is possible that the prosecution will take the view that Mick's conviction should be revealed during examination-in-chief. It is for an offence of dishonesty, which could bear on his credibility as a witness, especially if he had pleaded not guilty and given evidence in his defence. If this view is not taken, the defence will have to convince the judge either that the evidence of the conviction is important explanatory evidence under **s100(1)(a)**, which is unlikely, or that it has substantial probative value in relation to a matter that is in issue in the proceedings and is itself of substantial

1 This paragraph highlights the law as it developed through the common law and as it is now contained in the **CJA 2003**.

2 This discussion demonstrates knowledge of the way in which the courts treat collateral issues; here a denial will result in rebuttal evidence being adduced to prove that the denial is in fact untruthful.

importance in the context of the case as a whole: see **s100(1)(b)**. Whether these conditions are satisfied depends on the nature of Len's case. He appears to be saying that Mick has deliberately given false evidence incriminating him, in which case the conditions would almost certainly be satisfied. Leave of the court will still be necessary under **s100(4)**. The second matter is that if Len adduces the evidence under **s100(1)(b)** he will have made an attack on another person's character, which will allow evidence of his own bad character, if he has one, to be given under **s101(1)(g)**. But since he has almost certainly brought this provision into play by his claim that Mick is a person whose testimony has been affected by a grudge, this additional attack is unlikely to have any separate significance.[3]

If the conviction is put and Mick denies it, it may be proved against him by virtue of **s6** of the **Criminal Procedure Act 1865**. Proof would be made by producing a certificate of the conviction under **s73** of the **Police and Criminal Evidence Act 1984**. But it is likely that counsel for the prosecution would forestall the need for this by making a formal admission of the fact, since the information will have come from him in the first place.[4]

## QUESTION 40

Amy is prosecuted in the Crown Court for assaulting Bella, her neighbour. She pleads not guilty. The case for the prosecution is that Amy punched Bella during a quarrel in the street, causing Bella to fall and break her leg. When Amy was interviewed by the police, she told them that Bella's allegation was untrue and that on the occasion in question Bella had been about to hit her, but fell after tripping over a paving stone.

Consider the evidential issues that arise in each of the following circumstances:

(a) Amy gives evidence in her defence. During cross-examination, she states for the first time that at the time of the fall Bella was drunk. Counsel for the prosecution says: 'You've just made that up a moment ago, haven't you?' Amy replies: 'No, I haven't. The truth is, that woman needed half a bottle of gin before she could get up in the morning.' Defence counsel later wants to call Amy's cousin, Eddie, to give evidence that shortly after the incident, Amy spoke to him about it and said: 'It was that bitch Bella's own fault. She was out of her mind with drink as usual.'

(b) Amy calls her husband, Charlie. He wants to refresh his memory about the incident, which he observed, from a diary that Amy keeps.

(c) After Charlie has given evidence, Amy's brother, Dan, is called. He is asked about the incident, which he observed, but says: 'I'm sorry. I'm trying hard to remember, but it's just gone out of my head.'

---

3 This paragraph demonstrates knowledge of the statutory scheme for adducing bad character evidence under the **CJA 2003**. It is important to realise the repercussions of adducing such evidence and state this; here the accused's previous bad character, if any, is likely to be open to be adduced too.

4 The prosecution has a duty to disclose to the defence any previous convictions recorded against their witnesses. See *Paraskeva* (1983).

## How to Read this Question

This question requires you to consider the following evidential issues: adverse inferences (**Criminal Justice and Public Order Act (CJPOA) 1994**) from any failure to mention facts when questioned; evidence to rebut an allegation of fabrication; whether witnesses can refresh their memories and from what source; and what happens when a witness becomes hostile or unfavourable.

## How to Answer this Question

Part (a) involves an allegation of recent fabrication; you should refer to *Oyesiku* (1971). It also raises the possibility that the prosecution might want to rely on **s34** of the **CJPOA 1994**. Don't forget to set out the *Petkar* direction. Part (b) is a straightforward question about the use of memory-refreshing documents. Part (c) raises a number of possibilities. You should discuss the law relating to hostile and unfavourable witnesses, refreshing memory during the course of giving evidence, and the possibility of using the provision of the **Criminal Justice Act 2003**.

## Answer Structure

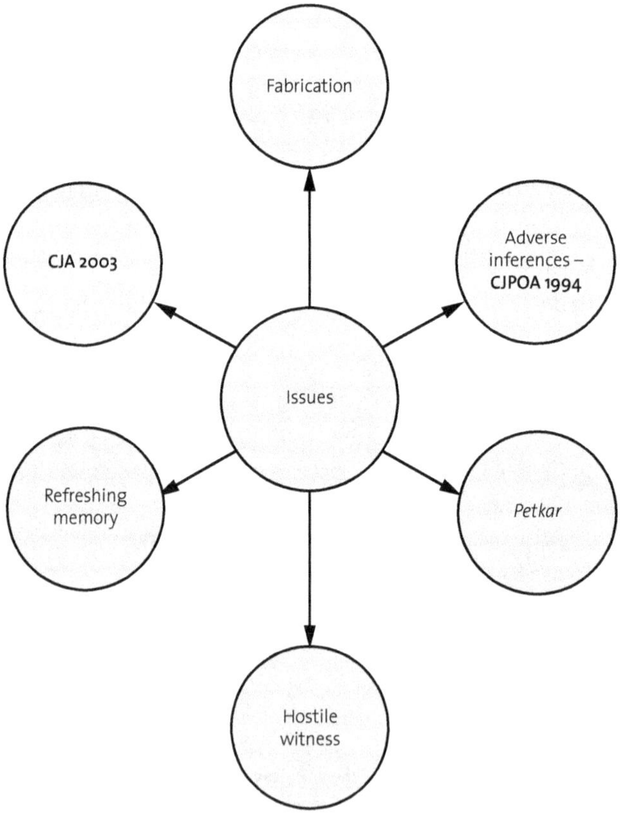


*This diagram outlines the main evidential issues that you should discuss in terms of the charge of assault against Amy.*

## ANSWER

(a) The general rule is that evidence of a statement previously made by a witness which is consistent with his present testimony is inadmissible. Thus in *Roberts* (1942), a trial for murder where the defence was that a gun had gone off by accident, the accused was not allowed to call evidence to show that two days after the incident he had told his father that the death had resulted from an accident.

Exceptionally, however, evidence of such a statement can be adduced under **s 120(2)** of the **Criminal Justice Act (CJA) 2003**, in order to rebut a suggestion that the witness's oral evidence has been fabricated. At common law such evidence was admissible to rebut an allegation of *recent* fabrication, which is the allegation on these facts. By **s 120(2)**, the earlier statement will be evidence of the truth of its contents. In *Oyesiku* (1971), for example, counsel for the prosecution challenged the evidence of the accused's wife on the basis that she had concocted a story with her husband after his arrest. It was held that the defence should have been allowed to show that she had made a previous consistent statement about the events to her solicitor at a time when she had had no opportunity to discuss matters with her husband because he was then still in custody.[5]

Amy was presumably interviewed by the police and failed to mention Bella's drunkenness at that stage. The prosecution could therefore ask the judge to give a direction under **s 34** of the **Criminal Justice and Public Order Act 1994**. If he does so, he must give directions on the lines set out in *Gill* (2001) and *Petkar* (2004), that is to say, he must identify the fact on which the defendant relies and which was not mentioned on questioning. He must direct the jury that it is for them to decide whether in the circumstances that fact was something that the defendant could reasonably have been expected to mention. He should tell them that if they think it was, they are not obliged to draw any inferences, but that they may do so. Further, he must tell the jury that a suspected person is not bound to answer police questions, that they must not convict solely or mainly on an inference drawn from silence, and that the jury must be satisfied that there is a case to answer before they can draw any adverse inferences from silence. Finally, he should tell the jury that they can draw an adverse inference only if they are sure that the defendant was silent because he had no answers, or none that would stand up to investigation.[6]

(b) By **s 139(1)** of the **CJA 2003**, a person giving oral evidence in criminal proceedings may, at any stage in the course of doing so, refresh his memory from a document made or verified by him at an earlier time if he states in his oral evidence that the document records his recollection at that earlier time, and that his recollection of the matter is likely to have been significantly better at that time than it is at the time of his oral evidence. Accordingly, Charlie can refresh his memory from the relevant entries

5 This paragraph outlines the position of the law, under the **CJA 2003**, relating to the exceptions to the rule against the admission of previous consistent statements. Often it is good practice to outline the general rule and its justification.

6 It is important, where authorities set rules or give guidance in relation to, as in this instance, the judicial direction, to state them as doing so.

made by Amy in her diary, provided he verified them at an earlier time. A witness who has used such a document must produce it for the inspection of the opposing party, who can cross-examine on it. It seems clear from *Senat v Senat* (1965) that counsel inspecting a document that has been used to refresh a witness's memory is not confined in cross-examination to those parts which were used for memory-refreshing purposes, provided it is relevant to go beyond them. But if cross-examining counsel does go beyond them, either party can apply to have the diary made an exhibit in the trial so that in due course the jury can take it into account as a whole when assessing the evidence. If the diary is made an exhibit, the entries used to refresh the witness's memory will, by **s120(3)** of the **CJA 2003**, be evidence of any matter stated of which oral evidence by the witness would be admissible.

(c) If Dan is simply suffering from a lapse of memory, he can refresh his memory from any written statement that he made earlier: see **s139(1)** of the **CJA 2003**. If Dan is not suffering from a lapse of memory, he may be a hostile witness, that is to say, a person who is not desirous of telling the truth to the court at the instance of the party calling him. A witness ruled hostile by the judge can be cross-examined by the party calling him, with a view to showing what he said in his written statement on an earlier occasion. The power is provided by both statute and common law. By **s3** of the **Criminal Procedure Act 1865**, the advocate calling the witness may, by leave of the judge, 'prove that he has made at other times a statement inconsistent with his present testimony'. If the witness, as seems to be the case here, does not provide enough 'present testimony' to be inconsistent with the previous statement, he can still be treated as hostile and cross-examined on the statement by virtue of common law (*Thompson* (1976)). It is possible that Dan is 'hostile' because he is afraid to testify on Amy's behalf. If that could be proved, it would be possible to apply to have the statement put in as a piece of documentary hearsay under **s116(2)(e)** and **(4)** of the **CJA 2003**. By **s119(1)**, such a statement will be admissible as evidence of any matter stated of which oral evidence by the witness would be admissible.[7]

## QUESTION 41

Konrad, aged 19, is charged with raping Letitia, aged 18. Letitia says that she met him for the first time in a public house, and that he invited her back to his flat for coffee when the pub closed at 11.00 pm. She says that after drinking coffee he tried to kiss her. She resisted, whereupon he flew into a rage, hurled her to the floor and raped her. When he had finished, he shouted, 'Get out! You're a whore!' When Letitia arrived home at about 3.00 am, she was met by her father, Herbert, who said, 'What time do you call this? I've been waiting up for you since 10.30. You'd better give a good account of yourself or you're out of this house for good tomorrow morning!' Letitia burst into tears and said, 'I've been attacked.' Herbert replied, 'I've told you time and again to come home early. I hope this teaches you a lesson. Now get to bed; I'll speak to you again tomorrow.' Letitia went to

7 This discussion demonstrates knowledge of the rules relating effectively to eliciting witness evidence. Do not be afraid to state that these rules also developed to support effective case progression.

college as usual the next day, but she was looking so tearful that her tutor, Megan, asked her what the matter was. She then told Megan that she had been raped by Konrad. Megan persuaded her to go to the police. She made a statement, and shortly afterwards Konrad was arrested.

At the police station Konrad said that he did not want legal advice. He was interviewed under caution, and at first denied meeting Letitia, but later in the same interview he admitted meeting her and having sex with her. 'But', he said, 'she was the one who started it. She was all over me, just begging for it. I should never have had anything to do with her.' Konrad wishes to give evidence in his own defence, and to call Naomi to say that she had often seen Letitia in public houses trying to pick up men. Konrad also wishes to call Jaspreet, who can give evidence that earlier in the evening of the alleged rape he had been in the same public house where Konrad later met Letitia. He said that Letitia, whom he had known only by sight, had approached him and persuaded him to have sex with her in one of the pub lavatories.

Konrad has no previous convictions.

- **Discuss the evidential matters arising.**

## How to Read this Question

This question centres on lies, good character and previous consistent statements. It is best to deal with each actor within the scenario individually.

## How to Answer this Question

The following points should be covered:

- Admissibility of what Konrad said to Letitia.
- Can Herbert give evidence of what Letitia told him?
- Can Megan give evidence of what Letitia told her?
- Warnings that should be given to the jury.
- The significance of Konrad's initial lie.
- Admissibility of Naomi's evidence.
- Admissibility of Jaspreet's evidence.
- Significance of Konrad's good character.

## Up for Debate

You will gain credit if you mention how *Vye* changed a trial judge's broad discretion to comment generally on an accused's good character to directing the jury on the relevance of it to the accused's credibility (limb 1) and propensity (limb 2).

## Applying the Law

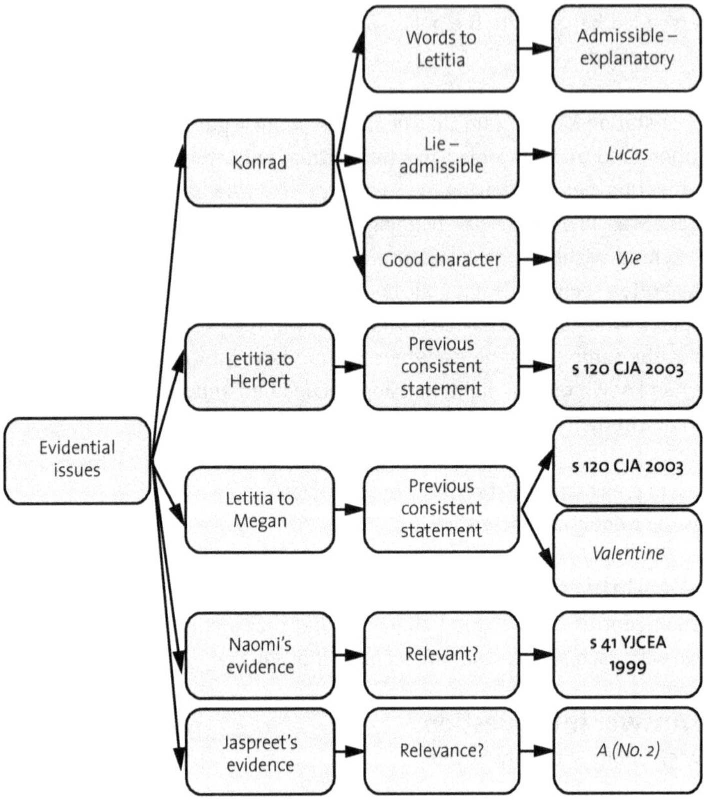


*This mind map outlines the main evidential issues that arise in this question including issues of lies, directions and evidential relevancy.*

# ANSWER

Letitia will be able to give evidence of her encounter with Konrad. There are no problems of admissibility. Konrad's words of invitation are not adduced as evidence of the truth of their contents, but as evidence of the fact that he uttered them, as an explanation of her decision to accompany him to his flat. His parting words are obviously adduced as evidence of his general violence towards her and are obviously not adduced as evidence of the truth of their contents.

The first substantial question is whether Herbert can give evidence that Letitia told him that she had been attacked. This will be admissible, if at all, as a previous consistent statement of the victim of a crime under **s120(4)** and **(7)** of the **Criminal Justice Act 2003**. By **s120(7)(c)** a complaint about conduct that would, if proved, constitute part of the offence is enough. So probably Letitia's statement that she had been attacked, though lacking in detail, will be enough to be admitted. However, the complaint, by **s120(7)(e)**, must not be made as the result of a threat, and Herbert's suggestion that she might have to leave home may constitute a threat and so make her statement inadmissible.[8]

Even if the complaint to her father is inadmissible, the complaint made to Megan will be admissible. It will almost certainly count as a complaint that was made 'as soon as could reasonably be expected' after the alleged offence. Letitia obviously felt unable to explain to her father in detail what had happened, and the Court of Appeal in *Valentine* (1996) recognised that victims of sexual offences often need time before they can bring themselves to tell what has been done to them, and some will find it impossible to tell a parent. In *O* (2006) the Court of Appeal said that evidence of more than one complaint can be admitted under **s120**. In particular, where a later complaint is made in different circumstances and to a different party, it can be admitted. So Letitia's complaint to her father, if admissible, will be no bar to the admissibility of her later complaint to Megan.[9]

By **s120(4)** the complaint is evidence of the matter contained in it, and so is not merely relevant to the complainant's credibility. But the jury must be warned that the complaint cannot amount to independent confirmation of Letitia's evidence because the evidence and the complaint come from the same source (*Islam* (1999)). Evidence of Letitia's distress, observed by both Herbert and Megan, will be admissible to show consistency with her description of the incident but does not amount to independent confirmation (*Islam* (1999)). In appropriate cases the judge should warn the jury of the risk that distress may have been fabricated (*Romeo* (2004)). Whether a warning should be given in this case will largely depend on the defence evidence and the arguments put forward on Konrad's behalf.

In his interview under caution Konrad lied at first about meeting Letitia. The prosecution can rely on this as evidence indicating guilt, but the judge must direct the jury as laid down in *Lucas* (1981) and *Burge and Pegg* (1996). The jury must be warned that the mere fact that the defendant has lied is not in itself evidence of guilt because defendants may lie for innocent reasons. Only if the jury is sure that Konrad did *not* lie for an innocent reason can his lie support the prosecution case. (It is assumed that Konrad in his interview admitted the initial lie. If he did not do so then or later, the jury would first have to be satisfied beyond reasonable doubt that he did lie.)[10]

Konrad's later admission of sexual intercourse, combined with the assertion that Letitia consented, amounts to a 'mixed' statement, which is admissible as evidence of the truth of all its contents, exculpatory as well as inculpatory (*Aziz* (1996)).

8 This part of the discussion evidences the law on the admission of previous consistent statements under the **CJA 2003**. It is important to be absolutely clear as to which of the exceptions contained in the statute apply, thus a thorough knowledge is required.

9 In this part of the answer the second statement is contrasted to the first in terms of the technical requirements of the law under the **CJA 2003**. Often it is important to highlight such differences as they may mean the difference between admission and exclusion.

10 This discussion highlights how the court deals with evidence of lies. It is important to state that the judicial direction (*Lucas*) must be given so that the jury can correctly use the evidence presented to them.

Konrad can, of course, give evidence in his own defence, but Naomi's evidence is unlikely to be admissible. It is unclear what she means when she says that she has often seen Letitia trying to pick up men. The facts observed by Naomi may not amount to sexual behaviour at all, in which case they will be irrelevant. If they do amount to sexual behaviour they will be excluded under **s 41** of the **Youth Justice and Criminal Evidence Act 1999** unless they can be brought within the exceptions in **s 41(3)(b)** or **(c)**. (The issue is clearly one of consent, as opposed to honest but mistaken belief in consent, so **s 41(3)(a)** does not apply.) There is no evidence that any of Naomi's observations took place within the 12-hour period on each side of the alleged offence – the time limits supported by the House of Lords in *A* (2001). Nor is there any evidence of features of Letitia's behaviour that might satisfy the test of similarity in **subs (3)(c)**.

The admissibility of Jaspreet's evidence is uncertain. The incident clearly falls within the contemporaneity test contained in **subs (3)(b)**. But the opening words of **s 41(3)** require that any evidence or question about a complainant's sexual behaviour should relate to a relevant issue in the case. The question, therefore, must be whether Letitia's sexual encounter with Jaspreet is relevant to the question of whether she consented to intercourse with Konrad. The prosecution might argue that just because she consented to sex with Jaspreet, it does not necessarily follow that she consented to sex with Konrad. This is right. But evidence does not have to be conclusive to be relevant. As Lord Steyn said in *A (No. 2)* (2002), all that is required for an item of evidence to be relevant is that it should have *some* tendency in logic and common sense to advance or defeat the proposition in issue. What the prosecution would have to argue is that her consent to have sex with one customer in the pub, whom she did not know, does not make it to any degree more likely that she was consenting when she had sex with another customer from the same pub, whom also she did not know, only a few hours later. Test it this way. Is evidence about Jaspreet capable of giving rise to a reasonable doubt about whether she consented to sex with Konrad? If it is, then it is relevant and should be admitted. It is likely that Jaspreet's evidence would be admitted.[11]

Because Konrad has no previous convictions he will be entitled to a direction in accordance with *Vye* (1993). His good character is relevant to his credibility as a witness and also when considering the likelihood that the allegations against him may be true.

11 This part of the discussion demonstrates knowledge of the test used to admit evidence relevant to an issue – here consent. It is useful to highlight the test as such – this can lead to perhaps not a definitive but a more decisive answer.

# 11 Opinion Evidence

## INTRODUCTION

From the standpoint of the examination candidate, opinion evidence is a tricky subject to prepare. Often evidence courses only briefly cover opinion evidence, if at all, and therefore it may appear as a minor part of a question dealing largely with other matters. Do not labour under any mistake for it is possible to devote an entire problem to this subject. It would even be possible to invite candidates to write an essay on some aspect of opinion evidence: for example, the current state of the so-called 'ultimate issue rule'. Of course, you should keep up to date with any proposals for law reform in this area, as you would in any other. But let's assume that you have ruled out the possibility of an essay question, or at least of doing it should one turn up. How should you cope with opinion evidence as part of a problem?

In the first place, you should be careful in analysing exactly what it is that the expert is prepared to say. Break it down into a number of separate propositions if need be, because some may be more readily admissible than others.[1]

Next, you need to clarify the basis on which the opinion has been formed. For example, how much is a psychiatrist relying on what a defendant has told him? If he relies too much, he may find himself simply repeating what the defendant has said; that, obviously, could be open to objection. You would also need to consider the hearsay provisions in the **Criminal Justice Act (CJA) 2003** (see **s127**).

Very often, the examiner will be vague about both these matters – exactly what the expert is saying and the basis for his opinion – and it will be for you to point out the difficulties.

Where you are dealing with the expert opinion of a psychiatrist or psychologist you should look at the issue to which it is directed. The reason is that evidence from either which does not amount to evidence of mental abnormality may be admitted to show, for example, the reliability of a confession. But where the issue in question is that of *mens rea*, it is most unlikely to be admitted (see *Coles* (1995)). Presumably, it is felt that to allow such evidence to be given would lead to experts deciding the issue that should properly

1 For an example of close analysis leading to rejection of psychiatric testimony, see *Hurst* (1995).

be left to the jury. Alternatively, there may be a fear that a stage would soon be reached where experts were called on each side, the jury would be left no wiser and the expense and length of proceedings would have been increased for nothing.

Although your problem is likely to involve experts who make a living from their expertise, you may have to advise in relation to a layman who appears to be giving an opinion. Don't forget that an amateur may be an expert or that an opinion can be given by a non-expert if it is simply a short way of describing facts: see **s 3(2)** of the **Civil Evidence Act (CEA) 1972** and *Davies* (1962).

**Checklist**

**Students should be familiar with the following areas:**

- opinion used as a way of conveying the sense of facts perceived;
- when expert psychiatric testimony is needed;
- who may give expert testimony;
- expert opinion on ultimate issues;
- expert evidence and the rule against hearsay – *Abadom* (1983); **s 30** of the **CJA 1988**; **s 1(1)** of the **CEA 1972**;
- advance notice procedures in civil and criminal cases.

# QUESTION 42

David and Jonathan are charged with murdering Salome, a prostitute. The prosecution case is that she was beaten and kicked to death by both the accused.

(a) David's defence is diminished responsibility. He says that he was one of Salome's regular clients and he acted as he did immediately after Salome said that if he did not give her £500,000 she would tell his wife of their relationship. David wishes to call Goliath, a psychiatrist. Goliath has prepared a report in which he says that he has examined David, that David described his horror at the blackmail attempt and became very emotional when speaking of his wife; in Goliath's opinion, David loves his wife dearly and would have been devastated by the break-up of their marriage. Goliath adds that in two other cases in his experience, the sudden shock of a blackmail threat led to violent physical retaliation. He states that this observation has been explained in several privately circulated papers by psychiatrists who have described experiments in which they observed patterns of bodily chemical reactions which appeared to be peculiar to blackmail victims. Goliath concludes his report by saying that in his professional opinion David is not insane within the M'Naughten Rules, but was suffering at the relevant time from diminished responsibility within **s 2** of the **Homicide Act 1957**. May Goliath testify as to all or any of these matters?

(b) Jonathan's case is that he had been with David and Salome on the occasion in question, but that he had had nothing to do with the attack. He says that when he saw what David was doing, he went into a state of shock and ran to the house of his girlfriend, Jezebel, a short distance away. Jezebel is a member of the police force. May Jonathan call her to say that when he arrived at her house, he was in a state of shock? He also wishes to call Zadok, a psychiatrist, who has examined him and who is prepared to state that in his opinion, Jonathan is a truthful man who has a peculiar horror of any sort of violence as a result of having been bullied at school. Will Zadok's evidence be admissible?

## How to Read this Question

This question requires you to consider the admissibility of the expert evidence of Goliath and Zadok. Take each in turn. You should break up the proposed opinion into parts and then deal with each, for instance, in relation to Zadok's opinion – can he be called to give evidence of Jonathan's truthfulness and his capacity for being violent?

## How to Answer this Question

(a) Since the expert's evidence is directed towards providing a defence of diminished responsibility for David, it is a good idea to outline briefly what this defence requires. The first paragraph does this, and shows that this is a case where expert evidence will be admissible in principle. But now you have to point out that there may be difficulties about the admissibility of what this expert is prepared to say. To do so effectively, you must break up what Goliath wants to say into separate heads, as follows:

- David's reaction to the blackmail attempt;
- David's reactions when speaking of his wife;
- Goliath's opinion that David loves her dearly;
- Goliath's opinion about the effect on David of the break-up of his marriage;
- Goliath's description of his own experience of similar cases;
- his reference to the psychiatric experiments reported in privately circulated papers;
- his opinion as to David's sanity;
- his opinion that David was suffering from diminished responsibility.

(b) The first matter to be considered is whether Jezebel's evidence is expert testimony at all. You then need to break up Zadok's opinion thus:

- his opinion that Jonathan was truthful;
- his opinion about Jonathan's capacity for violence.

### Up for Debate

Criticism levelled at expert opinions includes their independence and the cost of instructing them. In addition, issues have been raised in relation to the competence of some experts, the potential need for regulation and the rules on who amounts to one for the purposes of the law. Highlighting these, as appropriate, will gain you some credit.

## Applying the Law

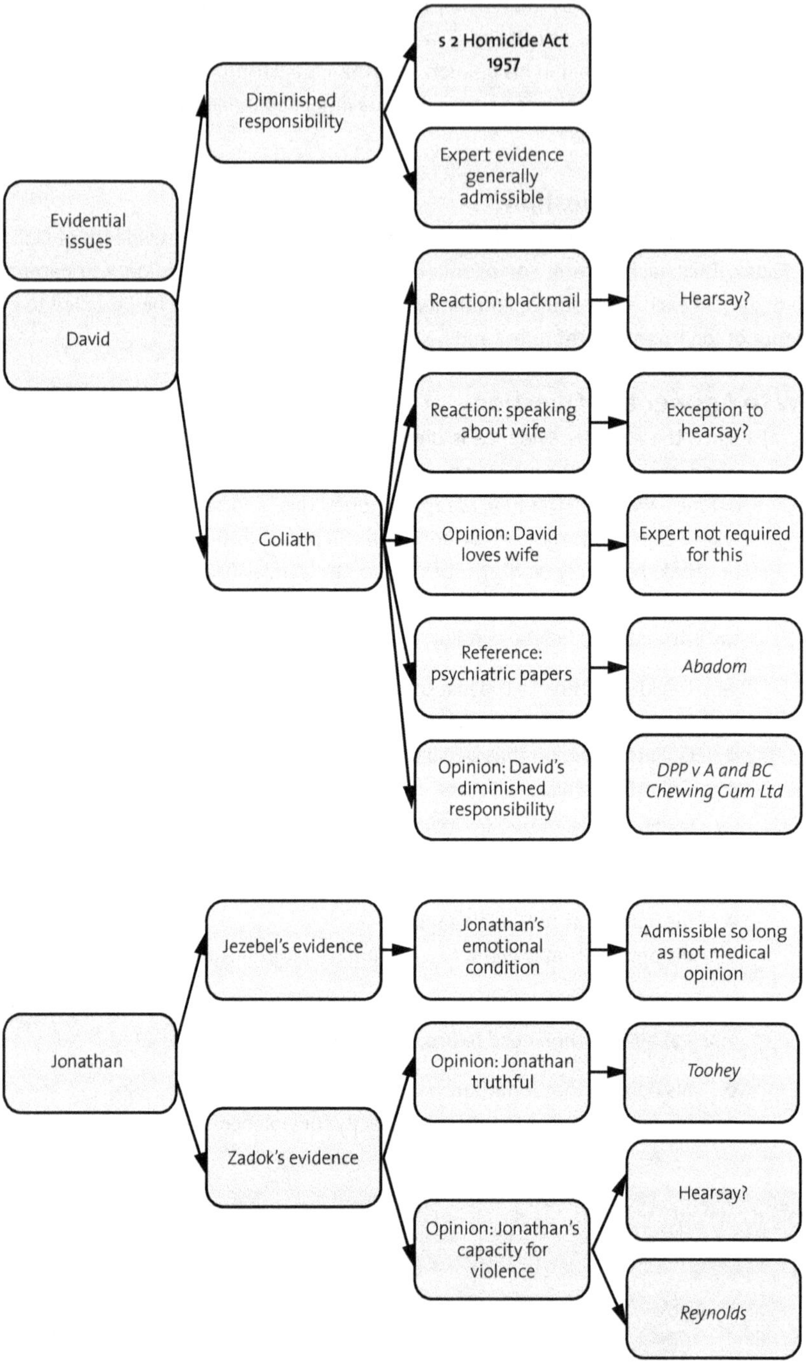


*This mind map illustrates the main points that you should raise in terms of the case against David and Jonathan.*

# ANSWER

(a) By **s 2** of the **Homicide Act 1957**, a person who kills another shall not be convicted of murder if he was suffering from such abnormality of mind as substantially impaired his mental responsibility for his acts. It is for the defendant to prove that he comes within the section. The requirement that some abnormality of mind be established makes it clear that this is the sort of case where expert opinion evidence is receivable. As was said in *Turner* (1975), the purpose of such evidence is to provide the court with information that is outside the experience and knowledge of a judge or jury. In *Dix* (1982), Shaw LJ said that while **s 2** of the **Homicide Act** did not in terms require that medical evidence be adduced in support of a defence of diminished responsibility, it made it a practical necessity if that defence was to begin to run at all. The question of admissibility in this case will therefore turn on the nature of the testimony that it is proposed that Goliath should give.[2]

It appears that the first thing Goliath wishes to do is to report the reactions of David when speaking of his wife, and to give his own opinion that David loves her dearly. He adds that David would have been devastated by the break up of his marriage, but whether this is an opinion formed as a result of what David told him directly, or as a result of what Goliath inferred from other things said by David, is unclear.

So far, it seems that nearly all this evidence would be inadmissible. To the extent that Goliath was repeating what David said to him, the evidence would be excluded by the rule against hearsay, although the fact that David became emotional when speaking of his wife would be admissible.[3] The questions of whether David loves his wife and what would have been his reaction to the break up of their marriage are not ones where the jury would require the special assistance of a psychiatrist. Thus, in *Turner* (1975), the Court of Appeal held that the trial judge had rightly excluded psychiatric evidence that the defendant had had a deep emotional relationship with his girlfriend, which was likely to have caused a blind explosion of rage after her confession of infidelity. As Lawton LJ said, the fact that an expert witness has impressive scientific qualifications does not by that fact alone make his opinion on matters of human nature and behaviour within the limits of normality any more helpful than that of the jurors themselves.[4]

Then Goliath wishes to say that in two other cases in his experience the sudden shock of a blackmail threat led to violent physical retaliation, and he refers to the experiments of

2 This discussion summarises the law applicable to diminished responsibility contained in the **Homicide Act 1957** and how the courts have interpreted **s 2** as practically requiring medical evidence in support.

3 What is relevant is David's state of mind at the time of the offence. Light can be thrown on this by David's emotional reaction when talking to Goliath about his wife, but not, according to English law at any rate, by his account to Goliath of what his state of mind was at the time when he killed Salome. If David wants this to go before the jury, he will have to testify.

4 This discussion makes a clear distinction of the types of things that jurors are able to consider without the need for an expert – the case of *Turner* supports this argument. Do not be afraid to state that historically one of the reasons for limiting expert evidence was the expense and time related to it.

other psychiatrists by way of explanation. The basic question here is the same: does the jury need the assistance of this scientific evidence to determine the particular matter under consideration? At this stage, Goliath's evidence is directed to the issue whether it is more likely than not that when David killed Salome he was suffering from such abnormality of mind as substantially to impair his mental responsibility.

Is Goliath prepared to adopt the explanation of his colleagues as his own? Unless he is, there is not much point in referring to their opinions. Assuming that he does, the argument for admissibility is stronger than in relation to his earlier opinions because this is something that would not be within the ordinary knowledge of jurors. In *Abadom* (1983), the Court of Appeal decided that an expert is entitled to draw on the work of others as part of the process of arriving at his conclusions. The fact that the work is unpublished is immaterial. Goliath may therefore rely on the privately circulated papers in forming his opinion and, as the court pointed out in *Abadom*, he ought to identify them so that the quality of his opinion may be assessed.[5]

However, it remains necessary to be cautious about admissibility. If the judge took the view that the scientists had merely been describing ordinary human reactions in scientific terms, he would very probably conclude that their discoveries would not assist the jury. The evidence would then be excluded.

Lastly, Goliath wishes to say that David was not insane, but was suffering from diminished responsibility. The question of David's sanity is not in issue, so the first part of this opinion would be irrelevant, and therefore inadmissible. Although experts may sometimes give opinions on the ultimate issue in a case, this is not one of them. The defence provided by **s 2** of the **Homicide Act 1957** involves more than a simple medical issue concerning the accused's state of mind. There is also the question of substantial impairment of responsibility and this is essentially for the jury to decide (*Byrne* (1960)).

However, in *DPP v A and BC Chewing Gum Ltd* (1968), Lord Parker acknowledged that although the question 'Do you think he was suffering from diminished responsibility?' was strictly inadmissible, it was allowed time and again without objection. Thus, on the assumption that there is some admissible evidence that Goliath can give, it is likely that he would also be allowed to say that in his opinion, David was suffering from diminished responsibility.

(b) Jezebel may certainly give evidence of Jonathan's physical and emotional condition when he arrived at her house; no special expertise is required to do this. If she wishes to give evidence that he was in a specific medical condition known as 'a state of shock', the fact that she is not medically qualified need not prevent her from doing so. It would be enough that she had acquired the necessary medical knowledge as

5 The authority of *Abadom* highlights how an expert may come to an opinion. This case also evidences the court's acceptance of the ways in which experts gain their knowledge – the notion of expert is far broader and not based solely on qualifications, so do not be afraid to state this.

part of her police training and experience. *Silverlock* (1894) is authority for the proposition that an appropriate professional qualification is not essential for an expert witness. In that case a solicitor who had studied handwriting as a hobby was allowed to give evidence as a handwriting expert.

Zadok will not be able to give his opinion that Jonathan is a truthful man. *Toohey v Commissioner for Metropolitan Police* (1965) establishes that medical evidence will be admissible to show that a witness suffers from some disease, or defect or abnormality of mind that affects the reliability of his evidence. But subject to this, it appears that only in the most exceptional cases will psychiatric testimony be admissible concerning the truthfulness of the accused.[6,7]

Two problems arise in connection with Zadok's opinion about Jonathan's capacity for violence. The first is whether it is in principle admissible at all. There is little to suggest that English courts are likely to follow the example set by the Supreme Court of Canada in *Lupien* (1970), which held admissible evidence showing that the defendant had a temperament that would have made his participation in a particular form of conduct very unlikely. In *Reynolds* (1989), the Court of Appeal took the view that psychiatric evidence about personal traits, such as the habit of fantasising, was inadmissible because the jury could use its common sense about such matters. It is likely that a court would regard an aversion to violence in the same light.[8]

Even if this basic problem can be overcome, a second one remains: on what basis was Zadok's conclusion reached? If it was merely on what Jonathan said to him during a consultation it would be likely to fall foul of the rule against hearsay. At least in *Lupien* (1970) the defendant had been subjected to psychiatric tests for the purpose of determining the issue in question.

6 One such case was *Lowery v R* (1974), where two co-accused blamed each other for a murder and the Privy Council held that the trial judge had properly admitted the evidence of a psychologist, who had carried out tests on both defendants, to show that the testimony of one was more likely to be true than that of the other. Nothing of the kind arises here; David accepts that he killed Salome and has not tried to implicate Jonathan.

7 This paragraph demonstrates knowledge of the issues relating to this area of the law of evidence and the fact that only in rare instances will expert testimony of truthfulness be admissible.

8 The case of *Reynolds* highlights the approach of the English courts in relation to evidence that they believe the jury to be capable of dealing with, without the need of expert evidence.

# 12 Privilege and Public Policy

## INTRODUCTION

The first thing you must get to grips with is the difference between the two concepts. A *privilege* is a right that the law gives to a person allowing him to refuse to testify about a certain matter, or to refuse to produce a document or piece of real evidence. *Public policy* (more commonly now referred to as 'public interest immunity') comes into the picture where it is thought that the disclosure of evidence would be damaging in some way to the general good. The most obvious example is where national security would be compromised if the evidence in question had to be given, or the disclosure made.

There are four privileges that you ought to study. The first is the privilege against self-incrimination. One theoretical topic that could come up as an essay question is whether such a privilege should exist at all. You should note that this is not the same question as whether the accused should have a right to silence. Some writers do refer to 'the privilege against self-incrimination' in the broad sense of a 'right to silence', but this is confusing and it will be better if you keep the two ideas distinct.

The classic context for the operation of the privilege against self-incrimination is a *civil* action where one of the witnesses is being cross-examined about conduct that would amount to a criminal offence. For example, suppose I sue a storage company for the loss of my valuable furniture which was in store with them, and it is my case that the furniture was destroyed when the company deliberately set fire to the premises to collect on an insurance policy. In those circumstances, the privilege might well be invoked at some stage of the hearing by a witness for the company who was being cross-examined.

You should note there are an increasing number of statutory exceptions to this privilege.

Legal professional privilege is also of considerable importance. Note the various circumstances in which this applies, especially those cases where the communications are not directly between lawyer and client, but between lawyer and third parties on behalf of the client.

This privilege can be 'waived' by accident. What happens is that, in any large action, the task of preparing documents for disclosure is so great that quite often one side shows the other privileged documents by mistake. By **r 31.20** of the **Civil Procedure Rules (as at April 2015)**, inadvertently disclosed privileged documents may only be used with the consent of the court. Some knowledge of the former law that governed the granting of injunctions to restrain the use of such documents is likely to be helpful in judging whether consent will be given.

Two more privileges ought to be studied. One is the limited privilege that has been given in respect of a journalist's sources. (See **s10** of the **Contempt of Court Act 1981**.) The other is the privilege that attaches to 'without prejudice' statements. With the latter, remember that if the negotiations result in agreement, there is no longer any need for 'without prejudice' protection. It follows that, if there is any subsequent litigation concerning that agreement, you are free to use the documents marked 'without prejudice' as evidence of the agreement and its terms (*Tomlin v Standard Telephones and Cables Ltd* (1969)). But note also *Rush and Tomkins Ltd v GLC* (1989), which makes evidence of negotiations inadmissible in any subsequent litigation connected with the same subject matter. This is particularly likely to affect a situation where a main contractor reaches a settlement with one of several sub-contractors.

Public policy questions are not ones that many candidates answer well, and unless you have also studied public law it is, perhaps, better to avoid the topic in the examination. I have nevertheless suggested in the checklist some areas with which you might make yourself familiar. The subject of police informers is interesting, topical and not too difficult to master. It is also a subject that might feature as part of a wider question.

### Checklist

**Students should be familiar with the following areas:**

- the privilege against self-incrimination;
- legal professional privilege;
- **s10** of the **Contempt of Court Act 1981**;
- 'without prejudice' statements;
- public policy considerations involving national security, affairs of state and the proper functioning of government and its services;
- public policy considerations in respect of information in the possession of the police relating to the investigation of crime;
- public policy considerations in respect of confidential or personal statements made in official reports or inquiries.

## QUESTION 43

'The fact that evidence which is relevant and otherwise admissible may be excluded by public policy or privilege gives to the two subjects an appearance of similarity that is misleading. The rules and their operation are quite distinct, and any superficial identity of result is more than outweighed by substantial and far-reaching differences.'

- **Discuss.**

## How to Read this Question

The question requires you to deconstruct the statement – the result (exclusion of evidence) does not render the two claims the same. In your answer you will need to weigh up the differences between public policy and privilege; the means by which a claim can be made and how they are determined, i.e. what the court considers and how it balances 'harm' etc.

## How to Answer this Question

Sometimes, the examiner sets quite a lengthy quotation as the subject for an essay. To write an effective essay, it is of course vital that you should read the quotation carefully, probably at least twice, in order to determine exactly what it means. All too often I have read scripts where it seemed as if the candidate had glanced at the quotation, had seen that it had something to do with public policy and had assumed he would pass if he regurgitated his lecture notes on *Conway v Rimmer* (1968), etc. I emphasise again that the examiner is looking for an argument, not an exposition of basic law. If you fail to provide an appropriate response, you will fail the question.

What is this particular quotation about? First, the writer refers to the fact that the rules of both privilege and public policy have the effect of excluding evidence that would otherwise be relevant and admissible. To that extent, the two sets of rules appear to be alike, but, he goes on, the fact that the rules have the same *result* does not mean that there are any other similarities. Similarity of result need not involve similarity in the way the result is reached. This is certainly true in some matters; is it true in this case? In other words, what are the differences and similarities between the rules relating to privilege and those relating to public policy?

It probably strikes you that the idea contained in the quotation is basically correct. But it is not very interesting to say so at once, and the key to producing a really competent answer is to argue a little *against* the idea contained in the quotation. This is done here by arguing that there is not only a similarity in outcome, but a similarity in the way the rules are operated.

You can then move on to make obvious points about waiver, use of secondary evidence and persons entitled to make the claim. You conclude by agreeing with the proposition contained in the quotation. But you do so with reservations, and have shown some independent thought on the subject.

In summary, therefore, the essay is constructed as follows:

- ❖ difference between outcomes and the means of achieving them;
- ❖ argument for similarity of means based on the balancing of potential harms;
- ❖ place of balancing interests in privilege and public policy;
- ❖ potential differences between privilege and public policy: waiver and use of secondary evidence;
- ❖ persons who can claim privilege and raise issues of public policy;
- ❖ concluding remarks on the quotation.

## Up for Debate

You can gain extra credit by mentioning recent cases in which public policy or privilege has been argued to prevent disclosure: for instance, *Commonwealth Affairs v Assistant Deputy Coroner for Inner North London* [2013] EWHC 3724 (Admin), and instances in which the defence can apply for a court's non-disclosure order to be reviewed (**s 8** of the **Criminal Procedure Investigations Act 1996**).

## Answer Structure

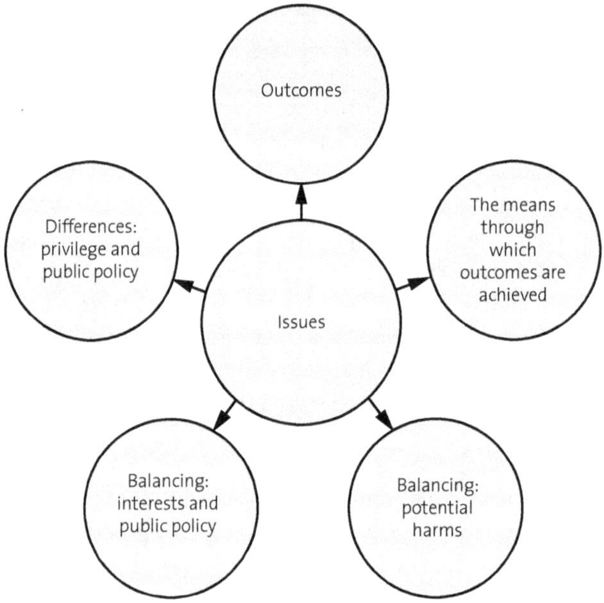


*This diagram illustrates those points that you should raise in your answer in terms of the differences between privilege and public policy.*

# ANSWER

Similarity of outcomes does not necessarily involve similarity in the way the outcomes under consideration were achieved. Dr Crippen died by hanging and Louis XVI lost his life by means of the guillotine. The outcome in each case was the same: death. However, the procedures preceding those outcomes and the methods by which death was achieved were vastly different. It does not, therefore, appear to be a very impressive argument for similarity between the rules relating to privilege and those relating to public policy that they achieve the same outcome.

However, it can be argued that there is more than identity of outcome, and that in fact there is similarity in the way the rules are operated. If a claim to privilege succeeds, it does so because when you balance the harm that will follow if the privilege is upheld against the harm that will follow if it is not, the latter is found to be greater. Yet this is the very same principle that operates in the sphere of public interest immunity.[1]

When privilege is being considered, this balancing exercise operates in a way about which it is difficult to generalise, but which may best be described as 'oiling the wheels of the administration of justice'. For example, for each party to have his case presented as well as possible within our adversarial context, it is necessary that the lawyers on each side be fully acquainted with all the relevant facts. To achieve this, it is vital that the client should be able to trust the lawyer. This could not be the case if what he said to his own lawyer could be used against him, and this gives rise to rules about legal professional privilege.[2]

The fact that justice can be done by disputants themselves, and not only by courts, is recognised by rules that encourage parties to settle their quarrels without recourse to litigation. So, for example, we find that there are rules that say that admissions made by parties while trying to reach a settlement cannot afterwards be proved against them if negotiations break down and the matter has to go to court.

On another level, there may be public interests that conflict with the doing of justice in a particular case. Thus, the public interest in the detection of crime or in the maintenance of national security may require non-disclosure of certain matters, even though this may harm an individual litigant by depriving him of vital evidence.[3]

In both types of case, there is a balancing of interests. Is the interest in rectitude of decision outweighed by the interest in keeping the administration of justice working as well as possible, both inside and outside the courts? Is the interest in doing justice to the parties in a particular case outweighed by some wider public interest? So far, it seems that although the situations giving rise to such problems of balancing may be very different, the principle that is operating in each case is essentially the same. Have we found a common feature other than outcome that would disprove the contention expressed in the passage quoted?

Closer examination suggests that although the balancing of interests is indeed a feature common to both the law of privilege and the law relating to exclusion on grounds of public policy, this does not disprove the contention. The reason for this is that it is too common a feature of evidence law, for it can be used to account for all the ordinary rules

1 This part of the discussion demonstrates knowledge in relation to the way in which the rules operate and their relative considerations. It is important in a question of this sort to be able to prove some substantive similarities to support the argument being made.

2 It is important to highlight the fundamental premise upon which such rules are based – here is one to promote candour between client and lawyer.

3 It is equally important in an answer of this sort to highlight the competing interests, here: national security as important over and above the likely harm to the individual. It would be salient to state that this is a somewhat Kantian argument – where the greatest good takes precedence.

of exclusion, such as those governing hearsay evidence or evidence of the accused's criminal propensity. The public may be said to have an interest in the full disclosure of relevant information in a criminal trial, but it also has an interest in rectitude of decision. This latter interest may be served better by concealing some information, because, if it were disclosed, its capacity to mislead the jury would increase the chances of mis-decision. Thus, it may be said that a balancing exercise takes place in which greater weight is given to one interest rather than the other, depending on the amount of harm likely to result.

On the other hand, there appear to be quite strong arguments to justify the contention expressed in the passage quoted.

Matters covered by public policy are those where the safety or general well-being of citizens is concerned. Privilege, by contrast, covers matters that directly affect only the particular litigant or witness. This gives rise to differences in the way in which the law deals with two subjects: waiver and the use of secondary evidence.

A party or witness who has a privilege may always waive it voluntarily and, in such a case, the once privileged document or testimony will be treated in the same way as any other evidence in the case. But, because public policy objections exist, in theory, for the benefit of citizens generally there is some difficulty with the idea that objections of this type can be waived. Thus, in *Rogers v Home Secretary* (1973), Lord Simon said that once the public interest which demands that evidence be withheld has been found weightier than the public interest requiring courts to have access to all relevant material, the evidence cannot in any circumstances be admitted. It is not a privilege that may be waived, either by the Crown or by anyone else.

However, in *Alfred Crompton Amusement Machines Ltd v Customs & Excise Commissioners (No 2)* (1974), Lord Cross thought that waiver could be allowed if a person or party, such as an informer, for whose benefit the objection was made volunteered to testify or disclose the evidence. One way of analysing such an odd situation would be to say that it was not a case of waiver at all, but one where the public interest had just disappeared, because the interest in question is that of protecting a person from having to disclose certain information *against his will*.[4] This approach was adopted by the Court of Appeal in *Savage v Chief Constable of the Hampshire Constabulary* (1997), where it was held that a police informer could waive his anonymity in order to sue the defendant on an alleged contract to make payments to the claimant in return for information.[5]

4 Lord Denning has on several occasions said that there could be waiver of objections based on public policy. In *Campbell v Tameside Metropolitan Borough Council* (1982), he proposed a distinction between claims affecting documents which must be kept secret on such grounds as those of national security or the preservation of diplomatic relations, and documents in a lower category which are kept confidential in order that persons should be candid in their reports or for other good reasons. In these latter cases, he suggested, immunity should be capable of being waived either by the maker or by the recipient of the document.

5 The authority of *Rogers* and *Alfred* should be used to highlight the court's approach to privilege and how the law was developing thereby.

The courts have recently brought the operation of public interest immunity more closely into line with that of privilege in respect of waiver. An important distinction used to be that, while a privilege could be waived, a claim to public interest immunity could not. As Lord Scarman said in *Air Canada v Secretary of State for Trade* (1983), when the Crown puts forward a public interest immunity objection, it is not claiming a privilege but discharging a duty. Similarly, in *Makanjuola v Commissioner of Metropolitan Police* (1992), Bingham LJ said that public interest immunity 'is not a trump card vouchsafed to certain privileged players to play as and when they wish'. He added that it could not, in any ordinary sense, be waived, because although rights can be waived, duties cannot. On that approach, it followed that where a litigant held documents in a class that was prima facie immune, he should (save in a very exceptional case) assert that they are immune and decline to disclose them. The ultimate decision about where the public interest lay was not for him, but for the court.[6]

However, this approach, coupled with a claim to immunity based on the class into which a document fell, rather than on its specific contents, led to undesirably wide public interest immunity claims by ministers. The practice was criticised in the Scott Report,[7] and the central government has now effectively abandoned class claims.

Further, in *R v Chief Constable of West Midlands Police ex p Wiley* (1995), the House of Lords held that a class claim cannot be made in respect of documents compiled as part of the investigation of a complaint against the police, and it seems likely that class claims generally will be reduced in future. After *ex p Wiley*, it is clear that if a minister believes that the overriding public interest requires government documents to be disclosed, he is not obliged to request immunity for them. It appears that ministers must now consider, before making a claim for public interest immunity, whether the public interest is better served by disclosure than by concealment. It looks very much as if they are expected to exercise a discretion in deciding whether or not to waive public interest immunity.

The second main difference between information affected by privilege and information affected by public policy is in relation to the use of secondary evidence.

When public policy requires that information be concealed, the documents, which are the immediate subject of the exclusion, are obviously affected but, in addition, it is not possible to prove their contents by secondary means. Privilege, however, attaches only to an original document or communication. Subject to the possibility of protection under the law relating to confidentiality, secondary evidence is in principle admissible. Thus, an opponent may be able to prove facts contained in a privileged document by producing a copy, or by calling a witness to give oral evidence of its contents.

6 This demonstrates knowledge of the law and the fact that the individual who claims professional privilege can choose to waive it. It is important to highlight that the same could not be stated in relation to matters of public policy until the decision in *Makanjuola* where the court stated that it was for the court, and not the individual in possession of the evidence, to decide whether it was privileged.

7 Report of the Inquiry into the Export of Defence Equipment and Dual-Use Goods to Iraq and Related Prosecutions, 1996, HC 115, 15 February.

A final point of distinction between claims based on privilege and claims based on public policy is that in the case of privilege the person who is entitled to the privilege must make the claim, but an objection made on grounds of public policy may be made by someone who is not even a party to the proceedings. The court may even do so of its own motion.[8]

Thus, it can be seen that, despite superficial similarities in both effect and operation, there are significant differences between the rules relating to privilege and public policy and between the ways in which those rules operate.

## QUESTION 44

Answer BOTH parts of this question:

(a) Francis is being prosecuted for possession of cannabis, which has been found at his house. When the police raided the premises, they discovered a small quantity of the drug wrapped in silver paper at the bottom of a pile of underclothes that lay on the floor. Francis denies the charge. He says that he is an asthmatic and unable to smoke, but that writers, artists and students are frequent callers at his house and that any one of them could have dropped the package. He suspects that the police were tipped off by George. George has been employed by Francis as a general handyman for the last eight years. In the past, he has been sentenced to terms of imprisonment; he is now an alcoholic and has often made false allegations against Francis when drunk.

Can the defence require the police to disclose the name of their informer?

(b) Harry is being prosecuted for supplying drugs. The only evidence against him is that of four police officers. Two officers, Ian and John, give evidence that while keeping watch in private premises, they observed Harry selling drugs. Two others, Kate and Larry, give evidence that while keeping watch in an unmarked police vehicle, they also observed Harry selling drugs.

Can the defence cross-examine Ian and John to discover the exact location of their observation point in order to test the quality of their observations? Can they cross-examine Kate and Larry to discover the colour, make and model of their vehicle and the times of their alleged surveillance?

### How to Read this Question

This question requires you to consider public interest reasons for withholding information relating to the investigation of crime and when the rules should be departed from, i.e. where the information is vital to prove innocence or to test evidence by cross-examination.

8 This discussion highlights the importance given to matters of public policy: it raises one of the major distinctions between the two claims.

## How to Answer this Question

This is a straightforward question involving cases in the public interest on non-disclosure of information concerning police investigations.

Part (a) deals with the traditional problem of the informer. The basic rule stated in *Marks v Beyfus* (1890) must be your starting point; it will be useful to refer to what Lawton LJ said in *Hennessey* (1978) about the reason for that rule. Don't rush things; deal with the basic rule first and turn to the exception only after that. Then comes the factual problem: is disclosure necessary to show the accused's innocence? The point is best made here by a comparison of *Agar* (1990) and *Slowcombe* (1991). Don't forget though to provide your own conclusion on the facts of this question; the cases you have cited are useful illustrations of a principle, but no more.

Part (b) is even more straightforward and is designed to test the candidate's knowledge of *Rankine* (1986), *Brown* (1987) and *Johnson* (1988).

### Up for Debate

You will gain additional marks for highlighting the overlap between the common law (open justice) and **Art 6** of the **ECHR**; you should also mention the authorities: for instance, *R v H* [2004] UKHL 3 and *Al Rawi and others (Respondents) v The Security Service and others (Appellants)* [2011] UKSC 34.

## Answer Structure

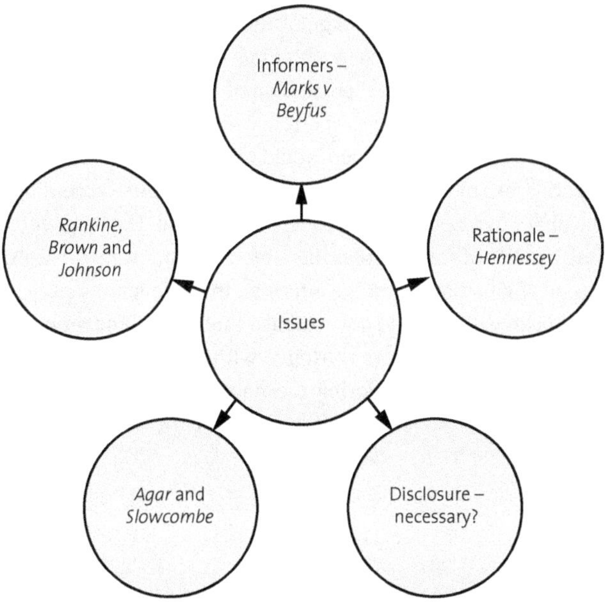


*This diagram highlights the main points that you should discuss in relation to the disclosure of an informant's identity and the exact location of discreet observation.*

## ANSWER

(a) The basic rule is that in public prosecutions witnesses may not be asked, and will not be allowed to disclose, the names of informers or the nature of the information given. Thus, in *Marks v Beyfus* (1890), an action for malicious prosecution, the Director of Public Prosecutions, who had been called as a witness, refused on grounds of public policy to give the names of his informants or to produce the statement on which he had acted in directing the earlier unsuccessful prosecution of the plaintiff. The trial judge upheld his objection, and the plaintiff was unsuccessful in his appeal. Lawton LJ stated in *Hennessey* (1978) that the rationale of the rule is that informers need to be protected, both for their own safety and to ensure that the supply of information about criminal activities does not dry up.[9]

However, in *Marks v Beyfus* (1890), Lord Esher qualified this basic rule by stating that it could be departed from if the disclosure of the name of the informant was necessary or right in order to show the prisoner's innocence. In such a case, one public policy would be in conflict with another, and the policy that said that an innocent man should not be condemned when his innocence could be proved had to prevail. However, it is for the accused to show that there is a good reason for disclosure (*Hennessey* (1978)).

An example of a case where disclosure was considered appropriate is *Agar* (1990). In that case, a prosecution for possession of drugs, the Court of Appeal said that the trial judge should have ordered the informer's disclosure because it was necessary for the support of the accused's defence that the informer and the police had acted together to frame him.[10]

But it may well be the case that knowledge of the informer will not affect the defence, and then disclosure will not be ordered. An example is *Slowcombe* (1991). Following a tip-off, the defendant had been arrested in possession of a shotgun outside a sub-post office. He claimed to have been recruited by V, and to have been told by him that there was an accomplice working in the post office who would hand over the money, but that the gun was necessary for the sake of appearances. The defendant argued accordingly that he was not guilty of conspiracy to rob, but only of conspiracy to steal. The judge refused a defence application to ask a police officer whether their informer had been V. The Court of Appeal upheld this decision. If V had not been the informer, the defendant's story could still have been true. If it had been V, this would not establish that the defendant had been told that only a theft was planned. V could have conspired with the defendant to commit robbery, but then have turned informer. Disclosing the name of the informer could contribute little or nothing to the issue the jury had to consider: might the defendant's explanation have been true?

9 It is good practice to use authorities, here *Marks* and *Hennessey*, to evidence the policy and rationale under which such privilege is based.

10 These last two paragraphs evidence the court's approach in relation to privilege where the evidence supports the accused's innocence.

The issue in the case of Francis is whether his explanation for the presence of the cannabis might be true. Knowing that George was the informer can contribute nothing to the resolution of this question. If Francis were to suggest that George planted the cannabis and then tipped off the police, the position would be different, but that does not appear to be his case.

It is unlikely, therefore, that the defence application would succeed.[11]

(b) It was held in *Rankine* (1986) that the rule in *Marks v Beyfus* (1890) also protects the identity of persons who have allowed their premises to be used for police observation, and the identity of the premises. Even if the accused argues that identification of the premises is necessary to establish his innocence (as it surely would be in this case), the judge may still refuse to allow the question to be put. For example, in *Johnson* (1988), where the accused was charged with supplying drugs, the only evidence against him was supplied by police officers who had kept observation from private premises. The defence applied to cross-examine about the exact location in order to test whether the officers could have seen what they said they did. The trial judge nevertheless ruled that the exact location should not be revealed and the Court of Appeal upheld this decision.[12]

But the prosecution must have first provided a proper evidential basis to support their claim for protection of identity. In *Johnson* (1988), Watkins LJ stated the following as minimum requirements:

- the police officer in charge of the observations must testify that he had visited all the observation places to be used and ascertained the attitude of their occupiers, both as to the use to be made of them and to possible subsequent disclosure;
- a police officer of at least the rank of chief inspector must testify that immediately prior to the trial he visited the places used for observation and ascertained whether the occupiers were the same as when the observation took place and, whether they are or not, the attitude of those occupiers to possible disclosure of their use as observation points.

In *Johnson* (1988), the prosecution called evidence as to the difficulty of obtaining assistance from the public and the desire of the occupiers, who had been occupiers throughout, that their names and addresses should not be disclosed because of fear for their safety. Assuming that similar evidence is available in this case, the defence will not be permitted to cross-examine Ian and John about the exact location of the premises they used.

11 But for what happened in the case on which this question is based, see D Farson, *The Gilded Gutter Life of Francis Bacon*, 1993, Chapter 12.

12 This discussion lends further support for the argument for privilege, here crime detection. From these decisions it is quite clear that the court understands the need to promote the willingness of the public to help without the fear of being exposed to fear or harm themselves.

But the object of keeping the identity of the premises secret is to protect the owner or occupier. Where this consideration does not apply, cross-examination may be permitted on detailed aspects of surveillance. Thus, in *Brown* (1987), where officers gave evidence that they had kept observation from an unmarked police vehicle, it was held that the defence was entitled to information relating to the surveillance and to the colour, make and model of the vehicle.

The defence will therefore be entitled to ask Kate and Larry about these matters.

# QUESTION 45

Cedric was employed by AB Ltd, a company engaged in the manufacture of meat pies. One day, his hand was caught in a mincing machine and he suffered grave injuries, because of which he decided to sue AB Ltd for compensation. When AB Ltd learned of the accident, they obtained a report from an independent safety expert in accordance with their usual practice when accidents occurred on their premises. Copies of this report were sent to the board of directors and to the legal department of the company.

Cedric wrote a letter to Derek, his solicitor, setting out his account of the accident in which he admitted that he had not complied with safety regulations when operating the mincing machine because he had been 'chatting someone up' at the time. Enid, Derek's secretary, took a photocopy of this letter and gave it to her lover Fabian, who is a director of AB Ltd.

Cedric wishes to obtain a copy of the safety expert's report. He suspects that his employers may have obtained a copy of his letter to Derek and is afraid that they may use it against him.

- **Advise Cedric.**

## How to Read this Question

This question requires you to assess whether the report and the letter are privileged so as to prevent disclosure. You will also need to discuss what happens if disclosure is made inadvertently and on how secondary evidence that relates to a privileged document is treated.

## How to Answer this Question

A relatively straightforward question about privilege. You need to discuss the following points:

- the safety expert's report – legal professional privilege in relation to third party communications;
- whether Cedric's admission is privileged;
- whether AB Ltd will be allowed to use the photocopy of the letter sent by Cedric.

## Up for Debate

You can gain extra credit by mentioning current authorities in this area of law. For instance, in *Oceanbulk Shipping & Trading SA v TMT Asia Ltd and Others* [2010] UKSC 44 the court held that facts, normally protected by the without prejudice rule, that are communicated between parties in the course of without prejudice negotiations are now admissible to aid the construction of an agreement. The court acknowledged that the rule is wider than it has ever been but its boundaries should not be diminished without good reason.

## Applying the Law

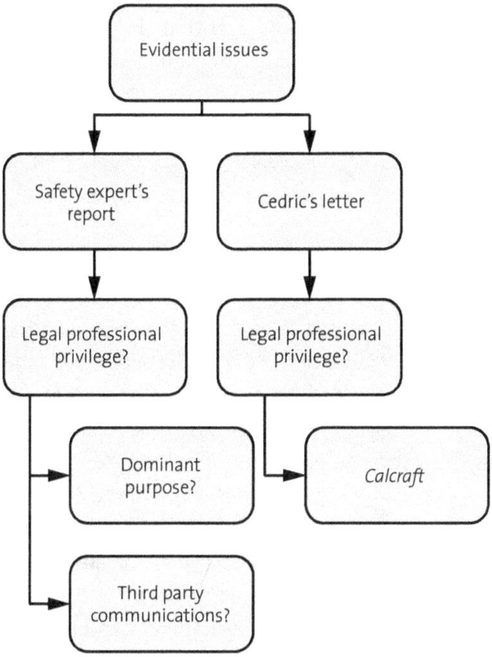


*This mind map outlines the factors that you should consider in terms of evidence potentially protected by legal professional privilege.*

# ANSWER

Communications made between a party and his legal advisers or his legal advisers and a third party will be privileged provided the dominant purpose in making the communications was to obtain or provide advice in connection with pending or contemplated litigation. The requirement that advice in such a connection be the dominant purpose of the communication was established by *Waugh v British Railways Board* (1980). In that case, the claimant sued the defendants under the **Fatal Accidents Act 1976** in respect of the death of her husband, which had occurred in a railway collision. Her advisers wished to obtain discovery of an internal report prepared by the defendants for submission to the railway inspectorate and the ministry. Another object of the report was to provide information for the Board's solicitor to enable him to advise the Board. The House of Lords held that the Board was not entitled to claim privilege in respect of this report. To attract such privilege, preparation for the purposes of intended or contemplated litigation had to be 'at least the dominant purpose' for bringing a document into existence. But the report in *Waugh* had been prepared not only for the purpose of litigation but for other major purposes in relation to the safe running of railways. Submission to the solicitor had not been shown to be the dominant purpose of making the report; therefore it was not privileged.[13]

Whether such a document is privileged will turn on the facts of each individual case. But, on the facts given, it looks as if assistance in litigation was only one of the objects of AB Ltd in obtaining the safety expert's report, and that the maintenance of safe working practices was equally important. The report is thus unlikely to be privileged.

All communications between solicitor and client made for the purpose of giving or receiving legal advice are privileged (*Waugh v British Railways Board* (1980)). It is clear that the letter that Cedric wrote to Derek was privileged for this reason.

However, privilege attaches only to the original letter sent by Cedric. In principle, secondary evidence of a privileged document is admissible. Thus, in *Calcraft v Guest* (1898), it was held that the defendant was entitled to put in evidence copies that he had made of certain proofs of evidence. By **r 31.20** of the **Civil Procedure Rules 1998**, inadvertently disclosed privileged documents may only be used with the consent of the court. But, this document has not been *inadvertently* disclosed. Use of a document that is an admissible piece of evidence may be restrained on the ground that it contains confidential information. In *Lord Ashburton v Pape* (1913), the plaintiff opposed the defendant's discharge from bankruptcy. The defendant obtained by trickery a number of relevant documents from a clerk in the employment of the claimant's solicitors. Having obtained them, he took copies. The Court of Appeal held that the plaintiff was entitled to an injunction requiring the defendant to deliver up all originals and restraining him from making any use of the copies or of the information that he had obtained. Provided the privileged documents or copies of them have not already been used as secondary evidence in the litigation, the party entitled to the privilege will be able to obtain a similar injunction (*Goddard v Nationwide Building Society* (1987)).[14]

Cedric's solicitors will therefore be able to obtain an injunction restraining the use by AB Ltd of the photocopy that was given to Fabian and of the information contained in it.

13 This paragraph demonstrates knowledge of the development of the law and its extent. In questions of this type it is often good practice to highlight the relevant rules before applying them to the scenario.

14 This discussion highlights how the law further developed, this time in terms of secondary evidence or inadvertent disclosure. Do not hesitate to outline the remedy available to prevent such disclosure: an injunction.

# Index

admissibility **1**; confessions **74, 107, 108–10, 111, 115–19, 119–23**; discovery **16–17**; evidence obtained by eavesdropping **122**; hearsay **53, 56–8, 61–2, 64–5, 79**; identification evidence **65**; improperly obtained evidence **119–23**; previous convictions **128–30, 133–6, 139, 143, 148–9, 150, 151–3, 162, 164, 167**; questions **1**; spontaneous exclamations **71**
alibis: false **62, 63, 64**; hazardous evidence **90, 94**
assault **172–5, 175–8**; basic issues **176**

Bentham, J. **50**
bugging evidence **119–20, 123**
burden of proof *see* proof
burglary **90, 115, 117–18, 160, 162–3**
business and other documents **60, 71–2**

cash discovery **9, 14, 15, 16–17, 76–9**
character evidence: basic issues **129, 146, 150, 153, 157, 161**; co-defendants **147–8, 156, 159**; collusion **136–40**; confession **156–60**; failure to testify **146–9, 152–6, 160–3, 168**; judicial directions **127, 132, 147, 149, 152, 159, 161, 168**; legitimate conduct **152–6**; lies/accusations of lying **133, 160, 162, 166, 169, 179–81**; pornography **129, 131, 140, 142–4**; previous convictions **129–30, 146–9, 149–52, 153–9, 162–3, 163–6** (*see also* previous convictions); propensity **128, 131–5, 143, 146, 148, 152, 155, 157–9, 162–6, 168–9**; relevance **127, 129–36, 140–4**; sexual inclination **140, 150–1**; statutory provisions **167, 178**; witness credibility **166–9, 172–5, 182**
childbirth, presumptions **40, 42**
circumstantial evidence **47, 67, 144**
civil action, burden of proof **28, 29–31**; affirming party **30**; civil/criminal distinction **30**; claim elements **30**; degree of probability **30**; movement between parties **31**; negligence **28–9, 31**
civil partners *see* spouses/civil partners, as witness
co-defendants **118, 147–8, 156, 159**
Coke, E. **50**
collusion **136–9**
common purpose, statements in furtherance of **72, 78–9, 100**
competence and compellability of witnesses: basic issues **38, 44**; civil trial **43, 45**; criminal trial **43–4**; spouses/civil partners *see* spouses/civil partners, as witnesses; statutory basis **37–8**
concepts, basic areas **5**
confessions: admissibility **74, 107, 108–10, 111, 115–19, 119–23**; basic issues **102, 107, 112, 116**; bugging evidence **119–20, 123**; character evidence **156–60**; and co-defendants **118, 160**; definition **9, 23, 34, 44, 53–4, 61, 89, 101–2, 108–9, 111–12, 114, 117, 125**; detention **109**; exclusion **101, 119–20**; exculpatory statements **101, 108, 110, 117**; hazardous evidence **92–3**; hearsay **72, 74–5**; impact **100–1**; joint enterprise **100–1**; legal advice **111–14**; mixed statement **101**; oppression **100–1, 106, 107, 108–9, 111**; police impropriety **119–21**; precedents **99**; recognising **100**; series of interviews **109**
Crippen, Dr **3–5, 194**
cross-examination, hearsay **59–60**

death, presumptions of: basic issues **37, 39, 46, 47**; circumstantial evidence **47**; conditions **47**; order of seniority **47**
deception, obtaining property by **163**

defendants: burden of proof **27–8**; separate treatment **14–15**
Dennis, I. **22–4**
description evidence **95, 97**
diminished responsibility **184–8**
discovery **9, 14–16**
drug offences **9, 14–17, 76–9, 119–23, 198–200**

eavesdropping, admissibility of evidence obtained by **122**
entrapment **124, 126**
exclusion of evidence: admissible evidence **120, 125**; confessions **101, 119–20**; discretion **123–6**; hearsay **79, 80, 81**; improperly obtained evidence **124**
exculpatory statements: confessions **101, 108, 110, 117**; hearsay **78**

fabrication, allegation **136, 176–7**
failure to testify **38, 102–4, 147, 153, 155**; *see also* silence, right to
false alibi **62, 63, 64**

golden thread principle **22**

handling stolen goods **172**
hazardous evidence: alibi **90, 94**; basic issues **83, 86, 88, 91**; confession **92–3**; informal warning **85, 90–2**; interview by police **89**; language **83–4**; mandatory warnings **84–5**; reasons **83–4**; relevance **92, 95**; similarity **87, 89**; statement to police **86–8**; trust **83**; *see also* identification
hearsay **5, 37, 53–67, 69–75, 77, 79–82, 87–8, 92–3, 114, 171, 178, 183–4, 186–7, 189, 196**; admissibility **53, 56–8, 61–2, 64–5, 79**; basic issues **53, 63, 68, 77, 80**; business and other documents **60, 71**; cash discovery **76, 79**; circumstantial evidence **67, 69**; common law rules **71, 74–5, 81**; common purpose, statements in furtherance of **72, 78**; confessions **72, 74–5**; cross-examination **59–60**; definition **53, 80**; exclusionary rules **79, 80, 81**; exculpatory statements **78**; false alibi **64**; historical development **79–82**; human rights issues **55–8**; implied assertions **54, 60–1**; inscriptions **62–4**; intention **78**; multiple **62, 72–3, 75, 87–8**; non-attendance **72–3, 74–6**; oral statements **62, 81**; overheard conversation **62, 65–6**; police observation **76, 81**; rationale issues **58–62**; real evidence, distinction **70**; relevance **62, 79, 81**; repetition **70**; *res gestae* statements **71–2, 81**; safety-valve exception **64**; spontaneous exclamations **71**; statement, definition **53**; tracker dog evidence **67–8**; and the unavailability exception **65**
human rights issues: hearsay **55–8**; statute interpretation, burden of proof **35**

identification: admissibility **65**; basic issues **95, 173**; description evidence **95, 97**; direction to acquit **85**; identification parades **81, 85, 97–8, 136, 172**; mandatory warnings **85**; mistaken **94–8**; photographic **85**; video identification **85, 97–8**; voice **66, 94–5, 97–8**; *see also* hazardous evidence
implied assertions **54, 60–1**
improperly obtained evidence **15, 118, 120–1, 124, 126**; admissibility **119–23**
indecent assault **57, 131**
indecent exposure **140, 141, 143–4, 145**
innocence, presumptions of **20–4, 32, 35, 37, 42**
inscriptions **62–4**

joint enterprise **72, 100–1**
journalists' privilege **192**
judicial directions: character evidence **127, 132, 147, 149, 152, 159, 161, 168**; identification, direction to acquit **85**; previous convictions **127–8, 149, 158, 166, 168**; proof **27–8**; in questions **1**
judicial notice: basic issues **11–12**; and evidence **13, 14**; fitness of the law **11–14**; mandatory application **13**; rationale **13**; scope **12**

legal advice **87–8, 105, 109, 111–14, 116–20, 122, 179, 204**
legal professional privilege **191–2, 195, 202–3**
legal relevance *see* relevance
lies/accusations of lying **133, 160, 162, 166, 169, 179–81**
lifestyle **9, 17, 77**

*mala in se/mala prohibita* **22**
mandatory warnings **84–5**
mistaken identification **94–8**
multiple hearsay **62, 72–3, 75, 87–8**
murder **3–4, 25, 62–3, 65–6, 69, 72, 92, 106, 140, 142–4, 177, 187, 189**

narrative **100**
negligence, burden of proof **28–9, 31**
non-attendance **72–3, 74–6**

opinion evidence: basic issues **183–4, 186**; diminished responsibility **184–9**
oppression **100–1, 105, 106, 107, 108–9, 111–12, 117**; definition **108, 117**
oral statements **81, 100**
outraging public decency **149, 156**
overheard conversation **62, 65–6**

Peirce, C.S. **141**
photographic identification **85**
planting of evidence **103, 115–16, 119, 201**
police: hearsay observation **76, 81**; impropriety **119–21**; informant's identity, disclosure **196, 198–202**; interview **87, 89, 105, 109–10, 113, 179, 181**; questioning, right to silence **105–6, 110–15, 115–19, 123**; statements to **86–8**
pornography **129, 131, 140, 142–4**
presumptions: arguments **40**; basic issues **37–8**; childbirth **40, 42**; death *see* death, presumptions; of innocence **20–4, 32, 35, 37, 42**; rationale **41**
previous convictions: adducing evidence **156–7, 159, 162, 164**; admissibility **128–30, 133–6, 139, 143, 148–9, 150, 151–3, 162, 164, 167**; cross-examination **148, 154, 158, 168**; duty to disclose **175**; and failure to testify **146**; judicial direction **127–8, 149, 158, 166, 168**; judicial discretion **155**; police observation **76**; propensity **128, 133, 135, 148, 158–9, 162, 164, 166**; relevance **132–3, 163, 168**
previous statements/complaints **88, 178**
privilege: civil actions **191**; journalists **192**; legal professional **191–2, 195, 202–3**; public policy, distinction **192–8**; self-incrimination **191**; without prejudice statements **192**
proof: basic issues **19, 24**; burden of **19–20**; civil action *see* civil action, burden of proof; civil/criminal distinction **19**; defendant's burden **25, 27**; defendant's peculiar knowledge **24**; ease of **24**; elements of offence/defences, distinction **22–3**; erroneous directions **28**; golden thread principle **22**; judicial direction **27–8**; *mala in se/mala prohibita* **22**; maximum penalties **23–4**; Parliament's responsibility **22–3**; presumptions of innocence **20–4, 32, 35, 37, 42**; prosecution/defence burden **20**; reverse **20–4**; self-defence **28**; standard of **19**; statutory *see* statute interpretation, burden of proof
propensity **128, 131–5, 143, 146, 148, 152, 155, 157–9, 162–6, 168–9**
property, obtaining by deception **163**
public policy **191**; informant's identity, disclosure **198–202**; privilege, distinction **192–8**

rape **10, 86–7, 89, 98, 118, 142–4, 171, 179**
real evidence **15–17, 67, 69–70, 83, 121, 191**
relevance: basic issues **6–7**; defendants **10**; definitions **6–7**; discovery **9, 14–17**; and duty to exclude **159**; hazardous evidence **92, 95**; hearsay **62, 79, 81**; judicial subjectivity **10**; lifestyle **9, 15, 17, 77**; minimum requirement **8–9**; previous convictions **132–3, 163, 168**; statutory framework **8**; usefulness of the concept **6–11**
*res gestae* statements **71–2, 81**
reverse proofs **20–4**
robbery **44, 123, 152, 154–6, 159, 200**
Roberts, P. **39**

sexual assault **134, 136, 140, 156**
shoplifting **145**
silence, right to **102–6**; basic issues **120**; burden of proof **104–5**; common law **102–4**; facts relied on for defence **118–19, 122**; police impropriety **105**; police questioning **105–6, 110–15, 115–19, 123**; *see also* failure to testify
similarity **87, 89**
spontaneous exclamations, admissibility **71**
spouses/civil partners, as witnesses: basic issues **48, 49**; civil partners **49, 51**; privilege **49**; public interest **50**
standard of proof *see under* proof

statements: common purpose, in furtherance of **72, 78–9, 100**; definition **53**; exculpatory **78, 101, 108, 110, 117**; mixed **101**; oral **62, 81**; to police **86–8**; previous statements/complaints **88, 178**; *res gestae* **71–2, 81**; without prejudice **192**; written **62, 72–3, 178**
statute interpretation, burden of proof **32–5**; basic issues **32–3**; deference to Parliament **35**; ease and difficulty **34**; elements of offence **33**; exceptions/ exemptions **33**; gravity of offence **34**; guidelines **34–5**; human rights issues **35**

Tapper, C. **39**
testimony: basic issues **171–2, 173, 179–80**; collateral evidence **173–4**; fabrication, allegation **136, 176–7, 181**; lies/accusations of lying **179–81**; memory refreshment **175, 176, 177–8**; previous statements/complaints **177–8, 179, 180**
Thayer, J.B. **6, 8**
theft: art gallery **110–15**; burglary and **90–4**; handling stolen goods **172**; shoplifting **145–9**
Thompson, Edith **4**
tracker dog evidence **67–8**
Twining, William **4, 37**

video identification **85, 97–8**
violence: capacity for **185–6, 189**; use or threat of **108, 154, 163**
violent disorder
voice identification **66, 94–5, 97–8**

Wigmore, J. **6, 8**
without prejudice statements **192**
witnesses: credibility **166–7**; *see also* competence and compellability of witnesses
written statements **62, 72–3, 178**

Zuckerman, A. **39**

For Product Safety Concerns and Information please contact our EU representative GPSR@taylorandfrancis.com
Taylor & Francis Verlag GmbH, Kaufingerstraße 24, 80331 München, Germany

www.ingramcontent.com/pod-product-compliance
Lightning Source LLC
LaVergne TN
LVHW011128300926
849160LV00008B/564
* 9 7 8 1 1 3 8 8 2 9 5 9 6 *